RELIGION BY REGION

Religion and Public Life
in the Midwest:
America's Common Denominator?

RELIGION BY REGION

Religion by Region Series
Co-published with the Leonard E. Greenberg Center for the
Study of Religion in Public Life at Trinity College
Mark Silk and Andrew Walsh, Series Editors

The United States is a nation of many distinct regions. But until now, no literature has looked at these regional differences in terms of religion. The Religion by Region Series describes, both quantitatively and qualitatively, the religious character of contemporary America, region by region. Each of the eight regional volumes includes overviews and demographic information to allow comparisons among regions. But at the same time, each volume strives to show what makes its region unique. A concluding volume looks at what these regional variations mean for American religion as a whole.

1. Religion and Public Life in the Pacific Northwest: *The None Zone*
   Edited by Patricia O'Connell Killen (Pacific Lutheran University) and Mark Silk

2. Religion and Public Life in the Mountain West: *Sacred Landscapes in Tension*
   Edited by Jan Shipps (Indiana University–Purdue University, Indianapolis) and Mark Silk

3. Religion and Public Life in New England: *Steady Habits, Changing Slowly*
   Edited by Andrew Walsh and Mark Silk

4. Religion and Public Life in the Midwest: *America's Common Denominator?*
   Edited by Philip Barlow (Hanover College) and Mark Silk

5. Religion and Public Life in the Southern Crossroads: *Borderlands*
   Edited by William Lindsey (Philander Smith College) and Mark Silk

6. Religion and Public Life in the South: *The Distinctive South*
   Edited by Charles Reagan Wilson (University of Mississippi) and Mark Silk

7. Religion and Public Life in the Middle Atlantic: *In Between*
   Edited by Randall Balmer (Columbia University) and Mark Silk

8. Religion and Public Life in the Pacific: *The Font of Diversity*
   Edited by Wade Clark Roof (University of California, Santa Barbara) and Mark Silk

9. Religion by Region: *Religion and Public Life in The United States*
   By Mark Silk and Andrew Walsh

Religion and Public Life
in the Midwest:
America's Common Denominator?

Edited by

Philip Barlow

and

Mark Silk

Published in cooperation with the Leonard E. Greenberg
Center for the Study of Religion in Public Life at
Trinity College, Hartford, Connecticut

ALTAMIRA
PRESS
A Division of
ROWMAN & LITTLEFIELD PUBLISHERS, INC.
Walnut Creek • Lanham • New York • Toronto • Oxford

Published in cooperation with the Leonard E. Greenberg Center for the Study of Religion in Public Life at Trinity College.

ALTAMIRA PRESS
A division of Rowman & Littlefield Publishers, Inc.
1630 North Main Street, #367
Walnut Creek, CA 94596
www.altamirapress.com

Published in cooperation with the Leonard E. Greenberg Center for the Study of Religion in Public Life at Trinity College.

Rowman & Littlefield Publishers, Inc.
A wholly owned subsidary of The Rowman & Littlefield Publishing Group, Inc.
4501 Forbes Boulevard, Suite 200
Lanham, MD 20706

PO Box 317
Oxford
OX2 9RU, UK

British Library Cataloguing in Publication Information Available
Library of Congress Cataloging-in-Publication Data

Religion and public life in the midwest : America's common denominator? / edited by Philip Barlow and Mark Silk.
p. cm.—(Religion by region ; 4)
Includes bibliographical references and index.
ISBN 0-7591-0630-4 (hardcover : alk. paper)—ISBN 0-7591-0631-2 (pbk. : alk. paper)
1. Middle West—Religion. 2. Religion and politics—Middle West. I. Barlow, Philip. II. Silk, Mark. III. Title. IV. Series.
BL2527.M53R45 2004
200'.977—dc22   2004019134

Printed in the United States of America
♾™ The paper used in this publication meets the minimum requirements of American National Standard for Information Sciences—Permanence of Paper for Printed Library Materials, ANSI/NISO Z39.48–1992.

DEDICATION

For William R. Hutchison

CONTENTS

Preface

Geographical diversity is the hallmark of religion in the United States. There are Catholic zones and evangelical Bible Belts, a Lutheran domain and a Mormon fastness, metropolitan concentrations of Jews and Muslims, and (in a different dimension) parts of the country where religious affiliation of whatever kind is very high and parts where it is far below the norm. This religious heterogeneity is inextricably linked to the character of American places. From Boston to Birmingham, from Salt Lake City to Santa Barbara, even the casual observer perceives public cultures that are intimately connected to the religious identities and habits of the local population.

Yet when the story of religion in American public life gets told, the country's variegated religious landscape tends to be reduced to a series of monochrome portraits of the spiritual state of the union, of piety along the Potomac, of great events or swings of mood that raise or lower the collective religious temperature. Whatever the virtues of compiling such a unified national narrative—and I believe they are considerable—it obscures a great deal. As the famous red-and-blue map of the 2000 presidential vote makes clear, region has not ceased to matter in national politics. Indeed, in this era of increasing federalism, regions are, state by state, charting ever more distinctive courses.

To understand where each region is headed and why, it is critical to recognize the place of religion in it.

Religion by Region, a project of the Leonard E. Greenberg Center for the Study of Religion in Public Life at Trinity College in Hartford, represents the first comprehensive effort to show how religion shapes, and is being shaped by, regional culture in America. The project has been designed to produce edited volumes (of which this is the fourth) on each of eight regions of the country. A ninth volume will sum up the results in order to draw larger conclusions about the way religion and region combine to affect civic culture and public policy in the United States as a whole.

The purpose of the project is not to decompose a national storyline into eight separate narratives. Rather, it is to bring regional realities to bear, in a systematic way, on how American culture is understood at the beginning of the twenty-first century. In line with the Greenberg Center's commitment to enhance public understanding of religion, these volumes are intended for a general audience, with a particular eye towards helping working journalists make better sense of the part religion plays in the public life—local, statewide, regional, and national—that they cover. At the same time, I am persuaded that the accounts and analyses provided in these volumes will make a significant contribution to the academic study of religion in contemporary America.

The project's division of the country into regions will be generally familiar, with the exception of what we are calling the Southern Crossroads—a region roughly equivalent to what American historians know as the Old Southwest, comprising Louisiana, Texas, Arkansas, Oklahoma, and Missouri. Since we are committed to covering every state in the Union (though not the territories—e.g., Puerto Rico), Hawaii has been included in a Pacific region with California and Nevada, and Alaska in the Pacific Northwest.

Cultural geographers may be surprised to discover a few states out of their customary places. Idaho, which is usually considered part of the Pacific Northwest, has been assigned to the Mountain West. In our view, the fact that the bulk of Idaho's population lives in the heavily Mormon southern part of the state links it more closely to Utah than to Oregon and Washington. To be sure, we might have chosen to parcel out certain states between regions, assigning northern Idaho and western Montana to the Pacific Northwest or, to take another example, creating a Catholic band running from southern Louisiana through south Texas and across the lower tiers of New Mexico and Arizona on into southern California. The purpose of the project, however, is not to map the country religiously but to explore the ways that politics, public policies, and civil society relate—or fail to relate—to the religion that is on the ground. States have had to be kept intact because when American laws are not made in Washington, D.C., they are made in statehouses. To understand what is decided in Baton Rouge, Louisiana's Catholic south and evangelical north must be seen as engaged in a single undertaking.

That is not to say that the details of American religious demography are unimportant to our purpose. That demography has undergone notable shifts in recent years, and these have affected public life in any number of ways. To reckon with them, it has been essential to assemble the best data available on the religious identities of Americans and how they correlate with voting patterns and views on public issues. As students of American religion know, however, this is far from an easy task. The U.S. Census is prohibited by law from asking questions about religion, and membership reports provided by religious bodies to nongovernmental researchers—when they are provided at all—vary greatly in accuracy. Most public opinion polling does not enable us to draw precise correlations between respondents' views on issues and their religious identity and behavior.

In order to secure the best possible empirical grounding, the project has assembled a range of data from three sources, which are described in detail in the Appendix. These have supplied us with, among other things, information from religious bodies on their membership; from individuals on their religious identities; and from voters in specific religious categories on their political preferences and opinions. (For purposes of clarity, people are described as "adherents" or "members" only when reported as such by a religious institution. Otherwise, they are "identifiers.") Putting this information together with 2000 census and other survey data, the project has been able to create both the best available picture of religion in America today and the most comprehensive account of its political significance.

Religion by Region does not argue that religion plays the same kind of role in each region of the country; nor does it mean to advance the proposition that religion is the master key that unlocks all the secrets of American public life. As the tables of contents of the individual volumes make clear, each region has its distinctive religious layout, based not only on the numerical strength of particular religious bodies but also on how those bodies, or groups of them, function on the public stage. In some regions, religion serves as a shaping force; in others it is a subtler conditioning agent. Our objective is simply to show what the picture looks like from place to place and to provide consistent data and a framework of discussion sufficient to enable useful contrasts and comparisons to be drawn.

A project of such scope and ambition does not come cheap. We are deeply indebted to the Lilly Endowment for making it possible.

Mark Silk
Hartford, Connecticut
May 2004

INTRODUCTION

NOT OZ

Philip Barlow and Becky Cantonwine

Officials imbibed enthusiasm when, in 1934, they laid the cornerstone of the capitol building in Bismarck, North Dakota. One earnest speaker prophesied that the town was destined to become the center of Western civilization. It hasn't worked out.

Like North Dakota, the Midwest has an identity problem. It also has an image problem. The two are related, but not identical, and each can be turned on its head to be or seem to be a virtue.

The identity problem derives from life in a vast, flat space that lacks a boundary, a culture, and a defined consciousness so contoured as that in, say, the South or New York or the Mormon corridor in the Mountain West. Within this great Midwestern expanse—the largest region in the nation—terrain and cultures range widely. Parts of its cultural north are *very* north, Canadian-like, or almost Scandinavian. Its southern parts take on characteristics of the South or, a century back, of the South and the anti-South. The physical, western halves of the Great Plains states are scarcely distinguishable from eastern Montana, Wyoming, and Colorado. And the populated states on the region's eastern boundary are "back east," a half-foreign land from a perch west of Topeka. The Ohioan Louis Bromfield's confusion about his state applies to broader (not all) aspects of the Midwest: "the farthest west of the east, and the farthest east of the west, the farthest north of the south, and the farthest south of the north."

The issue can be bared soberly—or otherwise, as by poet Dave Etter's "Henry Lichenwalner" in *West of Chicago*:

> Here in Alliance, Illinois,
> I'm living in the middle,
> standing on the Courthouse lawn

11

in the middle of town,
in the middle of my life,
a self-confessed middlebrow,
a member of the middle class,
and of course Middle Western,
the middle, you see, the middle,
believing in the middle way,
standing here at midday
in the middle of the year,
breathing the farm-fragrant air
of Sunflower County,
in the true-blue middle
of middle America,
in the middle of my dreams.

All this might yield, in some, a pale malaise. But the problem is often invert-ed, becoming the seed of confidence. As John Fenton writes in *Midwest Politics*: Unlike folks in Texas or Vermont, who identify strongly with the Lone Star State or New England, "most Midwesterners think of themselves as Americans. They live in America, for the Midwest *is* America" (italics added). The Minnesota his-torian Annette Atkins argues that even Midwestern language is widely taken as the standard dialect of the nation. The news anchor and South Dakotan Tom Brokaw addresses the country in his native Midwestern tongue; Dan Rather took speech lessons to conquer his Texas drawl. Moreover, a measure of pride is taken for granted in a region that provides the nation its bread and for a century sup-plied its economic thrust.

Too chronic to be a "crisis," the Midwestern identity problem thus consists of being lost in the middle—feeling forgotten, not clearly formed, undistinctive. Its redeemed mirror image (or conceit) is that the region defines the nation. There may always be Disneyworld, Broadway, or Hollywood—good for vacations. But the "heartland" is the country's mainstream—its normality, core, and microcosm; its representative and steady essence.

Beyond identity is image, also an issue in the Midwest. L. Frank Baum drew on (and, ambiguously, added to) its rural version: You do not understand, said Dorothy, in Oz, to the Scarecrow,

"because you have no brains. No matter how dreary and gray
our homes are, we people of flesh and blood would rather live
there than in any other country....There is no place like home."
The Scarecrow sighed. "Of course I cannot understand it,"
he said. "If your heads were stuffed with straw, like mine, you
would probably all live in the beautiful places, and then Kansas

would have no people at all. It is fortunate for Kansas that you have brains."

The rural Midwest and the Plains in particular are thus "not Oz." Seen through this lens they are unimaginative, puritanical, conservative, boring—a place for Muggles. In turn, such bloated Midwestern cities as Detroit, Cleveland, Toledo, and Gary constitute the "Rust Belt;" decrepit, dirty, tired places that used to drive America's old-fashioned industries, like steel, before the progress of computers and modern technology. The Midwest in this hybrid imagery becomes "flyover country," the void between the coasts. The coasts are where the chic and interesting people live, where the real action happens in news, entertainment, and the arts. Something of this perspective is apparent when *Time* reports on an important Picasso exhibit when it appears in New York—not when it opens earlier in Minneapolis.

On the other hand, this image can morph into a badge of honor. News media, scholars and others may see the Midwest as uninspiring shades of beige or gray, but they also frequently view it as virtuous. Its very lack of sophistication and cosmopolitan bustle spare it much temptation and corruption—Carl Sandberg's "Chicago" conjuring an exception that proves the rule. It is fodder for debate whether the Iowa painter Grant Wood, who came from a Quaker family, was, in his famous "American Gothic," celebrating or mocking that pitchfork-bearing farmer and wife (or father and spinster daughter). In either case, while the couple may not have much fun, one imagines them honest, hard working, frugal, self-effacing, dependable, and not likely to put up with nonsense. Though everyone notices that times are a-changin', that television and the Internet and American mobility are eroding aspects of regional distinctions, the Midwest retains its own character. It is often portrayed as the bastion of values associated with a rural past of austere means, inhabited by people who distinctively value community, practicality, church, family, decency, hard labor, neighborliness, privacy, and resolve in adverse conditions.

The myth of the Midwest, then—sensed and asserted sometimes from within and without—is that the region is bland but virtuous, and that its identity is weak, though tough to define precisely because it actually is the nation's Heartland, the real America. Nor are such stereotypes wholly lacking in plausible sources.

Even brief reflection, however, should rupture these daydreams, leaving one humble at the prospect of uttering anything accurate and worth saying about the contemporary and disparate 60 million citizens who inhabit Ohio, Indiana, Illinois, Michigan, Wisconsin, Minnesota, the Dakotas, Iowa, Nebraska, and Kansas. Was it the Midwest—or was it America—whose inchoate character was given form by Frank Lloyd Wright's prairie-informed change of architectural perspective? Can we think humorless a land that contributed Johnny Carson and

David Letterman to the nation's late evenings? Or construe as homogenous a region that produced both Phyllis Schlafly and Betty Friedan, the Republican Party and Students for a Democratic Society, Bob Dole and Jesse Ventura, Billy Sunday and Malcolm X? The region's people are many, its terrain vast. As we try to link them, some modern-day Tertullian is sure to ask, "What hath Cleveland to do with Omaha?"

In pondering a response, the chapters that follow offer many connections and contrasts, wrestling also with what does and does not render the Midwest different from other regions. In varying ways and degrees, they take into account the relative newness of the land for non-native peoples; the swiftness of the region's development; the consequences of the fleet pace with which the land was divided and the cities industrialized; the links with the nineteenth century's westward expansion—its destiny seemingly manifest—and the civil war that reshaped the region and the nation. The point of this book, however, is not a regional history, but a historically informed account of the religious heart of the heartland. How do Midwestern religion and culture affect one another? How is this disclosed in the public realm? And what about this manifestation is distinctively Midwestern?

The table of contents suggests the salient aspects. Philip Barlow begins by sketching a demographic portrait of the region in both its secular and religious dimensions, providing a statistical context for reading subsequent chapters. In the process, he examines hard numbers to test the notion that the Midwest comprises America's common denominator. Identifying a cluster of traits that distinguish religion in the region as a whole, he then illustrates Midwestern typicalities and diversities with a detailed look at four states—Michigan, Illinois, Kansas, and South Dakota—each representing a specific subregion.

Mark Noll examines the "earnest, evangelical, and energetic" Protestantism emerging from the mingled influences of early Midwestern settlers and of events and trends experienced by their descendants. The great national contribution of these believers, Noll writes, has been "faithful self-discipline of moral purpose." Their great contribution to religious life has been "faithful development of stable churches for stable communities." Noll draws on denominational and ethnic demographic data to comment on bridges between these groups and public life. He points to long-term influences on, and changes in, those public roles, speculating that the growing megachurch movement may be the newest chapter of a history founded strongly in Methodist community building.

The unique concentration of Lutherans in the upper Midwest dictates independent attention to them. In "The Lutheran Difference: What More Than Nice?" DeAne Lagerquist analyzes "the Lutheran difference" in the mode and attributed meaning of public activities. Beyond statistics testifying to their impressive presence, Lagerquist cites Lutheran leadership in education, sacred music and architecture, social service, and political life that have emerged from Martin Luther's visions of service and from cultural and historical factors shaping the various Lutheran bodies since the Reformation. Suggesting that "the Lutheran way is to address the whole person and the whole situation, to link person to principle, and to act simultaneously as citizen and believer," Lagerquist argues for a diffusion of Lutheran ways in upper Midwestern culture that in some ways parallels Mark Noll's insights into Methodist influence elsewhere in the region.

Jay Dolan writes of the "Different Breed of Catholics" who have flourished in the Midwest. Reflecting the openness of the land and the innovative spirit of those who settled it, these believers have varied in their distinctiveness over time. Dolan explains how these differences relate to the post-Civil War industrial development of the region and to the presence of especially influential ethnic groups. An openness to reform exceeding that in earlier and more urban regions long characterized the Midwest, but has narrowed in recent decades. The account closes by profiling Midwestern versions of national issues: numerical decline of clergy and of women religious in parochial schools, debate about tuition vouchers used at those schools, the sexual abuse scandal, and denominational social activism.

A mix of religions new to America has arisen in recent decades with the arrival in large numbers of adherents from the Middle and Far East. In "Religion and Recent Immigrants," Raymond Williams describes the result: a distinctive new ferment in American civic life. Departing from the pattern established in previous essays, Williams suggests that the experience of these new immigrants is not distinctly different from that in other regions, but constitutes local expressions of a national story. "The most important factor in shaping American Christianity and the future of American religion," he writes, "is the changing pattern of immigration that through the centuries selected people from different countries with a variety of religious affiliations." First examining the history of American immigration, he then reports how individual immigrants or families affect and are affected by the societies where they settle. Williams points to specific areas through which these impacts occur and to agencies, such as schools and interfaith councils, that facilitate a reopening of the negotiation of the religious and moral foundations of the region's civic life.

Chicago anchors and radiates influence into the Midwest and beyond. Its contemporary reality also erodes popular images of the Midwestern "Rust Belt," for it is exceeded nowhere else in its rapid transformation from the modern industrial city to the global, post-industrial, post-modern city of the future. Elfriede Wedam and Lowell Livezey argue as much by offering the only chapter in this eight-volume series that explores a single metropolis: "Religion in the *City on the Make*." Examining religion there in "the new context of technological change, global demographic shifts, cultural transformation, and political realignment," they look closely at the roles of congregations in several neighborhoods with diverse economic, ethnic, and political components. Reporting on the importance of four dimensions of urban space (centrality, sense of local place, political culture, and diversity), the authors argue that "religion as a public, cultural, and moral force competes vigorously with political and economic power in shaping the *kind* of place Chicago is."

Finally, looking for patterns of regional distinctiveness more locally than in sub-regions entailing several states, Rhys Williams considers urban, suburban, and rural forms of religious expression in ways no other chapter in the Religion by Region series attempts. Williams is sensitive to the difference and intersections between physical place and symbolic location. After contrasting empirical realities with popular conceptions of the Midwest's past and present, he reminds us that despite the seeming stability of religious traditions, "everyday, lived religion...depends crucially on place to constitute what it is"—and thus is influenced by where it is practiced. Urban religion is diverse, influenced by high population, and entrepreneurial. Suburban forms are colored by migration from cities, and are neither as homogeneous as they once were nor as they are sometimes portrayed. Rural religion is more conservative than its metropolitan cousins, but is still diverse and sometimes innovative in seeking survival amid rural decline.

Peter Williams brings the volume to summation by reminding us of what the earlier essays have shown: that in studying public religion in the Midwest, with its debatable definitions, we should look not for a single essence but at the particular mix of participants and the particular dynamics at work. He offers brief historical synthesis, stressing the importance of religious freedom from the earliest governance of the Northwest Ordinance, a pattern that differed from regions settled earlier. In this context, Williams shows how individual denominations were more or less suited to thrive in these middle lands. Looking then at specific examples of growing Midwestern pluralism, Williams concludes that these entwined themes have, at the beginning of the twenty-first century, resulted in a regionally distinctive religious and civic culture.

These eight chapters, taken together, offer an account of religion in the public life of the similar-but-different Midwest. For those hoping better to understand the vast and unevenly surprising Heartland, the book is intended both to provide a resource and to provoke further inquiry.

RELIGIOUS AFFILIATION IN
THE MIDWEST AND THE NATION

The charts on the following pages compare two measures of religious identification: self-identification by individuals responding to a survey and adherents claimed by religious institutions. The charts compare regional data for the Midwest and national data for both measures. The sources of the data are described below.

On page 18
Adherents Claimed by Religious Groups

The Polis Center at Indiana University-Purdue University Indianapolis provided the Religion by Region Project with estimates of adherents claimed by religious groups in the Midwest and the nation at large. These results are identified as the North American Religion Atlas (NARA). NARA combines 2000 Census data with the Glenmary Research Center's 2000 Religious Congregations and Membership Survey (RCMS). Polis Center demographers supplemented the RCMS reports with data from other sources to produce estimates for groups that did not report to Glenmary.

On page 19
Religious Self-Identification

Drawn from the American Religious Identification Survey (ARIS 2001), these charts contrast how Americans in the Midwest and the nation at large describe their own religious identities. The ARIS study, conducted by Barry A. Kosmin, Egon Mayer, and Ariela Keysar at the Graduate Center of the City University of New York, includes the responses of 50,283 U.S. households gathered in a series of national, random-digit dialing, telephone surveys.

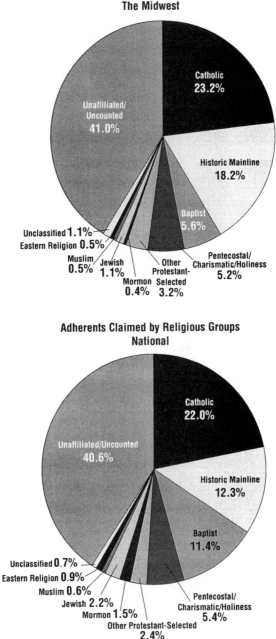

Adherents Claimed by Religious Groups
The Midwest

Catholic
23.2%

Unaffiliated/
Uncounted
41.0%

Historic Mainline
18.2%

Baptist
5.6%

Unclassified 1.1%
Eastern Religion 0.5%
Muslim
0.5%   Jewish
1.1%

Other
Protestant-
Mormon   Selected
0.4%   3.2%

Pentecostal/
Charismatic/Holiness
5.2%

Adherents Claimed by Religious Groups
National

Catholic
22.0%

Unaffiliated/Uncounted
40.6%

Historic Mainline
12.3%

Baptist
11.4%

Unclassified 0.7%
Eastern Religion 0.9%
Muslim 0.6%
Jewish 2.2%
Mormon 1.5%
Other Protestant-Selected
2.4%

Pentecostal/
Charismatic/Holiness
5.4%

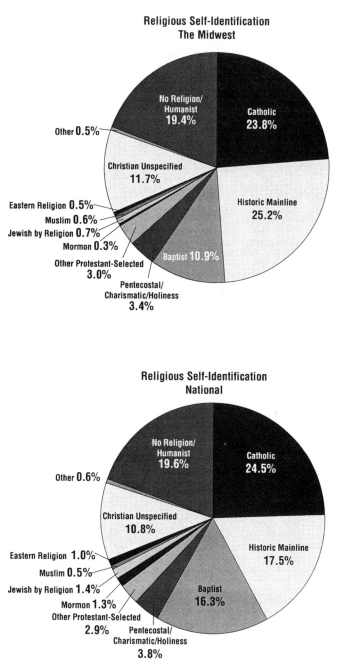

Religious Self-Identification
The Midwest

No Religion/
Humanist
19.4%

Catholic
23.8%

Other 0.5%

Christian Unspecified
11.7%

Eastern Religion 0.5%
Muslim 0.6%
Jewish by Religion 0.7%
Mormon 0.3%
Other Protestant-Selected
3.0%

Historic Mainline
25.2%

Baptist 10.9%

Pentecostal/
Charismatic/Holiness
3.4%

Religious Self-Identification
National

No Religion/
Humanist
19.6%

Catholic
24.5%

Other 0.6%

Christian Unspecified
10.8%

Eastern Religion 1.0%
Muslim 0.5%
Jewish by Religion 1.4%
Mormon 1.3%
Other Protestant-Selected
2.9%

Historic Mainline
17.5%

Baptist
16.3%

Pentecostal/
Charismatic/Holiness
3.8%

Chapter One

A Demographic Portrait:
America Writ Small?

Philip Barlow[1]

"Middletown" was the code name bequeathed in 1929 to Muncie, Indiana, by the researchers Robert and Helen Lynd. In that year, the pair published a pioneering community study that became a sociological reference point for the character of American life. *Middletown: A Study in Modern American Culture* proved seminal—and controversial—in ways its authors had not envisioned. Three-quarters of a century later, the Lynds may be seen to have spawned an entire subfield: "Muncieology." Beyond students, scholars, and concepts, Muncieology is embodied (in various languages) in hundreds of essays, articles, dissertations, monographs, follow-up studies, documentary films, Web sites, and a Center for Middletown Studies at Indiana's Ball State University.

Widely celebrated, the Lynds's work was also criticized. So relentless was the criticism on one point, indeed, that in a speech 55 years after the original study, Helen Lynd denied that she and her husband (a Protestant minister) had claimed that Middletown was a typical city. This was true in some respects, but her denial was also belied by the Lynds's original book. The two main criteria for the selection of Middletown had been "that the city be as representative as possible of contemporary American life" and that it be "compact and homogeneous enough to be manageable in such a total-situation study." In areas such as climate, rate of growth, industrialization, and "middleness"—a perceived absence of extreme problems or virtues—the Lynds found Muncie well-suited to their needs. It also fit their seventh criterion for representativeness: "the city should, if possible, be in that common-denominator of America, the Middle West."

Asserting that any particular locale represents the nation, then, can raise hackles. Yet such claims have often been attached to Muncie, to Indianapolis, to

Peoria, and to other cities, to various Midwestern states, and to the region as a whole. Is it demographically true? Is the Midwest the most representative region in the land?

Secular Profile

In important respects, the answer is yes. But the "yes" requires interpretation and challenge, as does the "no" that could also be proffered. Nonetheless, it is not wholly without cause that politicians or merchants pondering a new idea or product ask, "Will it sell in Peoria?" There does in fact exist a sense in which the Midwest tends closely to mirror the composite United States. Data from the 2000 census, including 34 categories detailing aspects of area, population, age, race, occupation, marital status, gender, and education, confirm that the Midwest more nearly than any other single region resembles the country as a whole.[2]

As we define it, the Midwest is geographically enormous. These 11 states contain almost one-quarter of the territory of the continental United States. The 60 million people who live in this vast expanse almost match the population of the South and exceed every other region. This large population, stretching across the center of the country, constitutes 21 percent of the U.S. populace—a sampling so thorough as to help explain why the Midwest so closely reflects the nation's demography.

This similarity begins with the states' typical size. Lacking both giants and dwarves because of the "when" and "where" of its settlement in U.S. history, the Midwest includes none of the country's 10 largest or 10 smallest states. The average size of its states (62,048 square miles) most closely of all regions approximates the national average. Similarly, the region's average population per state (5.345 million) makes it the nation's most "normal." Its population density of 86 people per square mile, while substantially below the national mean (139), approximates the national median: four regions are more densely packed, three are less so.

Midwesterners correspond most closely of all regions to U.S. numbers in gender distribution and in nearly every age category. Typical numbers of births occur here, and the percentage of the population less than 18 years of age most closely resembles that in the United States. While a significant portion of the population leaves the area upon reaching adulthood, the population rebounds in the 45-64 age group to proportions closer to the nation's than those in any other region. It maintains this parallel through the end of the human life span. Midwesterners also most closely approach national norms in the percentage of its population who are married, who have never married, who are divorced, and who are widowed.

The extent of Midwesterners' education, along with their occupations, is also strikingly close to the composite nation's. The 23 percent of its citizens who have achieved at least a bachelor's degree is closer to the national rate than that of any other region. The portion over 25 years of age who lack a high school diploma (16 percent) is closer than any but the Mid-Atlantic region. Perhaps as a consequence, Midwesterners are quite typical of Americans at work. The region varies no more than 0.5 percent from the nation in its percentage of service workers, sales and office personnel, and construction and maintenance laborers. It is also quite representative of the nation in its percentage of professionals and those in management. A notable exception to this parroting of the country is in the production and transportation workforce, where the Midwest sports a significantly higher percentage than any other region. Even this, however, may result from the region's centeredness; Chicago's O'Hare airport, for example, has long been the world's busiest.

Although a coastal outsider may fancy neo-*American Gothic* farm couples populating the landscape, the Midwest has a smaller percentage of those employed in farming, fishing, and forestry than five of the country's other seven regions. This is a function in part of the disappearance of the family farm and the growth of mega-agribusiness, requiring more machinery, more technology, larger farms—and fewer people. While Midwestern land devoted to farming increased by 27 million acres between 1964 and 2001, the number of farms shrank from 1,130,000 to 698,000. The U.S. remains the granary of the world, and in 2001 the Midwest produced more than half the nation's wheat, nearly 8 billion of its 9.5 billion bushels of corn, and 2.3 billion of its 2.9 billion bushels of soybeans.

It is racially that the Midwest varies most widely from the United States as a whole. While not starkly unusual, the region differs from the nation's overall racial composition more than do the Mid-Atlantic, Southern Crossroads, New England, and South regions. It is less Asian (1.9 percent of its population) than most regions, more Caucasian (84 percent) than any region but New England (87 percent; U.S.: 75 percent), and has especially few who identify themselves as being multi-racial or of a race other than the numerically dominant categories noted here. With 10 percent of its populace being African-American, the region has a larger share than four regions, though a smaller share than the South, Mid-Atlantic, and Southern Crossroads. The Midwest has fewer Hispanics (5 percent) than all other regions (U.S.: 13 percent), though this is less atypical than may at first appear: several regions fall within 2.5 percent of the Midwest's proportion. American Indians make up 0.9 percent of America's population, while the Midwest has only 0.6 percent. This, however, is a greater percentage than in five other regions. The Midwest is sharply the lowest of regions in the percentage of its inhabitants who are foreign-born. The 5.7 percent of its populace born in a foreign land, indeed, is less than two-thirds the proportion of the next lowest region (the Pacific Northwest, 9.5 percent) and about one-fifth the proportion of the Pacific region (25.3 percent).

Within the Midwest terrain, populations and cultures range widely—and these variations help define the region. The Plains states (Iowa, Kansas, Nebraska, and the Dakotas) are distinguishable from the states adjoining the Great Lakes (Minnesota, Wisconsin, Michigan, Illinois, Indiana, and Ohio). Alternatively, the states could rationally be divided east and west of the Mississippi River, by northern and southern tiers, by political orientation, or by other traits.

At 12.5 million people, Illinois is the region's most populous state. North Dakota, with 642,000, is the least; fewer than 10 people inhabit each square mile there, a rate less than half that of Nebraska. The Midwest is nine times more densely inhabited, the nation 14 times, and Ohio 28 times. During the past decade, population growth in the 50 states has been fastest in the West and South. Ranked according to rate of annual percentage increase, Midwestern states are largely in the bottom third. The fastest growing is Minnesota—ranked twenty-first; the slowest is North Dakota—ranked fiftieth. The region as a whole grew 7.78 percent between 1990 and 2000, while the United States grew 13.2 percent.

Seventy-five percent of Midwestern citizens reside in urban areas, 4 percent below the national average. These urban centers are anchored by metropolitan Chicago's 8.4 million people, and include metropolitan Detroit (4.7 million), Minneapolis/St. Paul (3 million), Cleveland (2.9 million), Cincinnati (1.7 million), Indianapolis (1.6 million), Milwaukee (1.6 million), and Columbus (1.5 million). On the plains, Omaha has 734,000 people in its metropolitan range; Wichita has 581,000; Des Moines has 463,000; and Sioux Falls, South Dakota has 177,000.

Religious Profile

The religious composition of this vast and diverse region is affected by yearly developments and the mobility of modern America. It is based, however, on layers of migration, immigration, and settlement that occurred in the nineteenth and twentieth centuries. As in its secular demographics, the region religiously is in some ways abnormally normal, the closest microcosm of the nation. In other respects, the Midwest is simply different.

The region abounds in Roman Catholics, Lutherans, and United Methodists who, respectively, represent 39 percent, 14 percent, and 7 percent of all religious adherents, according to 2000 figures reported by the denominations themselves and supplemented by demographers to account for uncounted groups (as reported in the North American Religion Atlas [NARA]). Those regional proportions are close to national ones for Catholics, somewhat low for Methodists (10 percent of adherents nationally), and dramatically high for Lutherans, who in the country as a whole make up less than half their Midwestern proportion.

A substantial number of Protestants in historically African-American denominations (primarily Methodist, Baptist, and Pentecostal) thrive in the Midwest, especially in urban areas. These constitute 11 percent of the region's religious adherents (markedly less than the 15 percent in the Southern Crossroads region or the 21 percent in the South, but more than any other region).

Other Midwestern Baptists claim 5 percent of the religiously affiliated, and Holiness and Pentecostal bodies represent almost another 5 percent. Presbyterians, German groups, Christian Churches and Churches of Christ, Disciples of Christ, Episcopalians, and the United Church of Christ (courtesy of a westward migration from New England during the early nineteenth century), make up a smaller but significant part of the religious populace, each from 1 to 3 percent. Jews comprise 1.8 percent of adherents: twice the rate of the Southern Crossroads, but less than any other region, including the South and the Mountain West. The Muslim population, at 0.9 percent of adherents in the Midwest, is similar to that in New England, less than in the Pacific and Mid-Atlantic, but greater than in the rest of the country. The region's proportion of Buddhists, Hindus, and other Eastern religionists relative to other adherents is the lowest in the United States—tied with the South and Southern Crossroads.

Compared to the United States, the Midwest is similar—more so than all other regions—in its proportion of adherents who are Catholic, Baptist, Holiness/Pentecostal, and those reporting no religious affiliation. It is closer than most regions to national rates of Muslims, Humanists, and unspecified Protestants. By contrast, it least resembles the nation in other respects, having a sharply thinner proportion of members of The Church of Jesus Christ of Latter-day Saints (Mormons) and Eastern religions, and a greater slice of historic mainline Protestants: Methodists, Presbyterians, Congregationalists, Disciples, and Episcopalians, as well as the ambiguously mainline Lutherans and northern (American) Baptists. Twenty-five percent of Midwesterners identify as mainline (compared with 17 percent throughout the United States), 12 percent as unspecified Protestant, and 1.3 percent as Humanists. Of those who could be categorized as mainline or evangelical, the Midwest is the only region with balance (53 percent mainline, 47 percent evangelical). New England and the Mid-Atlantic are heavily mainline (respectively 73 percent and 69 percent); the other regions are sharply evangelical, (ranging from 65 percent to 76 percent).

Beyond this preliminary relational sketch, several dimensions render the Midwest's religious complexion distinctive. These include the existence in the region of the nation's Bible Suspender; the dominating presence not simply of Catholicism, but of a certain kind of Catholicism; the uniquely Midwestern concoction of what we shall call "Catholics and . . .;" the fact of a Lutheran cultural domain, one of several identifiable Midwestern sub-regions; a series of historical and contemporary idiosyncrasies in the demographics of the region's Protestant and immigrant religions; the impact of various denominational headquarters in the Midwest; and the variations among the 11 states that contribute to this whole, suggested here by a detailed look at four sample states: Michigan, Illinois, South Dakota, and Kansas.

In addition to what space allows for developed attention here, we note also that Chicago is unique to the Midwest— so much so that an entire chapter is devoted to a model of its types of churches and their roles in the public sphere. And unlike, say, Alaska or the Mountain West, where vast spaces are uninhabited and the population is virtually confined to residence in specific spheres, the Midwest is characterized by its own more diffuse patterns of rural, suburban, and urban life, whose dynamics in the religious and public realms are treated in a separate chapter by Rhys Williams. Hence, in addition to what follows in this essay, the table of contents of the volume by itself implies something of what is distinctive about the religious Midwest.

Those unattached to or uncounted and undocumented by some organized religion participating in national surveys constitute a sizeable group: 41 percent of the Midwest's population. Since most of these people are not irreligious, but organizationally unattached, this constitutes the largest "religious" category in the Midwest; Catholics are second at 23 percent. Indeed, the "Nones" (no religious preference) are the fastest growing "religious" category in the nation. They are predominant in every region except New England and the Mid-Atlantic, where they are a close second to Catholics. For this reason, one must distinguish between a percentage of religious adherents and a percentage of the total population when an author in this book and the series of which it is a part, allude to such matters.

In every region, the numbers of "Nones" are sharply lower—about half— when gauged by how people identified themselves in a 2001 telephone poll conducted by the American Religious Identification Survey (ARIS). The numbers are not sharply at odds with other methods of calculation for most religious groups, though analysts sometimes cluster related denominations differently. But the "Nones" are an exception. This may be because individuals do not, by this method, get lost, as they may from denominational records for various reasons, including movement from one location to another. On the other hand, such people may have little active connection with a denomination; clearly, there is a rising tide, especially among those in their late teens and twenties, who construe themselves as "spiritual, not religious," holding little institutional commitment. "Nones" may be moving by stages into or away from a denomination; they may be active seekers or lightly attached to a vestige of their parents' or grandparents' loyalties. This is uncertain, though, and more study is needed on this increasingly numerous body of Americans. The two methods of calculating their numbers must therefore balance rather than trump one another. Even by telephone survey, however, the "Nones" in the Midwest (20 percent of respondents) exceed all individual denominations except Roman Catholics. Their proportion in the populace is lower than in four other regions, higher than in three, and virtually identical to that in the composite United States. Their existence in the Midwest, however, is unevenly spread—and this is important for understanding the region.

The skeptical H. L. Mencken captured public fancy in the mid-1920s by coining the term "Bible Belt," a region that has been and could be defined variously. Traditional and popular notions have since confined the terrain primarily to the Deep South, roughly from eastern Texas to the Carolinas, excluding Florida. So far as areas of highly concentrated church-synagogue-mosque-temple membership serve as definition, however, the traditionally conceived "belt" (the obverse of the "None Zone") is in fact attended by both a "twisted suspender," running vertically in the center of the nation from the Canadian to the Mexican borders, and a "boutonniere" farther west in Mormon Utah and southeast Idaho.

The majority of the national suspender is in the Midwest. It may be apprehended visually through a map in Edwin Gaustad and Philip Barlow's *New Historical Atlas of Religion in America* (p. 352). Here the suspender is defined as a large vertical pattern of counties whose proportion of citizens attached to a church or religion exceeds 75 percent (and, as a penumbra, 65 percent). Running south and slightly east, it covers the whole of North Dakota and western Minnesota, down through eastern South Dakota and northern Iowa. It then twists somewhat westward in its southern descent, encompassing eastern Nebraska and most of Kansas before proceeding out of the region south into Oklahoma and Texas. The figures behind this map do not of themselves demonstrate a high percentage of conservative and fundamentalist evangelicalism, as flourishes in the traditional Bible belt. They do, however, reveal that high rates of connection to organized religion are, contrary to popular imagination, higher in a broad vertical swath in the Midwest than in the horizontal, mythic Bible Belt of the South.

Not only in the Bible suspender but throughout the region, Roman Catholics' presence has long had an impact. Reacting to waves of new immigrants, Henry Bowers, a paranoid intimate of the former mayor of Clinton, Iowa, who had been defeated by the Irish labor vote, gathered a half-dozen associates in March 1887 to organize the nativist American Protective Association. The association, soon half-a-million strong from Detroit to Omaha, pledged its members never to vote for a Catholic nor to hire one when a non-Catholic option existed. Happily, most Bowers-like sentiments have dissipated. With 39 percent of all religious adherents, today's Midwest is dramatically more Catholic than the South (13 percent) and significantly more than the Southern Crossroads (27 percent), the Pacific

Northwest (30 percent), and the Mountain West (35 percent). Roman Catholics in fact constitute the largest denomination in every Midwestern state, and they remain largest in every state except North Dakota even if one combines independent Lutheran denominations.

What is distinctive here, however, is not so much Catholic numbers. It is, instead, the legacy of the *type* of Catholics who came to settle and their engagement with a region that developed at a different time, in a different manner, and with different results than elsewhere. In ways that Jay Dolan treats in a separate chapter, this difference includes especially the early and continued dominance of Midwestern German Catholics, who created a regional Catholicism open to reform and experiment, in marked contrast to the Irish-controlled Catholicism of the Northeast, the French Catholicism of Louisiana, or the Hispanic Catholicism of the Southwest. Irish (especially in Chicago and St. Paul) and other ethnic Catholics have been important in the Midwest, but not as important as the Germans, whose influence can be sensed by conjuring images of Milwaukee and Cincinnati.

This insight has a cognate. The religious kaleidoscope that increasingly draws scholars' and the nation's attention is a diversity for which our language has been too crude. American "diversity" itself has traits. While it has dynamics tending toward a "melting pot," it has additional dynamics, and the overall result is not a melting pot. Inter- and intra-regional diversity yields, rather, a patchwork. Even more, the diversity is marbled, layered, uneven. There is a diversity to this diversity: it is different "here" than "there," different "now" than "then." All this has implications for religion's expression in, and encounter with, local, state, and regional public spheres. The localized manifestations of this "diversity-with-traits" in the Midwest are glimpsed in the pages that follow, but one dimension of it, applied nationally, illustrates the point and can better equip one further to probe the nature of Midwestern religion.

Although the United States is noticeably more diverse than it was a generation ago, this diversity negotiates against enduring regional and local hegemonies, or at least dominances. It remains the case that almost every American state is numerically dominated by a few denominations. Several states, indeed, approach monolithia: Rhode Island is almost as Catholic as Utah is Mormon. But virtually *every* state is so constituted that no more than the three largest denominations within its bounds comprise more than 50 percent of declared religious believers. Frequently this is true of merely the *two* largest denominations (Catholics and Baptists [or Holiness/Pentecostals] in much of the Far West and Southwest; Baptists and Methodists in the South) or even a single denomination (Catholics in all the states of New England). The two or three largest denominations also form majorities in every region; a single one does so in three: New England, the Pacific, and the Mid-Atlantic.

It is not yet clear how the recent child-sex scandal will affect American Catholic membership, but in 2000 the Roman Catholic Church in the United States claimed 62 million members. This is more than three times the number of Southern Baptists, the nation's next largest denomination. Catholicism is the largest denomination in most—and among the three largest denominations in 90 percent of—U.S. counties outside the South and parts of the Southern Crossroads. The source of religious culture in any region outside the South and the northern reaches of the Southern Crossroads is apt to be "Catholicism and —." and it is the *combination* of Catholicism and some other religious influence or influences that most shapes the public religious sensibility in most areas of the United States. Just as the compound of sodium and chloride makes salt, whereas sodium and pentothal make truth serum, so the Catholicism-and-Judaism that presides in even so diverse a place as New York City creates a public culture in ways related but contrasting to the Catholic-and-Baptist forces that rule in Louisiana or the Catholic-Mormon-Baptist dominance in Arizona. In the upper Midwest, "Catholics and—" ends with "Lutherans"—creating a strong, particular culture fondly caricatured by Garrison Keillor. This Lutheran contribution to a unique zone is sufficiently significant to warrant independent focus by DeAne Lagerquist in a chapter that follows.

Demographic idiosyncrasies involving other Protestants distinguish the Midwest. One is a broad horizontal belt across the middle of the country in which Methodists are the largest of all denominations. Looking west, this belt begins in Delaware and Maryland, where Methodism gained its toehold at the end of the eighteenth century. It grows prominent in Ohio and through the Midwest, and then traverses the continent to the western borders of Kansas and Nebraska at the foot of the Rockies. It is a vestige of the more prominent belt of predominance apparent in the first half of the twentieth century, which in turn is a vestige of a nineteenth-century continental Methodist flood. United Methodists in the contemporary Midwest (apart from African-American Methodists, whose numbers are fugitive) represent 7 percent of all adherents—less than in the South (10 percent) and Southern Crossroads (8 percent), but more than elsewhere. While actual numbers of Methodists are heavier in the more populated eastern seaboard, the concentrated belt of east-west Methodist predominance relative to all other adherents remains a particular feature of the Midwest.

By contrast, the Midwest has a notable shortage of Baptists for a region that borders the South and the Southern Crossroads. Baptists (16 percent of the total population, according to ARIS) are by far the largest Protestant body in the United States; in the Midwest they are a substantial but smaller 11 percent. This relative paucity is true of the region as a whole and of each individual state, no one of which achieves the national average in proportion of adherents who are

Baptist. Of Southern Baptists in particular the case is striking. There are more members of the Southern Baptist Convention in the state of Mississippi than there are in the 11 states of the Midwest. Still, because so many Baptists occupy the South and Southern Crossroads and because comparatively so few do elsewhere, their numbers in the composite United States are skewed, making the Midwest most closely resemble the nation.

Another distinction of the region is the strong presence of the Dutch Reformed, whose dominant U.S. cluster lies in western Michigan. As distinct from the smaller concentration of Dutch Reformed in New York and New Jersey, heirs of an era when New York was New Netherlands, Reformed adherents in Michigan have retained much of their Dutch heritage. When the conservative Reformed are linked with conservative confessional churches, such as the non-ELCA Lutherans, and with conservative Congregationalists who never merged with the liberal United Church of Christ, the Midwest's distinctiveness further bares itself. This grouping constitutes 7 percent of all adherents in the region—more than twice that of any other region, more than five times the proportion of most.

Amish and Mennonite communities in the Midwest are the largest in the country. A good many still reside in New York and Pennsylvania, but the Midwest has 50 percent more, with especially strong concentrations in Kansas, Indiana, and Ohio (which has the largest Amish community in the world). Neither in Pennsylvania nor New York nor anywhere else in the country are Pietists and Anabaptists the largest religious grouping in a county. In the Midwest, however, they are largest in 10 counties. The region also has, in South Dakota, the nation's largest concentration of Hutterite Brethren.

The Midwest is also Disciples of Christ terrain, a group who in Des Moines in 1884 first published the *Christian Outlook*, later rechristened *The Christian Century*, which matured to become the preeminent magazine among liberal American Protestants. The Disciples' conservative cousins, the Christian Churches and Churches of Christ, are Midwestern to their core, with an especially heavy presence in Illinois, Indiana, and Ohio. The two denominations are not only stronger here than in other regions; in dozens of Midwestern counties this Restorationist family is the largest of all religious groupings. (The "Churches of Christ," as distinct from the related "Christian Churches and Churches of Christ," are clustered more thoroughly in the South.)

A nineteenth-century rival to this Restorationist family, the Mormons, are a significant (nearly a quarter-million people) but comparatively lighter presence in the region today: 0.7 percent of all adherents (0.3 percent by phone survey). One year after founding a church and publishing the Book of Mormon in New York, Joseph Smith moved west and spent the balance of his career in Ohio, Missouri, and Illinois. A historic temple at Kirtland, Ohio, and especially the newly reconstructed one at Nauvoo, Illinois, center and showpiece of nineteenth-century Mormonism, annually attract tens of thousands of pilgrims and tourists, Latterday Saint and otherwise. After Joseph Smith's death, those who formed The Reorganized Church of Jesus Christ of Latter Day Saints (as of 2001, the Community of Christ) did not follow Brigham Young west. This body's headquarters, formerly at Lamoni, Iowa, where the church maintains a college, are just beyond the Kansas border in Independence, Missouri. Thirty-seven thousand of its 99,000 U.S. members live in the Midwest, with another 20,000 in Missouri.

Denominational Headquarters

It was hard for antebellum citizens in Missouri or Illinois not to notice the Mormons. The presence of some denominations' headquarters in the modern Midwest can, however, affect the public without public awareness. Besides politics and other matters, a headquarters may affect local, state, or area economies and culture. An example: As the nearest urban center, Louisville very much influences the so-called "Kentuckiana" region, including southern Indiana, just across the bridges spanning the Ohio River. In June 2001, the Louisville *Courier-Journal* reported on the economic impact of the presence of the headquarters of the Presbyterian Church (USA). Separated since the Civil War, northern and southern Presbyterians merged in 1983. They sought eventually to consolidate their New York and Atlanta offices in a neutral city. At their 1987 General Assembly in Biloxi, Mississippi, the denomination chose Louisville over Kansas City because of the effective pitch of city officials, which promised to save them millions of dollars, included the donation of buildings, and featured a video presentation showing a downtown rally in which a multi-faith crowd of 5,000 Louisvillians urged the Presbyterians to come. They did.

Several years later, by the time the denomination held its first General Assembly in Louisville in 2001, attendees found a steadily improving neighborhood by the Ohio River and new businesses that city leaders, encouraged by their successful courtship of the Presbyterians, were able to lure to town. Church statistics noted that the presence of the denomination brought economic implications. In 2000, this included a $30-million payroll that produced $1.2 million in state and local payroll taxes. For the following year, the church budgeted $1.6 million in local hotel costs for meeting rooms, meals, and overnight stays for visiting church workers and guests, as well as $3.1 million in airline costs. The headquarters attracted a significant talent pool to the vicinity, with impact on the city and on local congregations. Among other things, it also raised the profile of Louisville Presbyterian Seminary and the students and personnel it was able to attract.

It remains for future students, reporters, scholars, and business interests to calculate the economic (not to mention cultural) effect on other cities and areas of additional denominational headquarters. In at least some instances, such as the Presbyterian case or the national center of the Islamic Society of North America in Plainfield, Indiana, the headquarters have been located in the Midwest precisely because of its geographic, moral, or symbolic "middleness." The Midwest harbors within its boundaries the headquarters of the largest branches of Lutheranism: the Evangelical Lutheran Church in America (ELCA) in Chicago; the Lutheran Church-Missouri Synod in St. Louis, across the Mississippi River from Illinois; and the Wisconsin Evangelical Lutheran Synod in Milwaukee. The headquarters of the United Church of Christ are in Cleveland; those of the Disciples of Christ are in Indianapolis. Others include the Nazarenes in Kansas City; the Brethren in Ashland, Ohio; The Church of the Brethren in Elgin, Illinois; the Church of God in Anderson, Indiana; and the Community of Christ in Kansas City (on the Missouri side at Independence). The Christian Reformed Church is centered in Grand Rapids, Michigan. Three of the six U.S. Synod offices of the Reformed Church in America are in Michigan, Iowa, and Illinois. In his chapter on immigrant religions, Raymond Williams notes several national centers in the Midwest in addition to the Muslim one in Indiana: Tibetan Buddhists, in Bloomington, Indiana; Kananya Indian Christians in Chicago; the Nation of Islam, also in Chicago; and the Baha'is in Wilmette, Illinois. Focusing on the religious-cultural negotiations among these groups rather than the economic point made here, Williams mentions also the non-territorial Korean Presbyterian Presbytery formed from Chicago.

As analogues to the meta-religious impact of these headquarters, one could attempt to gauge the modern cultural and economic—not simply the educational and religious—consequence of the presence of religiously affiliated colleges and seminaries that sprang up throughout the Midwest, especially in the nineteenth century. One should keep this in mind when noting the presence of specific colleges cited in several chapters of this book. The main campus of Reform Judaism's seminary, Hebrew Union College, remains in Cincinnati, where Isaac Mayer Wise planted it in 1875. Lutherans by themselves have two dozen affiliated schools in the region. Catholics have almost three times that many—and Notre Dame by itself exudes an influence beyond South Bend and into the region and nation. Another example, beyond seminaries and colleges, is the Lilly Endowment, one of the largest private philanthropic institutions in the world. The Endowment's philosophy is very publicly tied to mainline Protestant concerns, and the institution leaves a large footprint—economic, educational, and otherwise—in and far beyond its Indianapolis home.

Four Case Studies

Later chapters in this volume, especially those on Catholics and Protestants, are demographically rich in their own right. Mark Noll's analysis of Protestants identifies four sub-regions in the Midwest. What follows here is a zoomed-in look at one state from each of these sub-regions. Two of the states rest on the Plains, two adjoin the Great Lakes. Illinois is the most populous state in the region; South Dakota is virtually the least. Michigan occupies the Midwest's northeast corner, Kansas its southwest. Together these four should convey some local particulars while symbolizing the region's diversity.

South Dakota

The Dakotas share much beyond a name. Both exhibit a sometimes proud, sometimes wounded sense of being forgotten by the rest of the country. "The American Outback" is how *Newsweek* characterized them a few years back. Their eastern halves have more in common with each other than with their respective wests. Some believe the original states should have been divided east from west along the Missouri River, not north from south along the line of a bureaucrat's imagination.

At less than 10 people per square mile, South Dakota is scarcely more densely packed than its northern namesake. Nearly the size of California, the Dakotas together are home to 1.4 million people (fewer, even if coupled with everyone in Montana, than the population of metropolitan Minneapolis/St. Paul). The county housing Rapid City gained 10 percent in population between 1990 and 2000; that of Sioux Falls gained 19 percent. But more counties are losing rather than gaining people, which has implications for the state's psyche. The Dakotas have always seemed a place to be *from*. Hazardous, flooding rivers and cyclical climatic extremes bring dry spells with drought, grasshopper invasions, dust storms, and prairie fires, as well as wet cycles with torrential rains, devastating blizzards, and floods. Eighty percent of those who engaged the Homestead Act (1863) left within 20 years, seeking more plausible terrain for survival. The contemporary state has the highest proportion in the Midwest of people under 18 years of age, but the lowest proportion of people aged 18–44 and 44–64. That is, many leave for wider opportunities when they come of age, an issue with which North Dakota also wrestles.

This dearth and instability of residents conditions the extent and nature of the public and religious institutions South Dakota is able to sustain (and which sustain it). Many small-town classrooms and many pulpits remain vacant or are staffed through revolving doors—a function both of harsh physical conditions and Dakota's agricultural and oil industry economy: boom and bust. On the other hand, such conditions may in their own way foster a religious sensitivity and network: the percentage of citizens religiously unaffiliated is only 30 percent, lower than any state in the region except North Dakota, and compared with 49 percent in Indiana and 63 percent in the Pacific Northwest. In any event, at the beginning of the twenty-first century, the Dakotas had the highest rates of poverty in the region, and South Dakota's rate (13.2 percent) was worse than North Dakota's (11.9 percent). People seem forever to be leaving the family farm, and lamentation is common as "agribusiness" displaces what for many has been a way of life. Nonetheless, South Dakota remains the most rural of Midwestern states; barely half of its citizens reside in urban areas, as compared with 61 percent in Iowa and 75 percent in the Midwest in general.

The Dakotas share the Midwest's lowest percentage (by far) of Hispanics, African Americans, Asians, and those born in any foreign country—and a dramatically larger share of Native Americans. North Dakota has eight times the regional proportion, South Dakota has sharply more; around 59,000, more than 8 percent of its populace. Caucasians and American Indians, indeed, comprise 97 percent of South Dakota's population. Much of the area's history derives from the sometimes redeeming, more often distressing, encounters among Lakota/Dakota/Nakota peoples, and of their constriction before the onslaught of white settlement and culture.

At its most dramatic, this engagement has been bloody. It is no accident that the state's southwest includes a state park, a city, and a county named Custer. Not 30 miles southeast of Custer County is Wounded Knee. There, in December 1890, American troops massacred approximately 350 Minneconjou Indians, some of whom were participants in the Ghost Dance movement. Some were also, amidst high tensions resulting from the recent assassination of Sitting Bull at the Standing Rock reservation, possessed of a sense of messianic power that led them to believe that ritual "ghost shirts" rendered them invulnerable to the bullets of the U.S. Seventh Cavalry. In 1973, Russell Means and Dennis Banks, leaders of the American Indian Movement, drew national attention by leading 300 Indians in seizing the hamlet of Wounded Knee as part of America's wider civil rights unrest. Less dramatic but more grinding are the persistent poverty, dependence, and despondency that still thrive in parts of the reservations, though a renaissance of cultural pride shines through in diverse ways.

The political movement toward sovereignty rests in part on a sense of cultural distinctiveness; control over land and collective identity relies heavily on religious expression for South Dakota Indian people. A renaissance of "traditional" Lakota/Dakota/Nakota practices thus arose in association with the political activism of the 1960s and 1970s, and these have continued to the present. Sweat lodges, vision quests, and Sun Dances have all reappeared. Spiritual expression has become critical to various kinds of healing practices, whether for individuals and sickness or for collectivities and social trauma.

The most enduring form of native spirituality in the modern era has been that associated with the use of peyote. For more than a century, this has induced tension with enforcement agencies and court battles in the Dakotas and in the country. In 1918, peyote practitioners drew on both native and Christian notions and incorporated as the Native American Church. Adherents in South Dakota are difficult to quantify, but interest in this and other expressions of native spirituality has grown for decades. Generally, they have had physical and spiritual relationships with the land. Places matter, as Rhys Williams argues later in this volume, and specific places for Native peoples may matter more acutely, as Philip Deloria points out in the Mountain West volume of the Religion by Region series. They may be holy, analogous to the significance of churches among Christians. South Dakota's Bear Butte, for example, is crucial in the cosmology even of Montana's Northern Cheyenne. American Indians naturally react with displeasure to outsiders' disturbance of sacred places, whether in the interest of science, tourism, or the search for oil. Arvil Looking Horse, nineteenth-generation keeper of the sacred White Buffalo Calf pipe, put it this way to the state legislature in February 2004: "The legislature should respect our homeland, the Black Hills, and all our sacred sites."

By the end of the nineteenth century Episcopalians had surrendered dominance on the eastern seaboard, while gaining ascendancy in a few scattered counties in Texas and in South Dakota. In Dakota their adherents were not primarily English, but Native American converts. In the Christian spectrum, Episcopalian orientation to ritual, mystery, and sacrament comported comparatively well with Native American sensibilities.

More than any other denomination, Episcopalians trained Indian clergy and missionaries. Many were trained in Episcopalian schools and returned to their people to serve as Indian clergy. In the austere and open spaces of Dakota they conducted services in Lakota and participated in powerful traditions of Indian-language hymn singing. Indian clergy, to draw on Philip Deloria again, found ways to transcend their denominations. The Brotherhood of Christian Unity helped support a Christianity that was truly Lakota/Dakota/Nakota. They controlled money, resources, and meetings within the state. This system began to crumble only after World War II, when the Church embraced an assimilation policy. Many Indian people, having traveled the world, returned then to the reservations.

Contemporary South Dakota is the only state in the country in which Episcopalians are in several pockets the largest religious group. Among Protestants, they are the largest denomination in more than a half-dozen counties. In one diocese randomly selected in 2004 in Sioux Falls, the bishop—himself an Indian—presided over a diocese consisting of 50-60 percent Native Americans.

Presbyterians, Methodists, the Evangelical Covenant Church, and various others have missions or outreach programs on or near Rosebud, Pine Ridge, and a half-dozen other reservations. Many, both on and off the reservation, are either critical of such efforts as acts of cultural imperialism or grateful for the active interest and care extended in spiritual and physical ways. In some instances, Indian officials of Indian Christianity have successfully retained older native cultural practices. It is not uncommon, indeed, for an Indian to maintain allegiances at the same time to traditional native spirituality, to the syncretic Native American Church, and to some form of the Christian faith.

As elsewhere in the upper Midwest, however, those who most obviously dominate the religious landscape are Roman Catholics, among whom are thousands of Indians, and Lutherans. Forty percent of the state's populace is of German descent, helping to explain this showing. Strength in numbers does not inevitably imply institutional strength, however. Despite having 35 percent of all adherents, the Catholic Church, as Jay Dolan notes in this book, is able to support parochial schools in only a fraction of its parishes in the state, which, in contrast to states bordering the Great Lakes, resembles "mission territory." Nonetheless, Catholics and Lutherans together have the allegiance of two of every three believers who are attached to an organized faith. When Wisconsin- and Missouri-Synod Lutherans are extracted from this conceptual alliance and grouped with other conservative Christians, they make up 12 percent of South Dakota's adherents. United Methodists, with 37,000 members, claim 7 percent of adherents, and Baptists 4 percent.

A German influence manifests itself beyond the Catholics and Lutherans. Pietists and Anabaptists have a strong relative presence, representing almost 10,000 people, nearly 2 percent of all adherents. This includes 5,400 communal Hutterite Brethren in 54 congregations, the largest gathering in the United States and the only concentration outside Montana. By purchasing a ranch near Bon Homme in 1874, the Hutterites, recently arrived from Russia, created the mother colony for a string of communes up the James River basin. As pacifists, they fled under pressure to Manitoba, Canada, at the outbreak of World War I, many returning afterward. Prospering by industry and frugality, the Brethren—even toward the end of the twentieth century—aroused fears among neighbors: that they would purchase too much land, become too affluent, or assert their communal living too aggressively. Contemporary Hutterites in South Dakota have a presence in more than two dozen counties. In Clark County, for example, there are virtually as many Hutterian Brethren as there are Catholics or Methodists. With 15 percent of all adherents, the Brethren claim an even larger share in Faulk County. German remains the official and liturgical language.

As with Episcopalians, the latter decades of the nineteenth century witnessed the end of Congregational predominance in most American terrain. Outside of

New England, where they were rapidly being overshadowed by Catholic immigration, Congregationalists were the largest group in more than one county only in the Dakotas. In South Dakota, they remain the largest Protestant denomination in Ziebach, Stanley, Jerauld, and Bon Homme counties. Sixteen-thousand strong, the United Church of Christ occupies a substantial 3 percent of the state's adherents.

Other bodies with more than 1 percent of the state's adherents are Holiness and Pentecostal groups (5 percent), the Presbyterian Church (USA) (2.4 percent), and Mormons (1 percent). Scarcely any Muslims are organized in South Dakota —one small mosque—and there are only three Jewish synagogues. One thousand Baha'is operate in nine clusters.

Kansas

Like the Great Plains generally, Kansas has an image problem for those preoccupied with attracting tourists. One version of this image is of a desolate place (because of or despite all those fields of hard red winter wheat, a crop first sown by Mennonite settlers in the 1870s, and a product in which the state still leads the nation). Through this lens, Kansas is rural, unimaginative, puritanical, conservative. It is hot and cold and dry, a breeding ground for tornadoes, blizzards, floods, and drought. It is the land of Carrie Nation, wielding her Prohibition hatchet. It is the proper object of the ode penned in its honor: *Home on the Range*. It has been a hard land, even for those who love it. The state psyche connects to survival in the harsh landscape and agricultural enterprises, despite airplane manufacturing (Wichita is the nation's center) and other manifestations of modernization. Something of this heritage is etched in the state motto, which translates as "To the stars through difficulties."

Against this portrait, however, real people—complex people—live here. If this seems to New Yorkers a home for Muggles, it has also been a radical land. Displacing the Kansa and other native tribes, the state was peopled not only by those seeking land, but by those contesting slavery in a prelude to the Civil War. Kansans in Argonia in 1887 elected the nation's first woman mayor. *Brown vs. Board of Education,* first filed in Topeka in 1951, outlawed segregation in American schools when it reached the Supreme Court three years later.

Life in such places as Wichita, Kansas City, and Topeka makes the citizenry of contemporary Kansas surprisingly urban—more so than other Plains states and more even than Wisconsin and Indiana. Seventy-one percent of Kansans live in urban areas, compared with 61 percent of Iowa residents, 52 percent of South Dakota residents, and 68 percent of those who live in Wisconsin. Despite this, Kansas is less than half as densely populated as the Midwest, less than a fourth as dense as the United States; most of the population lives in the state's eastern third. Kansans are also comparatively well educated. Literacy rates have been

among the highest in the nation since statehood in 1861. Twenty-six percent of
people over age 25 possess at least a bachelor's degree—a figure higher than the
national average, and, in the Midwest, one that trails only Minnesota and Illinois.
The population is more mobile than that of any other Midwestern state. Kansas
youth emigrate at high rates in search of diverse opportunities, and 10 percent
more Kansans than Midwesterners lived in a different state five years previously.

Ethnically and racially, Kansans do help to define Midwestern patterns and
stereotypes. The state is typical of the Midwest in its high rate of Caucasians (86
percent compared to 83 percent regionally and 75 percent nationally), its low rate
of Asians (1.7 percent, 1.9 percent, and 3.6 percent respectively), African
Americans (5.7 percent, 10 percent, and 12.3 percent), Hispanics (7 percent, 5.1
percent, and 12.5 percent), and people born in a foreign country (5 percent, 5.7
percent, and 11 percent). On the other hand, a Kansan is 150 percent more likely
to be Native American than a typical Midwesterner, nine times less likely than a
South Dakotan, and exactly as likely as a randomly chosen American (among
whom 0.9 percent are American Indians).

Kansas is geographically and psychically at farthest Midwestern remove
from contemporary New England, but has inherited, say observers, a good measure of Puritan sensibility from disproportionately influential early immigrants.
Difficult to prove in objective ways, many analysts argue that Midwestern rural
and middle-class values are pronounced in the local culture, with emphasis on
frugality, honesty, hard work, resolve in adverse conditions, and family loyalty
(the state has the highest percentage of married people in the Midwest and the
lowest percentage who have never married, though they divorce at a rate approx-
imating the regional average).

Kansas lies on the edge of the Southern Crossroads region, where, as in the
South itself, Baptists rule. In Missouri, Kansas's eastern neighbor, Southern
Baptists are the largest denomination in three-quarters of all counties. South of
Kansas, in Oklahoma, Southern Baptists are predominant in virtually all counties.
Yet the denominational and cultural boundaries, while weakening, are still drawn
surprisingly sharply along ostensibly artificial state boundaries: in all of Kansas,
despite growth, Southern Baptists are the largest denomination only in
Montgomery County on the state's southern border. Baptists constitute an impres-
sive 12 percent of the state's religious adherents, but among Protestants a resilient
Methodist hegemony is even more striking. Methodists are the largest or next-
largest denomination in most Kansas counties and constitute 14 percent of all
those aligned with organized religion, without even counting the historically
African-American Methodists, whose numbers are difficult to ascertain.

One can strategically glimpse something of the religious makeup of the state
by comparing it with Nebraska, which shares its northern boundary and with

which it seems stereotypically interchangeable to those at far remove. In contrast to Nebraska's 35 percent, 44 percent of the population in Kansas is religiously unaffiliated—by far the highest proportion of all the Plains states. (As noted earlier, the figure is smaller in the ARIS data gathered by phone survey.) At 27 percent, the lowest in the region, Kansas also has a sharply slimmer proportion of Roman Catholics as a percentage of all adherents, while Nebraska (34 percent) is closer to the regional average of 39 percent. Nebraska also provides a buffer from the Lutheran dominance of the upper Midwest. In only three Kansas counties (McPherson, Russell, and Smith) is the Evangelical Lutheran Church of America (ELCA) the largest denomination; 17 counties in Nebraska make that claim. All Lutheran groups combined total 106,000 adherents in Kansas, slightly more than one-third the number in less-populous Nebraska. On the other hand, the percentage of Kansas Baptists relative to total adherents (12 percent) is four times that in Nebraska. (The contrasts between the Lutheran and Baptist weighting reflect the relative proximity of the two states to northern and southern geography and culture.) Compared to Nebraska, Kansas has three times the proportion of Disciples, five times the proportion of Pietists and Anabaptists, twice as many Jews, and a 50 percent greater share of African-American Christians. It has nearly twice the proportion of Holiness and Pentecostal groups, including 32,000 Nazarenes, whose national headquarters lies in Kansas City.

Beyond what has already been noted, Kansas has, in relation to the region as a whole, proportionately fewer Catholics, Lutherans, Muslims, Jews, and conservative confessional and Reformed groups. As a percentage of adherents, it has relatively more Methodists, Baptists, Mormons, Presbyterians, Pietist-Anabaptists, and Holiness-Pentecostal groups. The smattering of Buddhists, Hindus, and smaller groups of adherents to other Eastern religions (1 percent of all adherents) is proportionately similar in Kansas and the Midwest. As elsewhere, independent megachurches attracting worshippers of several thousand each week thrive in Kansas, including the Full Faith Church of Love in Shawnee Mission. A German heritage (in religious terms, a Catholic, Lutheran, and Mennonite one) is diffuse in the state. Pennsylvania Dutch River Brethren colonized at Abilene; one of their descendants, an Eisenhower, became the nation's president. A Swedish (Lutheran) legacy is discernible at Scandia and Lindsborg. A black heritage (Baptist, Methodist, Pentecostal) is evident in Topeka, Leavenworth, Lawrence, Nicodemus, and Fort Scott. A Mexican one (Catholic, Pentecostal) is tied especially to railroads (Kansas has had more miles of track in service than any other state) and migrant farm workers.

Religion in the public arena has entered Kansas's past and present in many ways and on many issues, including prohibition and school vouchers. The complex realities behind simplistic images attached to the state can be illustrated by a widely publicized move in August 1999 by the Kansas Board of Education that renewed controversy over the teaching of evolution in the public schools. Earlier in the decade the Christian Right had captured the state's Republican Party organization. Building on that success, conservative Christian strategists in the 1998 elections had achieved a slim majority on the board of education. The board and the conservative Christians who helped elect them were preoccupied with an array of issues, including the elimination of sex education in the public schools, the urging of Christian messages in public schools to teach morality, and consideration of "intelligent design" when teaching of human beginnings—an alternative to the general theory of evolution.

In 1999, the board enacted science standards inaccurately interpreted by many as banning the teaching of evolution in state schools. National reportage and editorial commentary, often misleading, was wide and potent, casting the state as dominated by Midwestern bumpkins. Headlines like "Kansas Deletes Evolution from Curriculum," "Ooze and Oz," and "Kansas Slides Down Evolutionary Chain" surfaced in such venues as the *New York Times*, the *Atlanta Journal Constitution,* and the *Washington Post.*

What is more characteristic of the state, however—and what the national media scarcely noted in follow-up—is that these moves by the school board took Kansans themselves by surprise. Indeed, in the wake of subsequent elections in 2000, moderate Republicans assumed command of the board and immediately approved revised science standards. Moreover, the earlier standards had not in fact prohibited the teaching of evolution but, instead, had discarded questions dealing with evolution from the state's science assessment tests (thus eroding incentive to teach the topic). The new board adopted standards that emphasized evolution. Moreover, a Gallup poll conducted in 2000 revealed that Kansas citizens resemble the rest of the nation in their beliefs concerning evolution. Forty-nine percent of them hold a creationist view, while 40 percent embrace a theistic evolution, and only five percent adhere to godless evolution. Despite this overwhelming theistic allegiance, Kansans apparently draw distinctions between their personal tenets concerning life's origins and their beliefs of what should be taught in science classes in their public schools. A *Kansas City Star* statewide poll revealed that less than a third of those surveyed supported the earlier board's move to discourage the teaching of evolution.

Illinois

Illinois hosts Chicago, and that changes everything. This birthplace of the skyscraper requires a separate chapter. The focus here is on the state, whose southern and northern halves Mark Noll assigns to two subregions.

No shortage of Midwestern places lay claim to being the "crossroads" and "cross section" of America, but Illinois' boast is as plausible as any. The most populous of the heartland's states at 12.4 million, it is a regional and national hub for air, rail, and water transport. During the bulk of the twentieth century, the nation's population center rested in or close to Illinois. Many observers—scholarly, political, and commercial—have argued that this fact signifies more than geographic happenstance. How an idea or a product sells in Peoria is no small matter before one launches a product nationally. The state's registered voters are persistently and remarkably balanced between the two major political parties; in three dozen presidential elections since the beginning of the Civil War, Illinois has voted the way the nation voted on all but three occasions. More than in virtually any other state in the country, the composite economy and occupational proportions in government, finance, trade, manufacturing, transportation, mining, and agriculture run closely parallel in Illinois and the United States. This is true also of levels of education, urban concentration, average household size, and median household income. By comparison to other Midwestern states, Illinois is proportionately the least Caucasian (73 percent) and the most African American (2.5 percent), Asian (3.5 percent), and Hispanic (12.3 percent; half of the region's 6 million Latinos reside in the state). It also has the highest proportion of those born in a foreign land; Catholic Mass in Chicago is offered in several dozen languages. Like the other demographic indices noted here, Illinois's racial and ethnic composition more nearly resembles the nation than it does other Midwestern states. In the words of the historian Cullom Davis: "Centrality, typicality, and middleness—terms commonly associated with the entire heartland region—apply with as much reason and with sharper focus to Illinois."

Most people who live here affiliate with a church. Only 34 percent do not—the lowest percentage among the Great Lakes states and, excepting the Dakotas, the lowest in the Midwest. Of the religiously affiliated, nearly half (48 percent) are Roman Catholic, a proportion as high as any in the region, and by far the highest number. Nearly two-thirds of adherents in Chicago's Cook county are Catholics, supplied especially by those of German, Irish, Latino, and Polish ancestry. Even when one includes DuPage county, with Naperville, the percentage of Chicago's adherents who are Catholic is 55 percent. A flood of Catholic immigration to the industrially and economically booming Great Lakes states in the decades surrounding the turn of the twentieth century provided a base for these numbers. In the majority of counties, especially in Illinois' northern half, there are even more Catholics, in relation to other religionists, than there were in 1970.

Illinois Protestants are led by historically African-American Methodist, Baptist, and Pentecostal churches (13 percent of the affiliated), Southern Baptists (6 percent), United Methodists (5 percent), and a considerable cluster of confessional and conservative Christians, comprising perhaps 9 percent of the affiliated. The liberal ELCA and the conservative Lutheran Church-Missouri Synod each claim 4 percent of the state's adherents; Lutherans as a whole have more than 1,100 congregations.

Several religious groups maintain headquarters in Illinois, a fact that, beyond mere numbers, lends public presence with economic, cultural, and sometimes political implications. With a population of 15,000, Joseph Smith's church-kingdom in and around Nauvoo was larger than Chicago or any other town in the state in the early 1840s, before the Latter-day Saints (Mormons) were expelled and launched on their trek to the Rocky Mountains. Without such a headquarters, there are 35,000 Mormons in Illinois today. Half of the 5,000 Baha'is in the state reside in the vicinity of the Baha'i national center at Wilmette. Chicago's 17 Hindu temples are not only a significant presence in their own right, but several of them serve as major centers that draw devotees from throughout the region and dispense guidance to temples in Cleveland, Columbus, and elsewhere in the Midwest, as Raymond Williams spells out in his treatment of immigrant religion in this volume.

More than 3 percent of all religious adherents in Illinois are Jewish, a proportion exceeding all other states in the region. Nearly 300,000 Jews worship in 161 synagogues, all but two dozen of them in Chicago. Nearly half that many Muslims, three-quarters of them in Cook county, reside in the state, along with 109,000 Buddhists, Hindus, Sikhs, Jains, and other Eastern religionists.

As elsewhere in the Midwest, denominationally independent megachurches have arisen, catering to the sensibilities and mobility of a new generation, often discarding old rituals and focusing on professional-caliber music. With as many as 20,000 in weekly attendance, the Willow Creek Community Church in South Barrington is a leader among many others in the state.

Michigan

Fewer of Michigan's citizens were living in a different state five years previously than is true of any other state in the region. It is a place with the least mobile population in the Midwest, yet Michigan is the nation's leading center for producing automobiles. Still, the state's modern economy enjoys a diverse foundation, including strong elements of agriculture and tourism, and in fact paralleling regional averages in every employment category. Ethnic diversity here hinges on the large number of African Americans (14.2 percent of the population compared to the nation's 12.3 percent and the Midwest's 10 percent). African Americans (along with some white "ethnics") dominate some of the state's major cities, including especially Detroit, where Democrats rule. It is no surprise that Motown music emerged from Motortown. The proportion of Michigan's populace who are Hispanic (3.3 percent) approximates that of the region, if one excludes Chicago, but this represents only one quarter of the proportion Hispanics occupy in the

United States. Four of five state citizens are Caucasian, slightly less than the 83.5 percent of residents throughout the entire Midwest. Despite variance in particulars, however, Michigan's composite demographics—accounting for dozens of such factors as race, population density, age, occupation, gender, education, and income—more nearly resemble the region as a whole than those of any other Midwestern state.

Considerable religious diversity thrives here. Almost half the population (47 percent) is religiously unaffiliated or uncounted, a percentage second in the region to Indiana. (The figures would be lower by self-report in phone surveys.) Six percent of those who are religiously affiliated belong to Holiness and Pentecostal churches, 12 percent to churches of the traditional mainline, and 4 percent are Baptists (apart from specifically black Baptists; see below). Michigan has seen the rise of a number of independent megachurches unattached to specific denominations, but tending toward a theological and cultural conservatism; their essential nature is sketched by Mark Noll in his discussion of Protestants in this volume. An estimated 81,000 Muslims reside in the state, three-quarters of them in Detroit and in adjacent Oakland and Washtenaw counties (housing Pontiac and Ann Arbor, respectively). Dearborn is home to the nation's second-largest Arab-American community (after that in New York City).

Here, as elsewhere, leaders launched voter registration drives in the post-September 11 era to give more Muslims a voice in the political system. One such drive, for example, took place in the suburbs of Dearborn during the first weekend in February 2004, coinciding with a major Islamic holiday when people traditionally visit friends and relatives.

Muslims represent 1.5 percent of all Michigan's religious adherents: the same percentage that inhabit Illinois, more than twice the percentage of any other Midwestern state, and a bigger piece of the Michigan religious pie than claimed by either the Episcopalians, the Mormons, or the United Church of Christ, though not so large a piece as Jews (2.1 percent). An additional 1 percent of the state's adherents affiliate collectively with Buddhism, Hinduism, and other immigrant religions originating in the Far East. Indicative of the large black population, the historically African-American churches, primarily Methodist, Baptist, and Pentecostal, include nearly 1 million members: 18 percent of all adherents. They exercise political influence diversely and are by far the largest grouping in the state, save only one denomination.

Michigan's 2 million Roman Catholics constitute the largest denomination in the state (38 percent of Michigan adherents). The upper peninsula is as Catholic and Lutheran as Wisconsin or Minnesota. Catholics are the largest denomination in 85 percent of its counties, are next largest virtually everywhere else, and comprise a full religious majority in some two dozen counties. There has long been a clergy shortage, and it remains to be seen what long-term effects the recent crisis over clergy sexual abuse will have on Catholic self-consciousness and behavior in the public sphere. However—as symbolized by the election of the state's Roman Catholic governor, John Engler, who served for a dozen years—Catholics in Michigan have traditionally wielded political clout, not only because of their numbers but also because, in recent times, they have become swing voters wooed by Republicans in the wake of an erosion of traditional Catholic loyalty to the Democratic Party. A growing cooperation has been forged between Catholics and Conservative Protestants on specific issues of public policy, such as their success during the 2000 election in getting vouchers for private schools on the ballot.

Although they number less than a quarter-million, more people in Michigan align with Reformed Christianity than in any other state in the country. Through their educational and publishing institutions, they exercise an influence well beyond their numbers. In colonial New York's antecedent, New Netherlands, Dutch Calvinists enjoyed a privileged, endowed establishment. Nineteenth-century schism in Holland brought an infusion of strict purists not to New York, but to western Michigan. The remains of further fissures coalesced into moderate and liberal (primarily the Reformed Church in America [RCA]) and conservative (especially the Christian Reformed Church [CRC]) expressions of the tradition. Unlike those on the East Coast, the Reformed faithful in Michigan retained much of their Dutch heritage. Following the Civil War, the RCA founded, in the town of Holland, Hope College and Western Theological Seminary. In Grand Rapids, the CRC created both Calvin College and Calvin Theological Seminary in 1876 and, in the publishing world, became an industry unto itself, spawning the prolific houses of Baker, Zondervan, and Eerdmans.

Even apart from the enormous influence Reformed sensibilities exercise in Grand Rapids and surrounding Kent County, the tradition constitutes not only the largest denomination, but claims more than half of all religious adherents in Allegan, Ottawa, and Missaukee counties, and is the second-largest group in several additional counties. In the twentieth and early twenty-first centuries, the RCA reached out institutionally toward other churches; it was a founding member of the original Federal (later National) Council of Churches. It reached out nationally and publicly through the positive-thinking radio-television-print ministries of Midwesterners Norman Vincent Peale and Robert Schuller (departed to California). The CRC, meanwhile, entwined itself in the public sphere through additional means: the secular gospel of Amway, the household products marketing venture founded by two CRC laymen and centered in Grand Rapids.

When these denominations of Dutch heritage are combined with smaller Reformed and related conservative churches, such as the Lutheran Church-Missouri Synod, the Associate Reformed Presbyterian Church, and the

Congregational churches independent of the liberal United Church of Christ, they constitute more than 10 percent of all Michigan religious adherents; their numbers approach a half-million.

The modern Christian Right has managed only uneven success in the state where the Republican Party was organized (1854). Constituting 15 percent of voters in the 2000 election, the Christian Right has, since the 1970s, achieved considerable—though still fragmented—organization and public presence (in part as a faction within the Republican Party), garnered state funds for charter schools, and influenced legislation restricting access to abortions. It has also had difficulty making its voice heard over the cacophony of the state's many powerful interest groups. It has met strong resistance in attempting to confine pornography, resist casino gambling, and win support for school vouchers for students attending private and parochial schools. Some of this resistance has come in the form of counter-mobilization by clergy on the political "left." An example appeared in *The Detroit News* on October 19, 2000, which reported on the gathering of representatives of the Washington-based Interfaith Alliance. The Alliance met in Grand Rapids shortly prior to the fiercely contested November election, publicly attacking the Michigan chapter of the Christian Coalition for placing voter guides in churches.

The Patchwork Middle

Our brief sampling of individual states from the Midwest's several subregions sheds additional light on regional traits, qualifies regional generalities, and suggests the diversity within, as well as of, the Midwest. A final kind of diversity is worth noting, one in which the region leads the country. To grasp it: imagine a map showing the largest religious denomination in every county in the country, with each denomination assigned its own color. (Better yet, consult one: Oxford's *New Historical Atlas of Religion in America* includes such a map for each 20-year period in U.S. history.) Despite the religious complexity we know is there beneath the surface—despite the United States' status as religiously the most complex nation in human history—the contemporary map and its 3,100 or so counties showing the leading denomination is stunningly simple. There are exceptions, but the South is colored relentlessly Baptist; the Mountain West has its thoroughly Mormon domain; most of the rest of the West and Southwest is Catholic, as is—with different racial and ethnic components—the Northeast and southern Florida and Louisiana. A receding belt across the Midwest and east to the Atlantic Ocean is Methodist, while the upper Midwest, where it is not Catholic, is Lutheran.

Against this simple picture, the semi-patchwork character in most of the Midwest stands subtly apart. Constellations of Reformed dominance, pockets of Pietist-Anabaptist predominance, sub-regions of Christians/Disciples superiority, Baptist swatches, an "oasis" of Holiness-Pentecostal counties, even an Episcopal one—all these interrupt the more common colors of Catholics, Lutherans, and Methodists. As a whole, the map of denominational predominance at the county level depicts a region more complex, more marbled, than in the rest of the country.

Conclusion

Much of modern America, including its scholars and media, is preoccupied with American diversity. Often this interest goes beyond a descriptive probe of variety and to a forthright pluralism—the advocacy and celebration of variety. Such concerns might play out diversely as future observers contemplate and report on life in the 11 states defined here as the Midwest. But those who assume the region to be boring might look within themselves for the boredom's source.

In important respects, both secular and religious, the Midwest is its own place, different as well as the same. In several respects, the Midwest lives up to its image as America's common denominator. This status is itself distinctive. In their secular profiles, most other regions have dimensions in which they are highly unusual compared to the nation: the South's extraordinarily rural landscape, for example, and its African-American population, which proportionately is nearly double the country's; and the Pacific's tremendously large range of ethnicities and races neither Caucasian nor African-American. The Midwest in important ways manages to be an amalgamation of the different eccentricities of each of the country's seven other regions.

In religious makeup, many traits help make the Midwest the Midwest: the presence of the Lutheran and Catholic-Lutheran zone in the region's upper reaches, the legacy of a distinctive kind of ethnic Catholic settlement, a unique vertical swath of high religious allegiance down the nation's center, the enduring horizontal Methodist belt, a constellation of individual idiosyncrasies in the demographics of the region's Protestant and immigrant religions, the presence and implications of many denominational headquarters, the existence of Chicago and other decidedly Midwestern patterns of urban and rural, secular and religious, interplay, and the considerable state and local variations within the region that contribute to this whole.

Attending to specific episodes and their implications for religion in the public realm—school vouchers, evolution in the schools, legal wrangling over the religious use of peyote—the thrust of this essay has nonetheless deliberately aimed at "what" and "who" and "where." The central question now becomes: So what? In what ways do these demographic realities, and others we shall presently encounter, impinge on and respond to the region's public realm? To these questions the subsequent chapters invite us.

Endnotes

1. I am indebted to Becky Cantonwine, Jenny Crye, and Ryan Jessup for invaluable research assistance in preparation of this essay.

2. Each region's statistics in 34 categories (including population density, racial composition, education, household income, type of employment, and urban-rural proportions) were weighed against national totals. The region most closely paralleling the nation in each category ranked 1, the second closest ranked 2, and so on. Thus, to determine how close a region is to the nation in terms of age, each region was ranked in each of several age categories (<18, 18-44, 45-64, 65+); the ranks were then summed. The region with the lowest total rank most nearly resembles the nation as a whole in the age of its population.

   Weighing the 34 various categories equally, the region with the summed ranking closest to 1 is the Midwest, making it appear to be the most nationally representative of eight regions in its secular demographics. The remaining regions, listed from most-similar to least-similar to the nation as a whole, are: South, Southern Crossroads, Pacific Northwest and Mid-Atlantic (tie), New England, Rocky Mountains, and Pacific.

   Like any method quantifying something subjective and complex, this one has constraints. Each category was considered equally important, for instance, and any data not included in the 34 categories carried no weight in the rankings. The results are suggestive, nothing more.

CHAPTER TWO

PROTESTANTS:
AN ENDURING METHODIST TINGE

Mark Noll

There are a number of remarkably interesting stories to be told about Protestants in the Midwest. Some have to do with the various Protestant groups themselves as they came into this central section of the country and then developed in different ways over the course of time. Some have to do with how Protestants of one sort or another have affected the public life of Midwestern states. And some stand out by comparison with what has happened in other parts of the nation.

Such comparisons might, in fact, give the impression that Midwestern Protestants are a pretty boring lot. In their history as well as in their contemporary life, one mostly looks in vain for the sort of dramatic public events that have lent color to other regions of the country. There is no striking Midwestern Protestant leadership, for example, in any of the nation's great wars (as Congregationalists from New England provided patriots during the Revolution; as Congregationalists and Unitarians offered the North during the Civil War; as Southern Presbyterians also provided their region during the same conflict; and as ministers from the two coasts mounted against the Vietnam conflict in the 1960s). There has been no unusual Midwestern Protestant stiffening of regional resistance to national culture, as white Baptists, Disciples, Methodists, Presbyterians, and other Protestants gave to the South for at least a century after the Civil War. Only a few internationally recognized leaders of moral crusades from the Midwest can be placed alongside the Rev. Dr. Martin Luther King, Jr., a Baptist pastor from Atlanta.

To be sure, it is not as though the history of Protestants in the Midwest is a bland history. It was, after all, in Cincinnati that Harriet Beecher Stowe, daughter of one famous Congregationalist minister-professor and wife of another, picked up almost all the information that she used for writing *Uncle Tom's Cabin* (published 1852), a novel that moved hearts and minds on the subject of slavery throughout the nation in the years before the Civil War. At the end of the nineteenth century, Chicago witnessed several events that in significant ways linked Protestant history and public history. In 1889, Jane Addams, a Presbyterian whose views were shaped in part by her Quaker upbringing as well as by the social pragmatism of the era, founded Hull House, which soon became a model for other efforts at comprehensive urban development.

Two years later a talented ballplayer who had grown up in Iowa left the Chicago Whitestockings to pursue full-time Christian ministry with the YMCA. Shortly thereafter, Billy Sunday began to preach as an itinerant evangelist (first stop, Garner, Iowa), and a new star had risen in the American religious firmament.

Five years after Sunday left baseball, a young Presbyterian layman from Omaha, Nebraska, William Jennings Bryan, delivered one of the most memorable speeches in American political history at the national nominating convention of the Democratic Party in Chicago. When Bryan took up the issue of the free coinage of silver, his memorable phrases rang with biblical as well as political conviction: "You shall not press down upon the brow of labor this crown of thorns, you shall not crucify mankind upon a cross of gold."[1] Sixteen years later Chicago was again the venue when, in August 1912, the New Yorker Teddy Roosevelt also invoked biblical language in accepting the nomination for president from the Progressive Party: "We stand at Armageddon, and we battle for the Lord."[2]

Early in the twentieth century, Columbus, Ohio, was the scene of ferocious public controversy because of Washington Gladden, minister of Columbus' First Congregational Church and moderator of the Congregationalists' national association. In 1905, Gladden led efforts to repudiate a gift of $100,000 from John D. Rockefeller to the American Board of Commissioners for Foreign Missions. To Gladden this was "tainted money" that bore the marks of rapacious business practices that no church should condone.[3]

A few years later, up-close observation of modern industrial life was the spark that transformed a Detroit-based minister of the Evangelical Synod of North America into a nationally recognized public theologian. When Reinhold Niebuhr came to Bethel Evangelical Church in 1915, he embraced the standard liberal theology of his era that pictured God as benevolently guiding the steady moral progress of the human race. After 13 years observing Detroit's labor-capital disputes at that urban church, Niebuhr was radicalized socially and sobered theologically. The result was trenchant criticism of the American economic order as partaking of genuine evil, and also effective advocacy of a "Christian realism" that depicted humanity as, under God, both uniquely gifted and uniquely sinful.

Niebuhr won renown for these views from his position as a seminary professor in New York City, but Detroit was the incubator in which they were hatched.[4]

In 1972, a different sort of public event drew attention to the Midwest. Amish parents near New Glarus, Wisconsin, refused to enroll their children in the local public high school in order to protect them from forces that might alienate the children from their agrarian religious community. When the state sued, the United States Supreme Court eventually decided the case, *Wisconsin v. Yoder*, with a unanimous decision that extended the protection of the First Amendment's free exercise clause to the Amish parents and their desire to raise children according to their religious views.[5]

There are many more unusually effective individuals or striking moments in the history of the Protestant Midwest, including as only a very partial list:

- D. L. Moody, who got his start as an internationally renowned evangelist during the Civil War era by working with street children in Chicago;
- Eli Lilly, an Episcopalian from Indianapolis who in 1876 founded Lilly Pharmaceuticals, and his grandson, also Eli, who in 1936 established the Lilly Endowment that from Indianapolis has long been the nation's leading philanthropy for encouraging the study of religion and promoting the integrity of American religious life;
- Carrie Nation, bold and big (nearly six feet tall), who launched her national crusade against alcohol from Medicine Lodge, Kansas, in the mid-1890s;
- Frances Willard, a calmer, more subtle, yet no less determined foe of alcohol and other forces that ruined the lives of women and children, a life-long Methodist who directed the Women's Christian Temperance Union, from Evanston, Illinois;
- Milton Wright, bishop of the United Brethren Church in Dayton, Ohio, whose earnest, no-nonsense approach to preaching, teaching, and church oversight was communicated to his sons Wilbur and Orville for use in a more secular sphere;
- John Harvey Kellogg and William Keith Kellogg, Seventh-day Adventists who in Battle Creek, Michigan, founded a cereal company as a way of supporting the dietary principles of their denomination;
- Thomas A. Dorsey, a black Baptist musician and publisher who from Chicago transformed the face of African-American church music, and then of all American music, by his promotion of gospel music (including "Take My Hand, Precious Lord");
- William Bell Riley, long-time pastor of the First Baptist Church in Minneapolis, who presided over a fundamentalist empire that through radio, students, and the printed page decisively shaped religious life in Minnesota, Iowa, Nebraska, and the Dakotas;

- C. L. Franklin (father of Aretha Franklin), for 33 years the pastor of the New Bethel Baptist Church in Detroit, who was as effective in leading community reform as he was as a pulpiteer;
- Billy Graham, the evangelist who finished his higher education at Wheaton College, outside of Chicago, and who began his career as a pastor, radio preacher, and itinerant in the Great Lakes region;
- Tom Osborne, legendary football coach of the Nebraska Cornhuskers, since 2000 a member of the U.S. House of Representatives, and a serious Methodist from Lemoyne in Keith County;
- Bill Gaither, the popular songwriter and recording artist from Monroe County, Indiana, whose more than 50 albums (with songs like "He Touched Me") have garnered numerous awards;
- Kathleen Norris, who from her home in Lemmon, South Dakota (Perkins County), has shown through a series of well-received books how her religious life as a Presbyterian could be revived by the open Dakota landscape and the enduring practices of Benedictine monasticism;
- James T. Meeks, pastor of the Salem Baptist Church in Chicago, one of the city's largest churches, a forceful civil rights advocate with the Rainbow-Push Coalition, an earnest evangelist, the founder of Salem Christian Academy, and since 2002 a member of the Illinois House of Representatives.

Out of the Midwest have also come some of the nation's presidents with the most significant connections to religion: Lucy Webb Hayes, the wife of Rutherford B. Hayes of Ohio, was a Methodist so strongly committed to temperance reform that during the years in which Hayes presided over the White House (1877-1881) it was said that the water flowed like champagne; James Garfield, Hayes' protégé, also from Ohio, was an ordained Disciples of Christ pastor and the only minister ever to have served as president (1881); Herbert Hoover, of West Branch, Iowa, carried the Quaker principles of his home into distinguished service in international relief after World War I before beginning his tenure as president (1929-33); and Ronald Reagan was strongly influenced during his boyhood in Dixon, Illinois, by the evangelical faith of his mother, a member of the Christian Church (Disciples of Christ), and then later during his tenure as president (1981-89) solidified a bond between the Republican Party and white evangelical Protestants.

It would, however, leave the wrong impression to imply that Midwestern Protestants have sought the dramatic gesture or the spectacular event. Their great contribution to national life has been faithful self-discipline of moral purpose; their great contribution to religious life, faithful development of stable churches for stable communities. In order to understand something of the background and present shape of Protestantism in the Midwest, it is useful to begin with a survey and then some comparisons of church styles that I call "proprietary," "ethnic," and "sectarian." Then a capsule history opens the way to understanding the particular religious sub-regions within this part of the country. That exercise, in turn, leads naturally into brief consideration of how the public life of the Midwest has been affected by the early preeminence of Methodism. Throughout, the purpose is not only to provide background context for contemporary events, but also to illuminate the extraordinary resilience to be discovered in the ordinary life of Midwestern Protestants.

Survey and Comparisons

Protestantism in the Midwest means first of all the **Lutherans**. In a 2001 telephone poll asking people to specify their religious traditions conducted by the American Religious Identification Survey (ARIS), six of the seven states in the country where Lutherans counted more than 10 percent of the respondents came from this Midwestern region.[6] An enumeration reported in the North American Religion Atlas (NARA), using for the most part figures supplied by the denominations themselves (and so more conservative than self identification, since the denominations count only people who actually show up in church or who are attached in some other measurable way as "adherents") underscores this Lutheran presence. These church adherence figures suggest that about 6 percent of the total population in the five Midwestern states east of the Mississippi are Lutherans, rising to 16 percent in the six states west of the Mississippi. In fact, so important are Lutherans in the Midwest that a separate chapter in this book is being devoted to them, which explains why they mostly drop out of the picture in this chapter.

But even after setting aside the Lutherans, there are still a lot of Protestants left—perhaps as many as 14 to 15 million non-Lutheran Protestant adherents in these 11 states. They worship in approximately 57,000 churches (Tables 2.1 and 2.2). For the sake of comparison, this is about the same number of churches that existed in all of the United States, for all denominations (including Catholics and Lutherans), in 1860. The number of Midwestern non-Lutheran Protestants today is approximately equal to the total populations of Sweden and Finland combined.

These Midwestern Protestants can be divided into the following groups, a division that is necessary in order to understand the great strength, but also the great diversity, of Protestants in this area of the country.

Methodists In the ARIS survey, 7.5 percent of Midwesterners identified themselves as Methodists, more than for any other region in the United States. Of the 11 states where at least 10 percent of respondents told researchers they were Methodists, five are in the Midwest (Ohio, Iowa, South Dakota, Nebraska, and Kansas). The United Methodist Church, by far the nation's largest Methodist denomination, has strong concentrations of adherents in the South. But its own

Table 2.1   Number of Adherents 2000 (NARA)

First column (in parentheses) and last column are total numbers, in thousands; the other columns show each religious sub-group's percentage of the total state population as provided by NARA; the "ethnic Prot." column is an estimate of the percentage of the state population belonging to ethnic, predominately black, churches.

State (Total pop.)	% Rel. Adhr.	% RC	% Luth[1]	% Other[2]	%Non-L Prots.	% Ethnic Prot.[3]	Total% Non-L Prot.	Non-L Prots.
East of Mississippi								
OH (11,363)	*53.7*	19.7	3.4	2.5	19.3	4.5	23.8	2,704
MI (9,947)	*52.7*	20.3	4.5	2.7	14.3	6.0	20.3	2,019
IN (6,082)	*50.6*	13.7	3.0	1.4	24.8	3.6	28.4	1,727
WI (5,368)	*65.3*	31.6	17.0	1.3	10.5	3.3	13.8	740
IL (12,420)	*65.5*	31.2	4.6	4.1	15.4	8.1	23.5	2,918
						Sub-total		10,108
West of Mississippi								
MN (4,921)	*64.9*	25.6	22.5	2.0	11.6	3.3	14.9	733
IA (2,924)	*62.1*	19.1	13.4	1.3	24.7	1.8	26.5	774
ND (642)	*75.3*	27.9	31.1	1.1	13.1	2.3	15.4	98
SD (755)	*69.6*	24.0	21.6	1.1	21.1	3.3	24.4	184
NE (1,712)	*64.9*	21.8	14.7	2.3	20.0	3.0	23.0	393
KS (2,686)	*56.0*	15.1	3.9	1.7	28.7	4.2	32.9	883
						Sub-total		3,065
						Total		13,163

1 Evangelical Lutheran Church in America, Lutheran Church—Missouri Synod, Wisconsin Evangelical Lutheran Synod

2 Bahai, Buddhists, Latter-day Saints, Greek Orthodox, Muslim, Orthodox Church in America, Jews, and .3 percent for each state as miscellaneous.

3 Figured at 30 percent of a state's non-white population.

records show that, after Oklahoma and Mississippi, there is a higher proportion of United Methodists in Iowa than in any other state, and that proportions of United Methodists in Ohio, South Dakota, Nebraska, and Kansas are also among the highest in the nation.

Additionally, several smaller Methodist denominations (especially the Wesleyan Church, particularly in Indiana, Minnesota, and South Dakota) and Holiness denominations that arose from Methodism (especially the Church of the Nazarene, particularly in Ohio, Indiana, and Kansas) have strong pockets of Midwestern adherents. Methodist, Wesleyan, and Holiness denominations are rarely flashy, but they sustain in various ways the legacy of their founders, John

Table 2.2   Number of Churches (NARA)

	Total chs	RC chs	Luth[1] chs.	Other[2] houses worship	Total chs. non-L Prot	% ethnic multiple[3]	Total non-Luth Prot. chs.
East of Mississippi							
OH	11,167	1,000	850	404	8,913	18	10,517
MI	7,527	888	907	332	5,400	37	7,398
IN	7,492	462	433	169	6,428	10	7,070
WI	5,181	879	1,598	182	2,522	26	3,177
IL	10,140	1,125	1,107	543	7,365	47	10,826
					Sub-total		38,988
West of Mississippi							
MN	5,115	730	1,789	163	2,433	23	2,992
IA	4,584	508	816	130	3,130	2	3,192
ND	1,507	261	560	45	641	12	717
SD	1,712	252	432	65	963	11	1,068
NE	2,612	368	571	110	1,563	10	1,719
KS	3,959	354	310	112	3,183	10	3,501
					Sub-total		13,189
					Total		52,177

1 Evangelical Lutheran Church in America, Lutheran Church—Missouri Synod, Wisconsin Evangelical Lutheran Synod.

2 Bahai, Buddhists, Latter-day Saints, Greek Orthodox, Muslim, Orthodox Church in America, Jews, and for miscellaneous non-Protestant house of worship 30 (for OH, MI, IL), 25 (for IN, WI, MN), and 20 (for IA, NE, SD, ND, KS).

3 Figured as the percentage of ethnic Protestant adherents (Table 2.1) divided by the percentage of non-Lutheran Protestants (Table 2.1) minus 5 percentage points so as not to exaggerate the number of churches for non-white Protestant groups.

and Charles Wesley—a deep respect for religious experience (even at the expense of precise doctrine), an unusual attention to the work of the Holy Spirit, and an energetic interest in practical good works.

Baptists There are also a lot of Baptists, with 8.2 percent of Midwesterners identifying themselves as such. But unlike the situation for Methodists, the Midwest is not the nation's most populous region for Baptists. Rather, the Southern and Southern Crossroads regions both report a much higher concentration than the Midwest. The ARIS survey found proportionately more Baptists in 17 other states than in the Midwestern states with the most Baptists (14 percent in Indiana, Michigan, and Ohio, and 13 percent in Kansas).

Baptists are also divided into more separate denominations throughout the Midwest than are Methodists. While the Southern Baptist Convention is strong in Kansas (3.8 percent of the state's population), and there are also many Southern Baptist churches in Indiana and Illinois, the denomination has only a negligible presence in Wisconsin, Minnesota, North Dakota, and Iowa. Other Baptist denominations show up with some force in several of the states, including the American Baptist Churches in the U.S.A. (in Ohio, Indiana, Illinois, Michigan, South Dakota, Iowa, Nebraska, and Kansas), the General Association of Regular Baptist Churches (in Indiana and Michigan), the Baptist General Conference (in Minnesota), the New Testament Association of Independent Baptist Churches (in Indiana), and the North American Baptist Conference (in North Dakota). Wherever Baptists are present they contribute a special stress on the need to be born again, a sometimes feisty insistence on the Bible as the sole religious authority, and a strong commitment to the autonomy of local congregations.

African-American Protestants The ARIS survey revealed that 6.3 percent of all Midwesterners reported themselves as associated with historically African-American Protestant churches, a percentage less than half of that reported for the South, and about two-thirds of the proportion in the Mid-Atlantic and Southern Crossroads regions. Although NARA carefully estimates the number of African-American Protestants, specific information is hard to come by for congregations of the National Baptist Convention, U.S.A., Incorporated; the Church of God in Christ; the National Baptist Convention of America; the African Methodist Episcopal Church; the National Missionary Baptist Convention of America; the Progressive National Baptist Convention, Inc.; the African Methodist Episcopal Zion Church; and the Christian Methodist Episcopal Church—all denominations well represented in Cleveland, Detroit, Indianapolis, Chicago, Cincinnati, Omaha, Wichita, and other urban areas, as well as in many smaller communities. And this is not to speak of the thousands of independent black congregations, many of them quite large and influential in their own locales. African-American churches have been a vital part of the region's Protestant history, at least since the great urban migrations early in the twentieth century.

Hispanic (and other ethnic) Protestants Efforts to provide precise information on Hispanic and other ethnic Protestant churches have been even less successful than for the largely black denominations. The ARIS survey revealed 1.1 percent of Midwesterners identifying themselves as Hispanic Protestant, the lowest percentage of any region, and another 1.2 percent as Protestants in other ethnic groups. For other ethnic Protestants, only New England reported a lower proportion than the Midwest, and in the Pacific region there was almost three times as many people (3.4 percent) who self-identified as ethnic Protestants as in the Midwest.

Again, although exact figures are not at hand, Hispanic churches, often Pentecostal, have been growing rapidly in areas of strong migration from Mexico and Latin America; a similar situation exists for communities with significant Korean, Cambodian, Russian, Ghanaian, and other immigrant populations, where churches are being formed at a very rapid pace.[7]

Presbyterians Only 2.7 percent of Midwesterners reported themselves as Presbyterians; still this is a higher proportion than anywhere else in the country except the Mid-Atlantic and Southern regions. The Presbyterian Church (U.S.A.), the nation's largest denomination in this religious family, is particularly well represented in eastern Ohio, which is adjacent to the nation's strongest concentration of Presbyterians in western Pennsylvania, as well as in Iowa, South Dakota, Nebraska, and Kansas.

Congregationalists Outside of New England, the historic center of Congregationalism, a higher proportion of the population in the Midwest (0.9 percent) call themselves Congregationalists than in any other region of the country. As with several of the Protestant denominations that originated on the East Coast during the colonial period, the United Church of Christ retains some strength in a belt that stretches from Ohio through into Illinois, and then across the Mississippi into Iowa, Nebraska, South Dakota, and Kansas.

Episcopalians Despite the presence of impressive Episcopalian churches in several large and mid-size Midwestern cities, the Episcopal position on the ground was never particularly strong in the Midwest. As with the Congregationalists, 0.9 percent of Midwesterners told the ARIS researchers that they were Episcopalian. With the exception of South Dakota, where there have been several successful Episcopalian missions to native Americans, this church does not enjoy the adherence of even 1 percent of any Midwestern state's population.

Disciples of Christ (and other Restorationist churches) The Restorationist movement arose in the early nineteenth century from efforts by leaders like Alexander Campbell and Barton W. Stone to foreswear traditional denominational labels, to follow no creed but the Bible, and to bring Christian belief and practice back to the standards of the New Testament. The Restorationist movement, which was always strongest in the upper South and the lower Midwest, subsequently divided into sub-movements: the Christian Church (Disciples of Christ), which came most to resemble other mainline Protestant denominations; the Christian Churches, which negotiated carefully between Restorationist traditions and modern life; and the Churches of Christ, which retained most directly the localist, anti-denominationalist traditions of the movement's founders.

In the ARIS survey, 0.4 percent of Midwesterners reported being Disciples of Christ, while it was not possible to get a reading on the number of those self-identified with the Christian Churches and Churches of Christ (because of confusion with respondents who labeled themselves simply as "Christians"). In NARA's reporting of adherents by denominations, the Disciples of Christ show a significant presence (more than 1 percent of the population) in Indiana, Iowa, and Kansas, and somewhat less in Ohio and Nebraska. Christian Churches and Churches of Christ are also well represented in Southern Indiana, with considerable strength as well in southern Iowa, Nebraska, and Kansas.

Pentecostals   From its origins at a revival in Los Angeles in 1906, Pentecostalism has become the most rapidly growing segment of world-wide Christianity. It is also one of the most difficult movements to chart accurately because so much Pentecostal organization is propelled by local leaders, and because the more recent Charismatic movement (which brought Pentecostal practices like healing, prophesying, and speaking in tongues into other churches) is mostly an informal set of emphases. Still, research of different sorts testifies to the significance of Pentecostalism in the Midwest—2.1 percent of those responding to the telephone poll called themselves Pentecostals or charismatics, which is exactly the national average.

The largest mostly white Pentecostal denomination, the Assemblies of God, has a substantial number of churches in all 11 Midwestern states, with the highest percentage of state populations in Minnesota (1.1 percent), North Dakota (1.6 percent), and Nebraska (1.1 percent). The Church of God (Cleveland, Tennessee), which is strongest in the South, also enjoys a considerable number of churches (228) in southern Ohio. Smaller pentecostal denominations and independent pentecostal churches are spread throughout the region. Charismatic and Pentecostal churches pioneered the new Protestant church music (electrified instruments, praise choruses, overhead projectors) that has become common everywhere in the region and the nation.

Independent Churches   Almost as hard to measure as African-American congregations are independent churches, of which there have historically been more in the United States than anywhere else in the world. In the ARIS telephone poll, 9.9 percent of the Midwestern population identified themselves as "evangelical," "nondenominational," or "Christian" without any other designation. A substantial number of these people participate in the life of independent congregations of one sort or another.

Early in the twentieth century, the fundamentalist movement led to the creation of many "Bible" or "community" churches throughout the Midwest, and independent churches have long been a feature of African-American urban communities as well. In the last quarter century, suburban areas around the country have provided the venue for a new style of church aimed at the unchurched or lightly churched population, organized to do away with church practices unfamiliar to rising generations, presented with professional attention to music and drama, and oriented toward making the Christian message applicable to the tensions, mobility, and trials of modern American life.

The Willow Creek Community Church in South Barrington, Illinois, with up to 20,000 worshippers each week (and several branch operations in other northern Illinois cities), has been a leader in this "megachurch" movement. But many varieties of this same kind of church fellowship can be found in and surrounding all major cities, and sometimes in rural areas as well. They are called by names (to take examples from the Chicago area) like Bountiful Blessings Ministry, Centro Cristiano Vida Abundante, Charisma Christian Ministries, Fountain of Life Church, Ginger Creek Community Church, Grace Community Church, Harvest Bible Chapel, Heart Song Community Church, New Abundant and Everlasting Life Ministries, and The Warehouse Church. Some of the largest of these newer megachurches, with weekly attendance of 2,000 or 3,000 or even more, include the Vineyard Community Church in Cincinnati; the Church of the Open Door in Crystal, Minnesota; Christ Universal Temple in Chicago; the Kensington Community Church in Troy, Michigan; the Christian Fellowship Church of Evansville, Indiana; and the Full Faith Church of Love in Shawnee Mission, Kansas.

In addition, there are a large number of denominational churches—like Church of the Resurrection United Methodist in Leawood, Kansas, the Emmanuel Christian Center in Minneapolis (Assemblies of God), or the Central Wesleyan Church in Holland, Michigan—that because of their size, programs, and emphases now also function like the newer megachurches.[8] As explained in the conclusion, these churches carry on significant aspects of Methodist tradition in Midwestern public life.

Mennonites (and other Anabaptists) Descendents of Europe's Anabaptist movements have never been numerous in the United States, but from the end of the seventeenth century (colonial Pennsylvania) there have been significant communities in North America of Mennonites, Amish, Hutterite Brethren, and other groups influenced by the Anabaptist movement ("Anabaptist" means "re-baptized" and was applied to early followers of, among others, Menno Simons, who looked upon infant baptism as the mistaken foundation for European "Christendom," which Anabaptists have always held to be the illegitimate binding together of church and state).

With their commitment to pacifism, Mennonites and Amish in the Midwest have suffered during earlier periods of national warfare. But their success as farmers, and later in movement to cities and suburbs, have earned Anabaptists the respect of surrounding communities. In Holmes County, Ohio, and Lagrange county, Indiana, the Amish today make up the largest single religious body. In addition, there are significant numbers of Amish and Mennonites in central

Illinois and east-central Iowa. Central Kansas is also the southern terminus of a "Mennonite Belt" that runs northward through Nebraska and South Dakota (where there are 44 Hutterite Brethren congregations, named after Jacob Hutter of the sixteenth century, who promoted a communal style of life) and on into Winnipeg, Canada.

Reformed denominations Like the Anabaptists, churches known as Reformed have never had an extensive presence in the United States, but as with the Anabaptists, the Midwest has been the home to significant concentrations of these Reformed Protestants.

"German Reformed" churches, of which there once were many in Ohio and the Dakotas, took part in a series of mergers that led eventually to the United Church of Christ, and so have been grafted onto the stock of traditional New England Congregationalism. But European Reformed distinctions—loyalty to the Heidelberg Catechism of the sixteenth century, unusual respect for pastors, some uneasiness with both mainline and evangelical styles of American churchmanship—remain alive in two denominations rising from Dutch immigration to the new world, the Reformed Church in America (with roots in the colonial period), and the Christian Reformed Church (which traces its ancestry to migrations of the mid-nineteenth century). These Reformed denominations are strong in western Michigan, central Iowa, and the Sioux country stretching from northwest Iowa into southeast South Dakota.

Smaller evangelical denominations The Midwest has also provided ample space for several smaller evangelical movements that spun off from the historic denominations, arose during the fundamentalist-modernist controversies of the early twentieth century, or owe their existence to religious developments in Europe. The Christian Missionary Alliance, with a concentration of churches in Nebraska, was founded in 1897 in order to stress missionary service abroad and holiness of life for all believers at home. Two denominations with Scandinavian origins that sponsor a number of Midwestern churches, often in the penumbra of the Lutherans, are the Evangelical Free Church and the Evangelical Covenant Church. Both began as pietistic movements within Scandinavian Lutheranism, but emerged as independent movements once settlers had arrived in the states. They are strongest in the Chicago area, Minnesota, and Nebraska.

To make sense of this parade of Protestant sub-groups that lie so thick, but also so diffusely, on Midwestern ground, it is important to risk a number of generalizations. The first and most obvious is that for the category "non-Lutheran Protestants" it is very difficult to make generalizations. The category is much more of a catch-all than for any of the other Christian groups surveyed in this book.

As an indication of this profusion, the NARA survey of denominational adherents for the year 2000 lists 24 different non-Lutheran Protestant denominations that had at least 1 percent of the religious adherents in at least one of the 11 Midwestern states (Table 2.3, page 63). NARA records smaller numbers for literally hundreds more Protestant denominations, and its researchers acknowledge that they miss many independent Protestant churches.

Yet once having recognized how difficult it is to make a useful generalization that could apply equally to, say, a Hispanic Pentecostal store-front church in Chicago; a grand and historic Methodist church in Indianapolis; a Mennonite church in rural Kansas; a Church of Christ congregation in small-town southern Iowa; and the Willow Creek Community Church in Barrington, Illinois, there are a few things that can be ventured.

In general terms, most of the Protestant churches in the Midwest (as elsewhere in the United States) can be described as either proprietary, ethnic, or sectarian.

Proprietary churches (a roughly equivalent term would be "mainline") include the Methodist, Presbyterian, Congregational, Episcopal, and Disciples churches descended from denominations that have existed for two, three, or even four centuries (the Disciples would be the exception, with a heritage extending back only 175 years). Because of their historic positions, these churches are usually wealthier (or have a history of relative wealth); they usually are centrally located in cities and towns; they have their greatest appeal to the middle and upper classes; they take the value of higher education for granted; they have been moderate or conservative in political outlook (and so are long-time allies of the Republican Party); they often are the churches of civic and professional elites; they are mostly Caucasian; and they have a long history of sponsoring civic institutions like colleges, hospitals, and retirement homes.

Religiously considered, the proprietary or mainline churches are stronger on Christianity as a civilizing force, while they tend to lay less stress on the need for conversion from sin and on the exacting demands of holy living. In the last few decades their position as denominations trying to be comprehensive for all people has led them into long, often contentious debate over sexual issues, especially whether to ordain practicing homosexuals for the ministry. Although these churches were not pioneers in ordaining women (Wesleyan, Holiness, and Pentecostal churches took that lead), they have been the denominations over the last half-century that have been most solicitous about promoting the equality of women in public life, including the leadership of their churches. The proprietary churches were the historic founders of religion in the Midwest, but they have declined considerably in recent decades.

Lutherans and also the Reformed often look like proprietary Protestants, but their history as immigrant churches can lead to significant differences, whether preserving some characteristics of European established churches where they are in an overwhelming majority (as in many parts of Minnesota, Nebraska, Iowa, and the Dakotas) or remaining somewhat standoffish from public life when they are in a minority. Quite a few Lutherans, and even more Reformed, also emphasize religious beliefs and practices similar to those promoted in the more evangelical sectarian churches. Historically, they are the Protestants most likely to establish private schools to serve their own constituencies.

Ethnic churches are harder to describe since African-American churches do not necessarily provide a template for Hispanic, Korean, or the other newer ethnic Protestants. For their part, black churches are usually located in cities; they tend to be Baptist, Methodist, or Pentecostal; they feature strong preaching and pastoral leadership; they take for granted the need to play an active role in economic affairs; and they are often sustained by a remarkably loyal corps of dedicated women. Whether they are well-financed or not (and some are), they are closer to the needs of the urban poor than are the predominately white churches.

In their religious beliefs and ethical practices, black churches are usually conservative. But because of the long history of estrangement from centers of economic power, their adherents provide key votes and (less frequently) important leaders for the Democratic party. Worship in black churches is usually more expressive than the worship of mostly white churches.

Other ethnic Protestant churches are often pentecostal or charismatic. Some (like the Korean) can stress correctness of doctrine. They are, of course, located in concentrations of immigrant and second-generation settlement (usually cities); many are led by entrepreneurial pastors; they often remain connected to churches and religious currents in the home countries; most that have existed for any time struggle over when and how to use English in their services; and they are growing very rapidly in size and in number.

The sectarian Protestants are characterized by religious beliefs and practices—and sometimes by ethnic or regional (especially Southern) distinctives—that separate them to one degree or the other from a majority of other Protestants or from most of their fellow American citizens. The list of distinguishing features is long and diverse. The key thing is not just that these items are part of church tradition, but that they are maintained as vital elements in defining what it means to be a true Christian, even if holding dogmatically to that commitment offends the sensibilities of other Christians or cuts against the grain of the broader American society.

Because sectarian churches define themselves by the truth claims for distinctive beliefs and practices, they have been wary about cooperation with other church bodies, often even other sectarian groups that to outsiders seem quite similar. As a partial list, the separating features include the following:

- insistence on a distinct born-again experience before being admitted into full church membership, for many Baptists and other bodies;

Table 2.3   Denominational adherence as % of state population—NARA
(Records all denominations with at least .5 percent of the state's total population; percentage provided is of state's total population.)

	OH	MI	IN	WI	IL	MN	IA	ND	SD	NE	KS
RC	19.7	20.3	13.7	31.6	31.2	25.6	19.1	27.9	24.0	21.8	15.1
Luth[1]	3.4	4.5	3.0	17.0	4.6	22.5	13.4	31.1	21.6	14.7	3.9
Un.Meth.	5.0	2.2	4.7	2.4	2.9	2.4	8.5	3.1	4.9	6.9	7.7
PrCUSA	1.4	1.1	1.2	.8	1.1	1.2	2.4	1.4	1.7	2.3	1.9
UCC	1.4	.6	.8	1.6	1.3	.9	1.7	1.0	2.1	1.4	.5
AoG	.6	.8	.9	.8	.8	1.1	1.0	1.6	1.0	1.1	1.0
ABptUSA	1.0	.6	1.9	-	.7	-	.9	-	.9	.7	2.4
SBC	1.6	.6	2.0	-	2.5	-	-	-	.9	1.0	3.8
Episc.	.5	.6	-	-	-	.6	-	-	1.5	.6	.6
ChC-ChsC	1.3	-	3.4	-	1.1	-	.9	-	-	.9	2.1
CC (Disc)	.6	-	1.4	-	-	-	1.9	-	-	.8	2.1
L-dS	-	-	.5	-	-	-	-	-	.8	.9	.8
RCA	-	.8	-	-	-	-	1.3	-	1.0	-	-
Ch of Naz.	.8	-	1.0	-	-	-	-	-	-	-	1.2
Wesleyan	-	.5	.6	-	-	-	-	-	1.0	-	-
ChsC	-	-	.6	-	-	-	-	-	-	-	.7
RegBptGA	-	.5	.6	-	-	-	-	-	-	-	-
CRC	-	1.1	-	-	-	-	.7	-	-	-	-
EFC	-	-	-	-	.6	-	-	-	-	.7	-
BptGenCf	-	-	-	-	.9	-	-	-	-	-	-
NABptCf	-	-	-	-	-	-	-	.8	-	-	-
FreeLuth	-	-	-	-	-	-	-	.7	-	-	-
HuttBrth	-	-	-	-	-	-	-	-	.7	-	-
C&MA	-	-	-	-	-	-	-	-	-	.6	-
ChG(Clvd)	.5	-	-	-	-	-	-	-	-	-	-
MennUSA	-	-	-	-	-	-	-	-	-	-	.5
NTBptF	-	-	.5	-	-	-	-	-	-	-	-

1 Evangelical Lutheran Church in America, Lutheran Church—Missouri Synod, Wisconsin Evangelical Lutheran Synod

Key to Denominations

Un.Meth. = The United Methodist Church
PrCUSA = Presbyterian Church (U.S.A.)
UCC = United Church of Christ
AoG = Assemblies of God
ABptUSA = American Baptist Churches in the U.S.A.
SBC = Southern Baptist Convention
Episc. = Episcopal Church
ChC-ChsC = Christian Churches and Churches of Christ
CC (Disc) = Christian Church (Disciples of Christ)
L-dS = The Church of Jesus Christ of Latter-day Saints
RCA = Reformed Church in America
Ch of Naz. = Church of the Nazarene
Wesleyan = The Wesleyan Church

ChsC = Churches of Christ
RegBptGA = General Association of Regular Baptist Churches
CRC = Christian Reformed Church in North America
EFC = The Evangelical Free Church of America
BptGenCf = Baptist General Conference
NABptCf = North American Baptist Conference
FreeLuth = The Association of Free Lutheran Congregations
HuttBrth = Hutterite Brethren
C&MA = The Christian and Missionary Alliance
ChG(Clvd) = Church of God (Cleveland, Tennessee)
MennUSA = Mennonite Church U.S.A.
NTBptF = New Testament Association of Independent Baptist Churches

- belief in the entire trustworthiness of the Bible (sometimes described as the inerrancy of the Bible), for many of the denominations;
- pacifism, for Mennonites;
- rejection of electricity and modern conveniences, for the Amish;
- speaking in tongues, for the Assemblies of God and other pentecostals;
- baptism by immersion upon profession of faith, for Baptists and some other groups;
- singing without instruments, for the conservative branch of the Churches of Christ;
- insistence that the King James translation of the Bible is the only acceptable version, for many of the groups;
- tee-totalism, for many of the groups;
- rejection of public education and the provision of alternate schooling at home or in private academies, for some of the groups.

(In these terms, Mormons, by upholding the distinctive beliefs and practices of the Church of Jesus Christ of Latter-day Saints, or Seventh-day Adventists, by meeting to worship together on Saturday, fit well into the sectarian pattern. And both of these hard-to-categorize bodies have become a major presence in these 11 states, with NARA reporting the number of Latter-day Saints in 2000 as 230,235, and the number of Seventh-day Adventists as 136,769.)

Many of the sectarian groups, but not all, are evangelical in the American sense of that term. (The European sense, which means roughly "Lutheran," is a different matter, but helps explain why the largest denomination in the United States with the word "evangelical" in its title, the Evangelical Lutheran Church in America, is usually not classified with the American evangelical denominations and movements.)

American evangelicals stress the need to be converted ("born again") from sin to God through Christ; they regard the Bible as the ultimate religious authority; they stress the need to share their faith with others that they too might be converted; and they hold that faith in Christ is the only way for humans to enjoy fellowship with God. Evangelical convictions are widespread in proprietary denominations, but they are usually not as central or all-defining as in the groups that use the term "evangelical" for themselves.

Whether sectarian bodies hold to evangelical beliefs or not, they tend to be less intimately connected to the civic and public life of their communities. Historically, they have not enjoyed the adherence of as many civic leaders as the proprietary bodies, although that situation is changing rapidly as more and more large sectarian churches grow up in specific communities. Historically, they have not been wealthy, although that situation too is changing fast. Politically, the sectarian groups have a long record of pietistic non-participation, or even (into the 1950s) of leaning toward the Democratic Party. But in recent decades, the politicization of some of these sectarian groups has played a major part in the rise of the New Christian Right.

Also in recent decades, many sectarian churches have come to sponsor their own private schools. It is, however, imperative to remember that the huge diversity among sectarian Protestant groups means that no simple ascription applies to them all on political, or almost any other, matters. To underscore the reality of sectarian Protestant diversity, the NARA survey of 2000 showed that in Ohio alone there existed a tremendous range of such groups that garnered at least 0.1 percent of the state's religious adherents (i.e., at least 3,000-4,000 adherents, with some much larger). These groups included the following:

- American Baptist Churches in the U.S.A.,
- Apostolic Christian Church of America, Incorporated,
- Assemblies of God,
- Baptist General Conference,
- Brethren Church (Ashland, Ohio),
- Christian and Missionary Alliance,
- Christian Churches and Churches of Christ,
- Christian Union,
- Church of God (Anderson, Indiana),
- Church of God (Cleveland, Tennessee),
- Church of Jesus Christ of Latter-day Saints (Mormons),
- Church of the Brethren,
- Church of the Nazarene,
- Churches of Christ,
- Churches of God—General Conference,
- Community of Christ,
- Conservative Congregational Christian Conference,
- Conservative Mennonite Conference,
- Evangelical Free Church,
- Free Methodist Church of North America,
- General Association of Regular Baptist Churches,
- International Council of Community Churches,
- International Church of the Foursquare Gospel,
- Mennonite Church USA,
- Missionary Church,
- National Association of Free Will Baptists,
- Old Order Amish,
- Pentecostal Church of God,

- Presbyterian Church in America,
- Salvation Army,
- Seventh-day Adventist Church,
- Southern Baptist Convention,
- Vineyard USA,
- Wesleyan Church.

The proprietary-ethnic-sectarian designations are not airtight. Some of the groups I have classified as sectarian, like the America Baptist Churches in the U.S.A., often act with proprietary concern. More conservative elements in the proprietary churches support evangelical, and hence sometimes sectarian, causes. African-American and other ethnic churches sometimes provide a full range of social and community services to their members and so act very much as the proprietary churches have often done throughout their history. Many of the ethnic churches are on their way to playing a more public role in either the sectarian or the proprietary style, and sometimes both.

Yet dividing Protestants into these three broad groups does offer a conceptual grid that is useful for understanding their presence in the Midwest. The non-Lutheran, proprietary churches do, in fact, often tend to act and think alike, although even among them the historic distinctions of the various denominational traditions can be salient. The diversity, especially among ethnic and sectarian Protestants, should always be kept in mind by journalists and others who are tempted to equate the actions of one particular group with all other "evangelicals," "fundamentalists," "black churches," or other frequently-used but woefully imprecise designations.

Capsule History

A one-paragraph summary of the Protestant history of the Midwest would go like this.

In the beginning were the Methodists, with Presbyterians and Baptists not too far behind, and the Congregationalists a significant presence as well. Then after the Civil War came a half-century of rapid population growth for the whole region. In that deluge were lots of Methodists, Presbyterians, and Congregationalists, but many more Catholics and Lutherans, and a full laundry list of others—Baptists, Jews, Moravians, Brethren, Mennonites, Disciples, and more. Over the course of the twentieth century the proprietary Protestants have continued to give ground to Roman Catholics, Lutherans, sectarian Protestants, and non-Christian groups, though their earlier hegemony is still visible in many smaller communities and particular sub-regions. Protestants in the Midwest have come to be fairly evenly balanced between proprietary and sectarian types, while the national importance of the region for American Protestantism as a whole is indicated not only by the gross numbers of self identifiers in the ARIS survey and by tabulations of denominational adherents, but also by the large number of Protestant colleges and seminaries, as well as the denominational headquarters in the region noted by Philip Barlow in his treatment of Midwestern demography.

Although it is long past time when a full-scale history of Protestants in the Midwest has needed to be written, the paragraphs that follow try to provide a little flesh for this bare-bones skeletal history.

The 1790s, when the Ohio River valley was for the first time fully opened to settlement, marked a new chapter in American religious history. Into the opening "Northwest," as it was then called, streamed representatives of many religious traditions, but the Methodists were there "firstest with the mostest."[9] The Ohio Territory offered to Methodists two advantages they had not earlier enjoyed: there was no inherited competition from the older established churches, and there were no slaves.[10]

In their first years in America, Methodists had been handicapped by the suspicion that they were stealing sheep from other church flocks, and they had been beset especially in the South by the strong testimony against slavery announced first by John Wesley and then maintained vigorously by Francis Asbury. On the Ohio frontier, these handicaps simply did not exist.

The Methodists' zeal to preach conversion, their strategy of establishing local classes wherever folk responded, and their savvy in keeping far-flung adherents linked by itinerant circuit riders made them the overwhelmingly dominant religious force in the newly opened territory. Success on a somewhat smaller scale soon came to the Disciples and Christians, who also were experts at self-mobilization. As it was in Ohio, so it continued to be in Indiana, Michigan, much of Illinois, and then over the Mississippi into Iowa, Nebraska, and Kansas.

Massive Catholic and Lutheran immigration created different conditions in the Upper Midwest, but from the Ohio River to well beyond the Missouri River, Methodists gobbled up territory and Methodists set the tone. Strikingly, many of Ohio's earliest political leaders—or their wives—were Methodists, which had not been the case in any of the original states. This early Methodist preeminence left a powerful mark on public life. In some interesting ways, to which we shall return, there is an echo of this early Methodist presence in the rapid expansion of the newer megachurches in the region.

In 1850, the United States census for the first time counted the churches (the last such effort by the census came in 1936). By 1850, the Midwestern states east of the Mississippi, as well as Iowa to the west, had received considerable settlement. The proprietary Protestant character of that settlement was indicated by the census enumeration of accommodations (i.e., "seats" available in the church buildings of the various denominations—the census did not try to count members, attendees, or adherents), as seen in Table 2.4.

Almost one-third of the accommodations for the entire region were Methodist, a proportion that entailed a broader Methodist influence then than a similar proportion of Catholic adherents in the Midwest exerts today, since in that earlier period there was much less competition from other cultural institutions or entertainment media. Presbyterians and Baptists each accounted for about one-sixth of adherents, and Congregationalists about one-fifteenth. The religious diversity for which the Midwest would be renowned was definitely visible by 1850, with Catholics, Lutherans, Quakers, Disciples, Reformed, Episcopalians, Moravians, and Universalists all having established a presence. But all of these other groups combined totaled far less than the Methodists.

Methodists, who in 1850 were still more sectarian and evangelical than they later became, had established the religious tone for the region. That tone would change greatly in decades to come, but the foundation was, and remains, important. In doctrine, Methodists stressed holiness of personal life (they were at the forefront of the era's temperance movements).

In society, the Methodists adopted a low-key presence but were energetic creators of public schools. They took steps to alleviate poverty, and they were more open to the leadership of women than the other historic Protestant denominations. In their internal organization, Methodists combined empowerment for the laity (the local class meeting where lay people took charge was still a force), with strenuous recruitment of able young men (itinerancy was still the expected path for a young preacher) and diligent oversight of the connection as a whole (bishops, elders, and settled pastors worked closely to coordinate the Methodist work).

In the terms used above, Methodists, carrying on with the great zeal they had shown in the United States since the end of the Revolutionary War, were at once sectarian, proprietary, and evangelical. Presbyterians, Congregationalists, and Episcopalians were then most likely to be proprietary and evangelical, while the Baptists and Disciples/Churches of Christ of the period were usually evangelical and sectarian.

In the 50 years from 1860 to 1910 the modern history of the Midwest began—economic, industrial, agricultural, educational, and also religious. The population of the five states east of the Mississippi jumped by a huge 163 percent in that 50-year period, while in the six states west of the Mississippi it increased an unbelievable 745 percent. (As a comparison, for the longer period from 1910 to 2000 the population of the five eastern states grew by only 147 percent, and the population of the six western states grew by only 63 percent.)

Great population growth does not necessarily entail dramatic changes in religious demography, but in the latter half of the nineteenth century it certainly did for the Midwest. In 1890, for the first time, the U.S. census counted church members instead of just accommodations.[11] Its very detailed figures from that year,

Table 2.4 Percentage of a state's total accommodations—1850 (Census)						
	OH	**MI**	**IN**	**WI**	**IL**	**IA**
Methodists	37.3	28.2	37.5	21.8	36.7	33.7
Presbyterians	18.7	18.8	14.9	8.7	17.1	18.2
Baptists	12.7	14.9	19.6	17.2	19.3	9.2
Congregationalists	2.9	8.7	-	11.3	3.2	11.0
Episcopalians	2.2	7.0	1.0	5.3	2.9	1.7
Christians	2.1	-	9.2	-	6.3	6.5
Quakes	2.1	1.2	6.3	-	-	3.6
All Others	10.6	5.1	5.3	4.8	5.1	3.4
RCs	5.2	13.4	3.5	25.5	6.0	10.4
Lutherans	6.2	2.7	2.7	5.4	3.4	2.3

which probably was the most thorough enumeration of American religious life ever done, revealed a very different pattern from only 40 years before. While in 1850 the Methodists had been the largest denomination in five of the six states then in the region (Wisconsin was the exception with its Catholic population), in 1890 the Methodists remained the most numerous church in only two of what had become the region's 11 states (Indiana and Kansas).

Yet, as an indication of Methodist strength in the rural and small-town Midwest, Methodists were still the largest denomination in about two-thirds of the region's counties.[12] Although Catholics were concentrated in fewer counties their numbers, fueled by immigration from Ireland, Germany, France, and Southern Europe, were now the largest in each of the nine other states (Table 2.5). The same surge of immigration, with the Scandinavian countries also contributing, had led to a great growth of Lutherans, who were now the second largest denominational family in Wisconsin, Minnesota, North Dakota, and South Dakota. The proportion of Presbyterians, Congregationalists, and Baptists had dropped, along with that of the Methodists. The denominations that had come into the region for the first time in any significant numbers between 1850 and 1890 included mostly groups of immigrant origin, mostly from Dutch (Reformed) or German (Church of the Brethren, German Evangelical Synod, Mennonites, United Brethren) background.

By 1890, the cultural landscape of the Midwest was transformed. Most obvious was the growth of manufacturing in Ohio, Michigan, and northern Illinois, with the rise of great industrial and commercial cities, preeminently Chicago, but also Cleveland, Cincinnati, Detroit, Milwaukee, Minneapolis–St. Paul, and Omaha. While agriculture remained strong throughout the region, and dominant

Table 2.5	Percentage of a state's membership—1890 (Gaustad & Barlow)										
	OH	MI	IN	WI	IL	MN	IA	ND	SD	NE	KS
Methodists[1]	24.7	21.0	32.1	10.2	17.1	7.2	25.7	9.5	16.1	25.2	34.1
Presbyterians	8.5	4.6	6.2	2.5	6.4	2.8	2.3	5.1	5.6	7.7	9.3
Baptists	5.6	6.9	10.1	3.0	9.1	3.1	6.1	3.9	4.7	6.9	10.2
Congreg.[2]	5.3	4.3	-	4.9	6.1	3.6	5.5	2.7	6.0	6.3	3.5
Episcopalians	1.5	3.2	-	1.9	1.7	2.1	1.2	1.5	3.1	2.1	1.1
Christians	6.6	1.0	14.3	-	5.1	-	5.6	-	-	4.0	7.5
All Others	12.7	9.0	14.2	3.7	5.3	2.8	12.7	2.2	7.1	7.3	9.4
RCs	27.7	39.0	17.1	44.9	39.5	51.0	29.5	44.4	30.1	26.5	20.1
Lutherans	7.4	11.0	6.0	28.9	9.7	27.4	11.4	30.7	27.3	14.0	4.8

1 Includes denominations that later joined The United Methodist Church.
2 Includes denominations that later joined The United Church of Christ.

in Indiana, southern Illinois, and all the states west of the Mississippi, the presence of booming cities testified to religious as well as economic change.

For the most part, proprietary Protestants remained more at home in rural areas, small towns, and mid-sized cities. The massive Lutheran immigration to the upper Midwest gave to that sub-region a type of Protestantism that was more inward-looking than the proprietary traditions and more communal than the sectarians. With the massive social and economic changes, a new day had begun for Midwestern religion—not by replacing the old but by overlaying what had earlier prevailed with a new configuration dependent on European patterns of community religious life.

The more than 100 years since the thorough census of 1890 have witnessed incremental adjustments rather than the dramatic change-over of the late nineteenth century (Table 2.6). The most reliable estimates of church adherence in 1990 showed that Lutherans had moved from strength to strength; they had become the largest Protestant presence in Wisconsin, Minnesota, Iowa, the Dakotas, and Nebraska, and had even exceeded the Catholic population in Minnesota and the Dakotas.[13] The Baptists were the only one of the older Protestant traditions to increase their proportion of Midwestern population. They had become the largest Protestant tradition in Ohio, Michigan, Indiana, and Illinois, but because of the multitude of Baptist denominations and their largely sectarian outlook, the Baptists exerted less influence on public life than the Methodists and other proprietary churches had done in earlier eras.

Methodists remained widely distributed, with at least 10 percent of the state's religious adherents in Ohio and Indiana (where they were the second most widely distributed Protestant body after the Baptists), Iowa and Nebraska (where they

Table 2.6	Percentage of a state's membership—1990 (Gaustad & Barlow)									
	OH	**MI**	**IN**	**WI**	**IL**	**MN**	**IA**	**ND**	**SD**	**NE**	**KS**
Methodists	12.9	6.8	14.3	4.9	6.5	5.1	16.3	4.9	9.2	14.5	17.8
Presbyterians	3.8	2.9	3.4	1.5	2.4	2.4	5.1	2.5	3.5	4.9	4.8
Baptists	13.5	11.3	15.1	3.8	11.9	2.9	4.1	2.9	5.2	5.0	15.9
Congreg	3.6	1.6	2.3	3.0	2.7	2.0	3.5	2.0	3.9	2.8	1.3
Episcopalians	1.3	1.5	-	-	-	1.1	-	-	2.5	1.2	1.4
Christians	4.6	-	11.0	-	3.2	-	4.7	-	-	3.3	9.2
All Others	13.4	15.9	20.1	7.3	11.7	7.6	11.8	6.9	11.3	10.0	14.2
RCs	39.4	49.9	26.5	49.2	52.7	39.1	31.0	35.8	30.3	33.3	27.3
Lutherans	7.5	10.1	7.3	29.9	8.9	39.8	23.5	45.0	34.1	25.0	8.1

were second after the Lutherans), and Kansas (the one state where Methodists remained the largest Protestant denominational family). The other proprietary denominations—Presbyterians, Congregationalists, Episcopalians, and now also the Disciples—were still a significant presence in the southern tier of the region, but they too were declining alongside the Methodists.

Among the era's most significant Protestant developments was the rise of African-American churches in the region's urban centers as the result of the great black migration northwards from about the time of the First World War. Also important was the rapid spread of sectarian churches, many of them evangelical, like the Nazarenes, the Free Church, or independent congregations, but also including others like the Mormons and the Seventh-day Adventists. And then from 1965 and the passage of a new immigration law, the Midwest has witnessed a swelling tide of ethnic churches that, like African-American congregations, flourish in the cities but that more rapidly than the black churches have also taken root in suburban and small-town areas.

The religious history of the Midwest since 1910 has reflected the region's broader history. Much of Michigan and Ohio, the Chicago metropolitan area of northern Illinois and northwest Indian, southern Wisconsin, the Twin Cities, and other major cities have participated fully in the great social movements of industrialization, suburbanization, immigration, economic shift toward information technology, multi-cultural diversity, and extremes of wealth and poverty. Church life in these areas has fared best when congregations respond actively and intentionally to shifting social and economic realities, whether African-American and other ethnic churches providing enclaves of support for mobile communities, or the newer seeker-sensitive churches offering much the same to mostly Caucasian audiences.

More traditional, predominately white churches have not done as well in

Table 2.7   State-by-state percentage of denominational strength—East of the Mississippi
(1850 census; 1890, 1990 Gaustad & Barlow)

	OH	MI	IN	IL	WI
United Meths.[1]	37-24-13	28-21-7	38-32-14	37-17-7	22-12-5
Pres, Episc., UCC[2]	24-15-9	35-12-6	16-6-6	23-14-5	25-9-5
Sectarian[3]	22-13-23	17-9-16	38-30-42	26-14-18	17-3-6
[Baptist]	13-6-14	15-7-13	20-10-15	20-9-12	14-3-4
All Others	4-10-8	3-5-7	1-9-4	5-5-8	5-1-5
RCs	5-28-39	13-39-50	40-7-27	6-40-53	26-45-49
Old Europeans[4]	8-10-8	4-14-14	3-6-7	3-10-9	5-30-30
[Lutherans]	6-7-8	3-11-10	3-6-7	3-10-9	5-29-30

1 Includes denominations that joined The United Methodist Church.
2 Includes denominations that joined The United Church of Christ.
3 Baptist, Christian Church (Disciples), Christian, Adventist, Pentecostal-Holiness, Independent, Universalists, Pietists,
   Anabaptists, Quakers
4 Lutherans plus Reformed

these venues. They have, however, remained anchors of tradition in the more agricultural states west of the Mississippi and in less urban parts of the states to the east. In the second half of the twentieth century, Iowa, North Dakota, South Dakota, rural Nebraska, rural Kansas, as well as rural areas of Indiana and Illinois, have been by-passed. Population in these areas has not risen but, in fact, is draining away from many areas. (The ratio of population between Midwestern states east of the Mississippi and those to the west went from 2.15:1 in 1890 to 3.35:1 by 1990.) In these situations, the churches—whether Catholic, Lutheran, proprietary Protestant, or sectarian Protestant—have had the task of providing stability for a rapidly aging population. Some have performed that service with creativity and integrity, others have simply held on (Tables 2.7 and 2.8).

From the late nineteenth century, the Midwest has also developed as the heartland of Protestant higher education in the United States. Proprietary Protestants were responsible for a raft of college foundings. Many of these schools now retain only tenuous connections with their founding denominations, but the roster is still impressive. At least 25 colleges and universities in this region are still connected to the United Methodist Church (including Illinois Wesleyan University in Bloomington, Illinois; DePauw University in Greencastle, Indiana; Morningside College in Sioux City, Iowa; Kansas Wesleyan University in Salina, Kansas; Adrian College in Adrian, Michigan; Hamline University in St. Paul, Minnesota; Nebraska Wesleyan University in Lincoln, Nebraska; Baldwin-Wallace College in Berea, Ohio; and Dakota Wesleyan University in Mitchell, South Dakota); at least

Table 2.8   State-by-state proportion of denominational strength—West of the Mississippi (1850 census; 1890, 1990 Gaustad & Barlow)

	MN	IA	ND	SD	NE	KS
United Meths.[1]	x-7-5	34-26-16	x-10-5	x-16-9	x-27-15	x-34-18
Pres, Episc., UCC[2]	x-9-6	31-10-9	x-9-5	x-15-10	x-16-9	x-14-8
Sectarian[3]	x-3-6	20-14-13	x-9-5	x-7-8	x-11-12	x-24-35
[Baptist]	x-3-3	9-6-4	x-4-3	x-5-5	x-7-5	x-10-16
All Others	x-3-4	3-9-4	x-2-3	x-2-6	x-6-6	x-2-4
RCs	x-51-39	10-30-31	x-44-36	x-30-30	x-27-33	x-21-27
Old Europeans[4]	x-27-40	2-11-27	x-31-45	x-30-37	x-14-25	x-5-8
[Lutherans]	x-27-40	2-11-24	x-31-45	x-27-34	x-14-25	x-5-8

1 Includes denominations that joined The United Methodist Church.
2 Includes denominations that joined The United Church of Christ.
3 Baptist, Christian Church (Disciples), Christian, Adventist, Pentecostal-Holiness, Independent, Universalists, Pietists, Anabaptists, Quakers
4 Lutherans plus Reformed

16 with the Presbyterian Church (U.S.A.) (including Millikin University in Decatur, Illinois; Hanover College in Hanover, Indiana; Coe College in Cedar Rapids, Iowa; Sterling College in Sterling, Kansas; Macalaster College in St. Paul, Minnesota; Jamestown College in Jamestown, North Dakota; College of Wooster, in Wooster, Ohio; and Carroll College in Waukesha, Wisconsin); and several others with Disciples, Congregationalist, or Episcopalian connections.

The region is also home to more than a third (37 out of approximately 100) of the member or affiliated colleges of the Coalition of Christian Colleges and Universities, which represents more self-consciously evangelical institutions— including three colleges called "Bethel" (Missionary Church in Mishawaka, Indiana; Mennonite in North Newton, Kansas; Baptist General Conference in St. Paul, Minnesota); three Nazarene institutions (Olivet in Bourbonnais, Illinois; MidAmerica in Olathe, Kansas; Mount Vernon in Mount Vernon, Ohio); four Reformed institutions (Christian Reformed—Trinity Christian in Palos Heights, Illinois; Calvin in Grand Rapids, Michigan; Dordt in Sioux City, Iowa; and one Reformed Church in America—Northwestern in Orange City, Iowa); several large nondenominational schools (including Wheaton in Wheaton, Illlinois; and Taylor University in Upland, Indiana); and colleges or universities representing at least a dozen other denominations.

The region, with Chicago at the center, has also been very well represented by seminaries and other schools for training candidates for the ministry. A partial list of the non-Lutheran Protestant denominations that still sponsor seminaries in this 11-state region (sometimes more than one per denomination) includes American Baptist, Baptist General Conference, Christian Church (Disciples of Christ), Christian Reformed Church, Church of God, Church of God (Anderson, Indiana), Church of the Brethren, Community of Christ, Episcopal, Evangelical Covenant, Evangelical Free Church, General Association of Regular Baptist, Grace Brethren, independent Baptist, Mennonite, North American Baptist, Presbyterian Church (U.S.A.), Reformed Church in America, United Church of Christ, and United Methodist.

The most recent changes in religious demography can be charted with the aid of two maps provided by the Glenmary Research Center—one presenting religious data from 1970, the other from 2000.

The Glenmary data (roughly equivalent to NARA) is limited by the omission of hard-to-find data regarding certain religious groups such as African-American Protestants; nevertheless, the maps are generally accurate and helpful. In these maps, the largest denominational family in each county is designated by a particular color. From a distance, this means that the Northeast, the Great Lakes, the Southwest, and the West are blue (for the Catholic church), the southeast is red (for Baptists), the upper Midwest is orange (for Lutherans), Utah with surrounding regions is gray (for Mormons), and traditionally a band from Delaware to Nebraska has been green (for Methodists).

By comparing maps from 1970 and 2000, it is possible to gauge at least something about larger trends in Midwestern religious demography.[14] The color-coding of counties in 2000 mostly reinforces the major generalizations outlined above (Table 2.9). More revealing is the record of change from 1970 to 2000. This comparison reveals that for the region's 940 counties, from 1970 to 2000 Roman Catholics gained as a proportion of all religious adherents in 124 counties (or 13 percent), while Methodists lost ground in 144 counties (or 15 percent). The states of the upper Midwest (Wisconsin, Minnisota, North Dakota, and South Dakota, and northern sections of Nebraska and Iowa) witnessed mostly a give-and-take between Lutherans and Catholics.

But for the rest of the region, Methodists fell away almost everywhere, while Baptists and Christians (Disciples) gained ground in Indiana, southern Illinois, and Kansas (Table 2.10, page 77). These changes, along with a few other shifts, also reflected in county-wide pluralities as well as many not registered on a county-wide basis, point to a continuation of the history descending from the late nineteenth century. Proprietary Protestantism, especially in its Methodist form, continues to decline, while sectarian Protestantism rises in strength, but not at a rate to come even close to displacing the Catholic and Lutheran churches as the predominant religious families of the region.

Table 2.9   Denominational Pluralities in Counties 2000 (Glenmary*)

This table enumerates the counties in each state where a single denomination or denominational family includes 25 percent or more of the church adherents. In parentheses are the number of counties where the denominational adherence exceeds 50 percent.

	RC	Luth	Meth	Christ.	Bapt.	None	Other[1]
East of Mississippi							
OH (88)	45(15)	2(1)	20	2	3	15	1
MI (83)	72(35)	3(1)	1	-	-	2	5
IN (92)	36(6)	1	8	16	4(1)	26	1
WI (72)	55(36)	17(7)	-	-	-	-	-
IL (102)	46(32)	3	8	11	22(13)	12	-
West of Mississippi							
MN (87)	28(9)	59(37)	-	-	-	-	-
IA (99)	35(5)	34(4)	14	2	-	9	5
ND (53)	15(11)	38(30)	-	-	-	-	-
SD (66)	32(5)	29(6)	1	-	-	-	4
NE (93)	32(11)	35(8)	17(3)	-	1(1)	4	4
KS (105)	40(3)	7	37(2)	2	8(1)	9	2

* Note: Because of difficulties in enumerating members of various African-American Protestant denominations at the county level, this table excludes traditionally African-American Protestant groups. However, the table remains generally accurate. It is based on data in Dale Jones, et al., *Religious Congregations and Membership in the United States, 2000* (Nashville, TN: Glenmary Research Center, 2002).

[1] OH: Mennonite 1
MI: Reformed 3(2), Mennonite 1, Pentecostal 1
IN: Mennonite 1
IA: Reformed 4(1), Latter-day Saints 1
SD: Episcopal 3, Reformed 1
NE: UCC 3, Christian and Missionary Alliance 1
KS: Mennonite 2

The Methodist (and Now Megachurch?) Impact on Public Life

In conclusion, it may be useful to speculate on how the strong Methodist foundation for Midwestern religious life has left its mark on public life, including politics. That Methodist foundation explains why Protestant life in the Midwest has been earnest, evangelical, and energetic, but not as sectarian as elsewhere in the country. Although the rise of Baptists and other similar groups in many Midwestern states is making this region more like other regions, the early Methodist history (as well as the strong Lutheran presence) continues to distinguish this region.

In particular, Methodists have been more individualistic than Lutherans but less so than Baptists. They bequeathed a more relaxed acceptance of organized philanthropy than encouraged by Baptists. They have been less oriented to class divisions based on wealth and status than Presbyterians or Episcopalians, less ethnically defined than Lutherans, and more likely to go with the flow of cultural change than either Baptists or Lutherans.

Of course, any claim about a lingering Methodist influence must be qualified by attending to what have become the important sub-regions of the Midwest. In Ohio, Indiana, and southern Illinois, the Methodist legacy remains significant, although it has given way rapidly to Baptist and Disciples growth in recent decades. This sub-region retains links to an older proprietary Protestant past because the number of Catholics and Lutherans is smaller here than anywhere else in the Midwest. It also contains some of the most Mennonite (or Amish) counties in the region.

In Michigan, Wisconsin, and northern Illinois, Methodist hegemony is now only a memory. Catholics and Lutherans represent the dominant religious traditions, but Baptists have been expanding in Michigan, and a wide variety of evangelical, ethnic, fundamentalist, and sectarian Protestant groups sustain a lively, if not large, presence in this sub-region as well. Many are headquartered in the Chicago metropolitan area. African-American Protestants are also especially strong in the Chicago area, which is also home to a wide diversity of other ethnic churches. The Dutch Reformed denominations enjoy a special regional presence in western Michigan.

In Minnesota, North Dakota, and South Dakota, all religious groups stand in the shade of the Lutherans. Proportionately considered, the proprietary Protestant denominations are about twice as strong in South Dakota as in the other two states, and the sectarian groups with historic ties to Lutheranism are strong in Minnesota (as well as the Chicago area).

A final sub-region is constituted by Nebraska, Kansas, and Iowa (actually, mid- to southern Iowa, since the northern third of Iowa resembles the upper Midwest with a strong Lutheran plurality). In all three states the presence of Methodism is still obvious, as is also the presence of the other proprietary denominations. Baptists, with the Southern Baptist Convention at the forefront, have been advancing rapidly in Kansas, as has the Christian Church (Disciples of Christ) in Iowa and Kansas. Similar to the situation in Ohio, Indiana, and southern Illinois, both proprietary and sectarian Protestant churches are a major cultural presence, since Catholics and Lutherans are not as widely dispersed here as in the rest of the Midwest.

For politics, the historic strength of proprietary Protestantism has certainly played an important role throughout the region. In recent years, non-Lutheran Protestants have contributed to the rise of the New Christian Right, but with less direct impact on the winning and losing of elections than in the South and

Table 2.10   Changes in Denominational Pluralities in Counties, 1970-2000 (Glenmary*)

This table records the number of counties per state where the leading denomination changed (or increased its plurality from 25-49 percent to more than 50 percent, or decreased its plurality from more than 50 percent to 25-49 percent) in the period from 1970 to 2000.

+ = new plurality or higher pluraliry; - = relinquished plurality or lower plurality

	RC	Luth	Meth	Christ.	Bapt.	Other[1]
East of Mississippi						
OH	+13 -5	+2 -2	+2 -21	+1 -0	+3 -1	+1 -0
MI	+15 -9	+3 -2	+0 -2	-	-	+2 -2
IN	+10 -3	-	+0 -22	+11 -0	+1 -5	+1
WI	+15 -4	+2 -15	+0 -1	-	-	-1
IL	+13 -3	+1 -3	+0 -18	+10 -0	+4 -0	-1
West of Mississippi						
MN	+9 -1	+2 -13	-	-	-	-
IA	+9 -3	+7 -3	+0 -27	+2 -0	-	+2
ND	+2 -3	+6 -3	-	-	-	-
SD	+10 -7	+4 -8	+0 -1	-	-	+1 -3
NE	+13 -6	+11 -7	+0 -22	-	-	+1 -3
KS	+14 -4	+3 -3	+5 -30	+2 -0	+15 -0	+1

* Note: Because of difficulties in enumerating members of various African-American Protestant denominations through history, this table excludes traditionally African-American Protestant groups. However, the table remains generally accurate. It is based on data in Douglas Johnson, et al., *Churches and Church Membership in the United States, 1971* (Atlanta: 1974); and Dale Jones, et al., *Religious Congregations and Membership in the United States, 2000* (Nashville, TN: Glenmary Research Center, 2002).

[1] OH: +1 Mennonite
MI: +1 Reformed, +1 Pentecostal, -1 Reformed, -1 UCC
IN: +1 Mennonite
WI: -1 UC
IL: -1 Presbyterian
IA: +1 Latter-day Saints, +1 Reformed
SD: +1 Episcopal, -1 Reformed, -1 Presbyterian, -1 Episcopal
NE: +1 Christian and Missionary Alliance, -3 UCC
KS: +1 Mennonite

Southern Crossroads, where non-Lutheran Protestant populations are not so heavily counterbalanced by Lutheran and Catholic voters.[15]

In the 2000 presidential election, as analyzed by political scientists including John Green at the University of Akron, white Protestants as a whole contributed disproportionately to George W. Bush's narrow victory. Using a discrimination between "mainline" and "evangelical," which corresponds roughly to the "proprietary" and "sectarian" categories employed here, Green and his associates concluded that evangelical Protestants who regularly attend church (high-commitment evangelicals) accounted for 32 percent of Bush's total votes, with another 8 percent from evangelicals who do not attend church regularly (low-commitment evangelicals), 10 percent from high-commitment mainline Protestants, and 11 percent from low-commitment mainline Protestants. (By contrast, the contribution to Al Gore's total from these four groups was, respectively, 6, 7, 5, and 8 percent. For another major contrast, African-American Protestant voters contributed 19 percent of Al Gore's total vote, while giving George W. Bush only 1 percent of his vote total.[16])

To these totals Midwestern Protestants contributed their fair share. Exit polling from election day, which employed a different set of data than that used by the John Green team, found that across the nation white Protestants of all sorts favored Bush over Gore by 64 percent to 34 percent (with 2 percent going to other candidates). In the Midwest, white Protestants of all sorts favored Bush over Gore by 61.5 percent to 36.5 percent (with 2 percent going to other candidates). The black Protestant vote went more strongly the other way (with the national tally favoring Gore by 92 percent to 7 percent, and in the Midwest by 94 percent to 5 percent). Since the Midwest cast about one-fourth of the votes in this election, the strong Protestant support for Bush (though slightly less than the national white Protestant average) contributed greatly to the final results.

In the last quarter century, the Republican presidential candidate has, in general, done better in the Midwest (with Wisconsin, Illinois, and Minnesota as the major exceptions) than nationwide (Table 2.11). The strong Protestant presence certainly has played a role in these outcomes, although care is needed in attempting to specify the exact dimensions of electoral influence.

It is illuminating, however, to set this recent history into a longer historical frame. Well into the twentieth century, the Midwest was not only the most Methodist region of the country, but also as measured by the results of presidential elections, it was just about the most consistently Republican as well. As Table 2.12 suggests, the Midwest as a whole was more solidly Republican than the nation in its presidential votes right up to the first election of Franklin D. Roosevelt in 1932. Again, as seen in Table 2.12, that Republican strength in presidential elections has continued in what could now be called "the Old Methodist Midwest" (Ohio, Indiana, Iowa, North Dakota, South Dakota, Nebraska, and Kansas), by comparison both to the nation and to what can be termed "the Lutheran and Catholic Midwest" (Michigan, Wisconsin, Illinois, and Minnesota). Such generalizations are compromised in part by the strong Lutheran presence in North and South Dakota, but there is a clear enough pattern to leave room for thought.

Such thought would certainly emphasize the Methodist roots for a moderately conservative Protestant ethos that has fostered a certain measure of corporate solidarity in the rural and small-town Midwest, but that has never taken hold to the

Table 2.11 Ratio of state Republican vote to national Republican vote in selected presidential elections, 1976-2000

Richard M. Scammon, et al., eds. *America Votes 24* (Washington, D.C.: *Congressional Quarterly*, 2001).

	1976	1988	1996	2000
East of Mississippi				
OH	1.01	1.03	1.01	1.04
MI	1.08	1.00	.95	.96
IN	1.11	1.12	1.16	1.18
WI	1.00	.90	.95	.99
IL	1.04	.95	.90	.89
West of Mississippi				
MN	.88	.86	.86	.95
IA	1.03	.83	.98	1.01
ND	1.08	1.05	1.15	1.27
SD	1.05	1.05	1.14	1.26
NE	1.23	1.13	1.32	1.30
KS	1.09	1.05	1.33	1.21
National Republican %	48.0	53.4	40.7	47.9

same degree in cities. That ethos flourishes by nurturing a broad Protestant (and Caucasian) pluralism, but with certain suspicion of religious and cultural groups coming from outside Protestant (and Caucasian) networks. This ethos is definitely moralistic, with an ingrained commitment to decency and public order, but at the same time it only rarely looks to government for the formal enforcement of morality (debates over prohibition and abortion have been the major exceptions).

The moderation of such a "Methodist ethos" can also be seen in the historic Midwestern Protestant support for local public schools, with the Lutherans and Reformed the exception to this rule. Likewise, it can account for a relatively moderate tone (by comparison to the coasts and the South) in support of and opposition to labor unions, in support of and opposition to American wars of the last half century, and in support of pro-life and pro-choice positions. The moderation is less obvious west of the Mississippi on questions of agricultural policy, but that too points to the distinctive character of the region. Without pushing such speculations too hard, it is still possible to see the results of recent presidential elections as indicating where this "Methodist ethos" has been maintained, and where it has faded.

A final speculation is to wonder if the megachurches of the Midwest are not re-packaging some of the Methodist ethos into new forms for the suburbs, where

Table 2.12   State-by-State Presidential Voting, 1856-2000
(Republican victories followed by Democratic victories)

Presidential Elections, 1789-1996 (Washington: Congressional Quarterly, 1997).

The Old Methodist Midwest

	National	OH	IN	IA	ND	SD	NE	KS
1856-1928	14-5	17-2	14-5	18-1	7-2	9-1	12-4	13-4
1932-1964	2-7	4-5	6-3	5-4	6-3	6-3	6-3	6-3
1968-2000	6-3	6-3	9-0	5-4	9-0	9-0	9-0	9-0

The Lutheran and Catholic Midwest

	National	MI	WI	IL	MN
1856-1928	14-5	19-0	16-3	16-3	18-0
1932-1964	2-7	4-5	4-5	2-7	2-7
1968-2000	6-3	5-4	4-5	6-3	1-8

In 1892, South Dakota split its three electoral votes among three candidates; in 1892, Kansas voted for the Populist James B. Weaver; in 1924, Wisconsin voted for the Progressive Robert La Follette.

Since 1856, there have been 16 "sweep" elections, where one party captured all Midwestern states, 13 times for the Republicans (1860, Abraham Lincoln; 1864, Abraham Lincoln; 1868, Ulysses S. Grant; 1872, Ulysses S. Grant; 1880, James Garfield; 1888, Benjamin Harrison; 1900, William McKinley; 1904, Theodore Roosevelt; 1920, Herbert Hoover; 1928, Herbert Hoover; 1952, Dwight Eisenhower; 1956, Dwight Eisenhower; 1972, Richard Nixon), and three times for the Democrats (1932, Franklin Roosevelt; 1936, Franklin Roosevelt; 1964, Lyndon Johnson).

they are strongest, but also in some urban and rural areas where they can also be found. Like the early Methodists, the megachurches are innovative in their efforts at reaching and sustaining adherents. Like the Methodists they have pioneered in the production and use of a new hymnody. Like the early Methodist leaders, many megachurch pastors have their fingers on the pulse of popular sentiment. Like most of the Methodists throughout most of their history, most of the megachurch pastors are skilled in presenting their views on religion and other matters with a minimum of public offense. With some exceptions, the megachurches are, in political terms, less obviously liberal than the proprietary mainline and less overtly conservative than the sectarian evangelicals.

It is an open question whether it will be possible soon to speak of a "megachurch ethos." If the megachurches of the Midwest continue to grow in absolute terms, but also relative to other Protestants, such an ethos might emerge. If it did, it would reflect a most interesting development in the religious history of an American region that, more than any other, has been shaped by the orderly energy of its early Methodist pioneers.

Endnotes

1. William Jennings Bryan, "Speech Concluding Debate on the Chicago Platform," in *The First Battle: The Story of the Campaign of 1896* (Chicago: W. B. Conkey, 1896), 206.

2. H. W. Brands, *T.R.: The Last Romantic* (New York: Basic, 1997), 719.

3. Jacob Dorn, *Washington Gladden: Prophet of the Social Gospel* (Columbus: Ohio State University Press, 1966), 240-50.

4. Richard Wightman Fox, *Reinhold Niebuhr* (New York: Harper & Row, 1985).

5. Steven D. Reschly, "Expanded Exercise: The Amish, Compulsory Education, and Religious Freedom," *Historic U.S. Court Cases: An Encyclopedia*, volume 2, ed. John W. Johnson (New York: Routledge, 2001), 978-82.

6. Information from ARIS, referred to also as the phone survey, is from Barry A. Kosmin, Egon Mayer, and Ariela Keysar, *American Religious Identification Survey* 2001 (The Graduate Center of the City of New York, 2001).

7. For some of the best available research on these groups, with some attention to the Midwest, see R. Stephen Warner and Judith G. Witner, eds., *Gatherings in Diaspora: Religious Connections and the New Immigration* (Philadelphia: Temple University Press, 1998); and R. Stephen Warner, Ho Young Kim, Kwang Chung Kim, eds., *Korean Americans and Their Religions* (University Park: Penn State University Press, 2001).

8. The names of these churches are taken from a listing of megachurches maintained on the website of the Hartford Institute for Religion Research (<hirr.harsem.edu/org/faith_megachurches> Aug. 5, 2003).

9. Helpful orientation to the distinctives of the region at this period has been provided by Timothy L. Smith, "The Ohio Valley: Testing Ground for America's Experiment in Religious Pluralism," *Church History* 90 (Dec. 1991): 461-79.

10. I owe this insight, and much else in what follows, to John Wigger, "Methodism and the Development of Ohio Valley Religion," Society for Historians of the Early American Republic, Ohio State University, July 19, 2003.

11. The following survey of the census comes from Edwin Scott Gaustad and Philip L. Barlow, *New Historical Atlas of Religion in America* (New York: Oxford University Press, 2000), 376-81 (figure C.17).

12. Ibid., 360 (figure C.4).

13. Ibid., 382-87 (figure C.18).

14. I would like to thank my assistant, Luke Harlow, for these summaries of the information on institutions of higher learning, and for much other help in preparing this essay.

15. Corwin Smidt and James Penning, *Sojourners in the Wilderness: The Christian Right in Comparative Perspective* (Lanham, MD: Rowman & Littlefield, 1997), 269-276.

16. For discussion, see James L. Guth, John C. Green, Corwin E. Smidt, and Lyman A. Kellstedt, "Partisan Religion: Analyzing the 2000 Election," *Christian Century* (March 21-28, 2001) 18-20.

CHAPTER THREE

THE LUTHERAN DIFFERENCE:
WHAT MORE THAN NICE?

L. DeAne Lagerquist

Lutherans first appear in United States history as a case of mistaken identity when Spanish general Peter Menendez explained his motives for slaughtering a group of French Protestants, as against *Luteranos*. Since that incident in the 1560s neither journalists nor historians have paid much attention to Lutherans, who seldom are people of influence and power, or victims of persecution, or exotic. Historians of American religion treat Lutherans as a benign exception to their interpretation of the whole. Until well into the twentieth century the coincidence of Lutheran church membership with ethnic identity and Lutheran preoccupation with internal theological debates contributed to their invisibility. Geographic concentration in rural areas and in the Midwest further shielded Lutherans from national notice by academics or media types.

Lutherans who appear in the news are seldom identified as Lutheran. Unlike Jews and Catholics, Lutherans have produced few fiction writers. Moreover, authors seldom identify a character as Lutheran, perhaps because to do so seems to convey so little. Most often the designation suggests only vague, inoffensive religiousness. In an exceptional novel whose main characters are all Lutherans, the conductors on a train filled with Lutherans traveling to a historic convention in Minneapolis observe: "Nobody could say that the Lutherans weren't nice."[1] But, once credit is given for niceness, what more is there to say?

Recently, Midwestern Lutherans—specifically Pastor Ingqvist and members of Lake Wobegon Lutheran—have gained visibility if not understanding. Weekly, Garrison Keillor delights radio audiences with stories about this small-town congregation and its Roman Catholic neighbor, Our Lady of Perpetual Responsibility. His humorous accounts of worship, potlucks, and family dynamics reflect upon the humanity of the congregants. These monologues are neither journalistic accounts nor scholarly studies and cannot be held to those standards of accuracy. Nonetheless, Keillor's observations provide opportunity to ponder the veracity of his portrayal and its applicability beyond mythic Lake Wobegon.

Overall, Lutherans in Lake Wobegon are nice enough: frugal, responsible, and wary of rapid change. They know who they are because they are mostly Norwegian (or their ancestors were) and because they are not Catholic. Beyond ethnicity and church membership, they have much in common with the Catholics, with whom they pretty much run things. There are still farms outside Lake Wobegon, so even town folks are in touch with rural life. Although everyone has relatives there, "The Cities" (Minneapolis and St. Paul) are a distant place, geographically and culturally.

But Keillor's stories suggest that Lake Wobegon's values and customs are not confined to this town. Indeed, he once observed, "Everyone in Minnesota is Lutheran, whether they are or not." In fact, only one Minnesotan in four or five is a Lutheran, though in 2000 every other person in 37 of the state's 87 counties was Lutheran. In only one county are Lutherans less than one in 20, closer to their proportion in the national population: just under 3 percent.[2] Nonetheless, the pervasiveness of Lutheranism in the culture is not determined by counting baptized heads or even bodies in pews on Sunday.

Keillor's assertion suggests questions that inform this exploration of Lutheran contributions to public life and social capital in the Midwest. In what significant way might everyone be Lutheran? What characteristics of personal or public life reveal Lutheran influence? Is there more to this than a suggestion that "Minnesota nice" is a spillover from its Lutheran citizens? Does Keillor's assertion imply that in Minnesota, and by extension in the Midwest, Lutheranism has infused the culture and become the mainstream even though elsewhere Lutherans long have been invisible? A general look at Lutherans in the Midwest provides the background for exploring the variety of ways Lutherans participate in and contribute to public life in education, arts, social service, and political life.

Counting heads does not reveal what Lutherans, their churches, or their theology have contributed to public life, but it does suggest why Lutherans warrant more attention in the Midwest than elsewhere. Lutherans are most concentrated in the upper Midwest, and here they supply the largest portion of the population. The proportion of Minnesotans who are Lutheran is surpassed by the one-third of North Dakotans who are and nearly matched by the one-fifth of South Dakotans. In three other states—Nebraska, Iowa, and Wisconsin—the Lutheran population hovers just under 15 percent. Minnesota has the largest number, over 1 million in more than 1,600 congregations; Wisconsin has the second most, with nearly 750,000 members in almost 1,200 congregations. Pennsylvania comes close to

Wisconsin in membership, but those 630,000 and more Lutherans, in 1,400 con-gregations, constitute only about 5 percent of the state's total population. Illinois also has over 1,000 Lutheran congregations; California and Ohio each have more than 800; but in these populous states Lutherans are a much smaller fraction than in the upper-Midwest.[3]

The Midwest is also the location of a preponderance of key Lutheran institu-tions: five major seminaries (with a sixth in Missouri), two dozen colleges, sev-eral large social service agencies, a publishing house, and Thrivent Financial Services, offering investment advice and insurance, and encouraging its mem-bers' involvement in their communities.

All these Lutherans belong to congregations in the two largest denomina-tions—the Evangelical Lutheran Church in America (ELCA) and the Lutheran Church-Missouri Synod (LCMS)—or to a dozen and a half smaller bodies, including the Wisconsin Evangelical Lutheran Synod, the Lutheran Brethren, and the Association of Free Lutheran Congregations. Since the 1890s the number of extra-local bodies has steadily reduced as ethnic and theological differences dis-appear or are given less significance.

All the groups originated in the Reformation associated with Martin Luther, though that heritage has been shaped by differing European histories and immi-grant experiences in the United States.[4] To many Americans, Lutherans present an odd, even perplexing profile: Lutheran theology has much in common with Reformed or Calvinist Christianity (e.g., Presbyterians); Lutheran worship pat-terns resemble Roman Catholics' more than other Protestants'; and Lutheran piety or spirituality has affinities with the evangelical movement.[5] This seeming-ly eclectic set of characteristics is consistent with the Lutheran claim to be a con-fessing movement within the church catholic, not primarily a social institution. Indeed, whether it is now a denomination, a set of churches, or a movement, Lutheranism began as a protest against abuses within sixteenth-century Roman Catholicism. Luther's criticisms of the Church, his theological insights and prac-tical reforms, and his biography all inform American Lutheranism today.

Although Luther is remembered as a pastor, theologian, and reformer, his father intended that he would become a lawyer. A moment of personal crisis turned young Martin to the monastery, where he struggled with late medieval reli-gious practice in an effort to become good, acceptable to God. Finally, while preparing to teach Bible at the University of Wittenberg, he rediscovered the pri-macy of divine grace as the basis of salvation. Clinging to this gift, he challenged Church leaders to preach the gospel of freedom rather than requiring obedience to human regulations and rituals. He particularly criticized the treasury of merit: the notion that Christians can store up merit to release others from punishment for their sins. Political princes and theologians joined in the religious protest. Some, however, judged Luther's reforms too moderate. Radical reformers, ancestors of the historic peace churches, objected to continued cooperation between civic and Church leaders; others, including followers of John Calvin, demanded a purer church that worshiped in an austere setting and exercised more control in the secular community.

The theology of this movement to reform the Church by making the good news, the *evangelium*, central was articulated in a series of public statements beginning with the Augsburg Confession presented to the Emperor in 1530 and collected in *The Book of Concord*. The movement spread through Europe, particularly Germany and Scandinavia, by official action and popular response. Leaders of the movement's second phase, Lutheran Orthodoxy, labored to define its theology more precisely. By the mid-seventeenth century pietist pastors turned their preaching toward parishioners' hearts and souls, evoking a warmer, personal response to the gospel. Pietism encouraged Lutheran involvement in foreign missions and charitable activities. Despite the activist impulse demonstrated in works of mercy, pietist reiteration of the primacy of divine grace in salvation fostered a Lutheran tendency toward political quietism and non-involvement. Many Lutheran immigrants to North America, from the colonial era forward, were profoundly shaped by pietism, though the precise expression and depth of influence varied. The impulses of each phase intertwine in contemporary American Lutheranism, with pietism especially strong in the Midwest.

In the mid-1700s Henry Muhlenberg attempted to gather scattered colonial Lutheran congregations into a unified body, still an unfulfilled goal. A century later, the several dozen Lutheran groups—distinguished by ethnicity, piety, and theology—could be lumped into three parties: The American or neo-Lutherans, with affinities to the mainstream of American Protestantism; the moderate Confessionalists, who made fewer theological accommodations to the culture; and the Old Lutherans, often recent immigrants committed to orthodox doctrine. Among Lutherans the labels conservative or moderate indicate attitudes toward confessional doctrine.

In the late nineteenth century the center of American Lutheranism shifted away from Pennsylvania to the Midwest, where newly arrived Scandinavian and German Lutherans settled, often in rural areas. These immigrant Lutherans clustered in the moderate-to-conservative range of this scheme. When they were able, they founded congregations where they worshiped in their native European languages, organized their congregations into cooperative synods, and sponsored schools and charitable institutions. However, not all German immigrants came as Lutherans, and neither all of those who did nor all Scandinavians remained Lutheran. Norwegians were most likely to remain Lutheran: about 25 percent did. A significant number of "Red" Finns replaced church with labor organizations.

As Lutherans became more American, gaining education and economic means, the churches moved toward each other. Negotiators repeatedly addressed typical Lutheran concerns such as the authority of the Confessions, the relative weight of grace and faith in salvation, and the basis of and limits to religious cooperation; however, they seldom took up issues that preoccupied other American Protestants, notably the fundamentalist-modernist controversy.[6] Publication of shared worship books, their experience working together in relief efforts during the World Wars, and a combination of social and geographic mobility contributed to a series of mergers and the current denominational configuration. Just over 60 percent of the more than 8 million Lutherans in the United States belong to the ELCA, established in 1988.[7] The ELCA includes the ecclesiastical descendents of colonial Lutherans, both American and Confessionalist branches, as well as many nineteenth-century immigrant bodies and additions from the African-American, Native-American, and recent-immigrant communities. (This merger obscures the strength of the moderate American Lutheran Church, 1960-1988, in the Midwest.) Another third belong to the LCMS, which continues the line of the Old Lutherans. The remaining 500,000 are members of the smaller, conservative groups that preserve old identities or resulted from new divisions. These are particularly evident in the upper Midwest, where most of their headquarters are located.

Since the mid-twentieth century Lutherans have shed the designation "church of immigrants" given to them by H. Richard Niebuhr in his 1929 classic *The Social Sources of Denominationalism*. Changes in institutional structure were accompanied by developments in ecumenical relationships and a shift toward the mainstream. One observer locates this move in 1958, when Franklin Clark Fry appeared on the cover of *Time*; then president of the United Lutheran Church and a leader of both the National Council of Churches and the Lutheran World Federation, Fry was known as Mr. Protestant.[8] Unlike the members of Lake Wobegon Lutheran, most Midwestern Lutherans now live in suburbs or bigger towns and cities. They belong to larger congregations whose ethnic identity is diluted by Americanization or expanded by recent growth. At Christ Lutheran in St. Paul, Minnesota, for example, members hear the annual Pentecost lesson in their native African, East Asian, and European languages and the weekly gospel in Cambodian. In the early twenty-first century, Midwestern Lutherans have wide ecumenical contacts; they regularly cooperate with many sorts of Christians and other citizens in projects ranging from Meals-on-Wheels to community Thanksgiving services.

However, not all Lutherans waded so far into the mainstream. The persistent divide between the ELCA and LCMS is marked by disagreements about women's ordination rooted in biblical interpretation and about allowable ecumenical cooperation rooted in interpretation of the Lutheran confessions. The ELCA's agreements with Episcopal and Reformed churches in the 1990s increased that distance and fomented internal dissent, including organization of Word Alone, a protest movement within the ELCA. Similar debates about abortion and homosexuality reveal internal differences about biblical interpretation and appear to widen the chasms between the parties. Recognizing these distinctions, the American Religious Data Archive places the LCMS and several smaller groups among the evangelical (in the American sense) denominations and the ELCA (evangelical in the Reformation sense) among the mainline. In 1972, Dean M. Kelly described Lutherans as newcomers to the mainstream; in 1987, Wade Clark Roof and William McKinney included them in the moderate mainline with Methodists, Disciples of Christ, Northern Baptists, and Reformed churches.[9]

How Lutherans are categorized depends upon how categories are defined, the weight given to theological principles and historical factors in the United States, and attention to contemporary social stance and status. Jackson W. Carroll and Wade Clark Roof note the coincidence of social establishment and the religious (Christian) mainline that they describe: "a religious concern arising out of the Magisterial Reformation for the well-being of the common good, an emphasis on public as well as private faith, and more recently in the American experience, the social location of these groups among the more socioeconomically privileged classes."[10] Lutherans cannot undo their past ethnic associations and theological preoccupations, nor can their ancestors be made into social elites, but the current inclusion of some Lutherans in the mainstream recognizes increasing orientation toward external matters and a growing willingness to make official statements, even to take collective action, in the public realm. Nonetheless, division of the Lutheran family of churches between the (moderate) mainstream and more conservative, evangelical parties of American Protestantism complicates efforts to generalize about Lutheran positions and actions on the basis of aggregated data.

Lutheran concern for the common good is not an entirely new development. Since the Reformation Lutherans have been concerned for the well-being of their co-religionists and others, and they have contributed to social welfare through congregational life, schools, and charitable ventures. These contributions continue from all sides of their confessional divides, though Lutherans occupy every side of contemporary political and cultural issues.

Robert Putnam's investigations of social capital—a combination of social networks, civic virtue, and quality of life—point toward the ways Lutherans participate in American public life, particularly in the upper-Midwest, where they are most concentrated. Putnam identifies eight Midwestern states, including those with the largest proportion of Lutherans, as having high to very high levels of social capital.[11] Of course this coincidence does not demonstrate that Lutherans alone produce this valuable resource, since these states share other significant characteristics.

Some observers point to the region's settlement by a productive combination of New Englanders and northern European immigrants who shared social values and a common work ethic.[12] Others credit the historic agricultural base of the region's economy. Still others attribute acts of generalized reciprocity to the necessity for survival in a harsh climate. Nonetheless, the coincidence of Lutheran concentration and high social capital is notable.

Putnam suggests that multi-stranded networks of social exchange are a key component in generating social capital. Drawing on sociological research, Charles T. Mathewes asserts: "the mainline's typical forms of involvement in civic life and public discourse are multitudinous and subterranean—of a different and more diffuse form than many social scientists and political pundits have imagined them to be."[13] So too with Lutherans. Even when individuals have not held highly visible positions of national government leadership, Lutheran congregations have nurtured these "dense networks of social exchange" through religious and social programs that provide for repeated and intensive interactions among members of all ages.

Such networks are vividly portrayed in profiles of three Lutheran congregations published in *The Christian Century* in 1950 and revisited by Randall Balmer in the 1990s.[14] The church building and its members have hosted ordinary and extraordinary gatherings marking key events in the lives of individuals and the community—wedding anniversaries and funeral lunches—and provided space for polling places, child care centers, and scout meetings. Membership in congregations and participation in activities such as choirs, women's societies, and youth groups reinforce local, exclusive belonging (what Putnam calls bonding); and at the same time these activities and groups provide the basis for bridging experiences such as synodical conventions and national youth gatherings, where members' views of the church and the world are expanded by personal contacts and exposure to notable presenters. So too, personal and collective support for charitable ventures promotes the common good through social welfare and health care, while also enlarging the supporters' circles of social interaction. Joint efforts to influence public policy are a more recent, and contested, development.

That Lutherans do these things certainly does not make them unique; other religious groups behave similarly. The "Lutheran difference" is likely to be found in Lutheran motivations for these activities, in their mode of action, and in the meaning attributed to their activities.[15] The historian Mark Noll suggests that Lutheran differences are based less in ethnicity or geography and more in Lutheran theology: specifically, its rootedness in the past; its ironic understanding of human political activity; and its teachings about the church, human nature, and salvation. Thus the following consideration of Lutheran activity in public life must include attention to theological accounts for the work, as well as to descriptions of the work done.

Education

Lutherans boast that their tradition began in the university. The specific university, founded in Wittenberg, was more on the medieval model than like a modern research university. Luther and his colleague Philipp Melancthon were also committed to a basic education for a wider segment of the population, including girls as well as boys. Informed by humanist values, the education was directed both to preparing students to make useful contributions to their communities, including as pastors, and to producing informed Christian faith. Commitment to an educated clergy and unreliable support from European churches prompted Lutherans in the United States to establish seminaries and colleges beginning in the early 1800s. Some colleges were founded specifically to supply students to seminaries; others had a more general mission—to educate students who would take up lay occupations as well as become future pastors. The theological notion that students should be equipped for responsible participation in the world was joined to a concern that immigrants and their children find ways to enter into American society in these schools modeled on the "old college" of New England.

Lutheran sponsorship of pre-college education was less widespread than Roman Catholic sponsorship, though it is now growing. In the immigrant era, Scandinavian Lutherans made use of the public, common school and provided religious education in special summer sessions or outside of school hours. By the mid-twentieth century, in small upper-Midwestern towns, that religious education often took place during "release time."

In contrast, many LCMS congregations sponsored schools for the children of the parish. The curriculum combined standard subjects with religious instruction. Use of German in parochial schools cultivated the students' connection to their ancestors and community, and made the schools targets of anti-German sentiments during the early twentieth century. More recently, the emphasis has shifted away from the school as a means to reinforce membership; particularly in urban settings, Lutheran elementary education is regarded as a service offered to the congregation's neighbors as much as to its own members. In 2002 the LCMS sponsored 1,038 elementary schools, up 100 from five years earlier. The ELCA sponsored 200. Of the students in the ELCA schools, approximately one-third were racial minorities, a proportion much higher than in the ELCA's membership.

In the early twenty-first century the LCMS and ELCA are affiliated with 38 colleges and universities, 23 of them in the Midwest.[16] Assimilation, church mergers, and expansion of American higher education since the GI Bill reshaped these schools into larger, more diverse institutions where the Lutheran enrollment seldom passes 50 percent. (Some observers are quick to point out that if one judges by the number of Lutheran students, the University of Minnesota may be the largest Lutheran institution.)

Although only 5 percent of Lutheran college students attend a Lutheran college, alumni of these schools provide important church leadership locally and beyond. Research conducted in 1998 for the Lutheran Education Council of North America (LECNA) provides comparisons between graduates (both Lutheran and not) of Lutheran colleges and public flagship universities (PFU). Graduates of Lutheran colleges were more likely than graduates of public universities to actively participate in their churches (LC 83 percent; PFU 66 percent) and to place a high priority on contributing to their community (LC 41 percent; PFU 26 percent). This difference is consistent with these graduates' evaluation of the degree to which their colleges helped them to develop moral principles to guide their actions (LC 80 percent; PFU 30 percent) and helped them develop a sense of purpose in life (LC 76 percent; PFU 57 percent).[17]

The actual contribution alumni make to their communities depends in part on their proportion in the population, a proportion that varies considerably in the Midwest. In Ohio, graduates of the two Lutheran colleges are a negligible percentage of the total and only about 6 percent of students enrolled in private colleges. In Nebraska, where Lutherans are 15 percent of the population, the three Lutheran colleges enroll only 1 percent of the total college population and 15 percent of private-college students. In Minnesota, the five ELCA and LCMS schools enroll approximately 13,000 students: 33 percent of private college students and nearly 10 percent of the total.

Charges of secularization and betrayal of mission stimulated the current debate about the purposes and character of education at church-related schools.[18] James Burtchaell argues that such schools, overly committed to quality as defined by the modern research university, have abandoned their distinctive Christian mission. In response Richard Hughes, Conrad Cherry, and Robert Benne probe the strengths of specific schools and traditions. Lutheran institutions (e.g. St. Olaf College, which appears in these four studies) share commitment to vocation and a rich tradition of interaction between the study and practice of religion. Lutheran teaching about vocation asserts that all people have gifts to be used for the benefit of their neighbors; the Christian does so in grateful response to God's saving gift of grace, not in an effort to earn divine favor. When a Christian acts responsibly in occupation, family, or community, that person fulfills a calling from God and does God's work of sustaining the world. This teaching has shaped Lutheran higher education and its commitment to both the liberal arts and application of learning, particularly in preparation for serving professions such as teaching and health care. Vocational thinking infuses campus cultures attuned to service during college and after in programs such as the Lutheran Volunteer Corps and the Peace Corps. Since this sense of responsibility extends to financial resources as well, perhaps the presence of Lutheran college graduates in Midwestern businesses helps to sustain the region's characteristic expectation of generous corporate giving.

The combination of vocation and service to the neighbor is one way to practice religion; frequent, public worship on campus—sometimes daily—is another. There students, faculty, and staff, whether Christian or not, are invited to hear the proclamation of the gospel so central to Luther's reform and are given means to express both sorrows and joys. In the classroom the proclamation and the theology behind it are the subject of scholarly investigation, not indoctrination. Interaction of intellect and action is central to Lutheran understanding of faith and to the critical engagement with culture that is a mark of the best of Lutheran education. Lutherans are typically reluctant to devise Christian approaches to academic disciplines and yet they maintain the vital importance of religion as a partner in scholarly investigation.

The Arts

Over three-quarters (78 percent) of Lutheran respondents to the LECNA survey who attended Lutheran colleges reported that college helped them to develop an appreciation of the fine arts. This fact points toward the arts, notably music and architecture, as an arena of American public life where Lutherans have made important contributions. In contrast to radical reformers, even compared to moderates in Geneva, Martin Luther affirmed the arts. When others painted over frescoes, removed stained glass, and forbade use of instruments, Luther—himself a musician—advised a more temperate course and encouraged members' active involvement in worship through congregational singing. The music of J. S. Bach, who served as a congregational musician, is regarded by many as an expression of Lutheran theology. In the United States, both Lutheran colleges and congregations have promoted choral music performance and participation. In architecture, Edward Sovik has provided leadership in modern church design.

Garrison Keillor and the fictional train conductors who observed the Lutherans' niceness draw attention to Lutheran singing. The form of Lutheran liturgical worship shares much with the Roman Catholic tradition, but Lutheran hymn singing perhaps has more affinity with the Methodists. Typically, Lutheran hymns and liturgy combine theologically rich texts with equally rich music. Publishing a common liturgy and hymnal has been a crucial step in each move toward institutional unity. Inclusion of English and American hymns in these books and in members' hearts signals transition from the era of immigration and into a church more at home in the United States. *With One Voice* (1995) included a global selection of hymns and new works. Among the latter were many by Marty Haugen, a Luther College graduate, whose work is used extensively by Catholics. Paul Manz, long-time cantor at Mt. Olive in Minneapolis, and John Ferguson, professor of music at St. Olaf College, have stimulated and shaped contemporary church music—both organ performance and congregational singing—inside and far beyond Lutheran circles.

Ferguson continues a tradition of faculty leadership. F. Melius Christiansen, founder of the St. Olaf Choir, was a generative force in twentieth-century American choral music. His influence spread through the choir's example, his students' leadership in congregations, schools, and communities; his summer institutes; and his compositions. Christiansen's notion that music, specifically choral performance, is fundamentally a way to serve God rather than to gain glory for the performers expressed a typical Lutheran conviction.[19] The current director, Anton Armstrong, has enriched the St. Olaf Choir repertoire with music from around the globe while continuing to include perennial favorites. For Memorial Day 2003, the college donated to U.S. military chaplains copies of the choir's *Great Hymns of Faith* recording. Armstrong is often guest conductor at events such as all-state high school choir concerts. While in some ears St. Olaf is synonymous with sacred, a cappella music, the music department conducts a music education program and sponsors instrumental ensembles. Alumni sing in many community and church choirs, including two professional choirs in Minneapolis/ St. Paul founded by alumni.

St. Olaf is not alone in the quality and influence of its music program. Christiansen's son, Paul, established a similar legacy at Concordia College in Moorhead, Minnesota, as has Weston Noble at Luther College in Decorah, Iowa. Since 1882 Bethany College, in Lindsborg, Kansas, has sponsored an annual performance of *The Messiah* that draws several hundred musicians from college and community. At the LCMS colleges, the repertoire may vary, but the dynamics are similar. The University of Minnesota faculty member Vern Sutton recalled Lutheran musicians' contribution to his Opera on the Farm project. In each location through the upper Midwest local singers were recruited for the chorus and lead roles. When asked about the difficulty of this he replied: "We had contacts in the towns, usually the high school music teacher who was always the choir director at the Lutheran church."[20] No doubt there is exaggeration in Sutton's remark, but in the upper Midwest the exaggeration points to a truth about Lutherans' musical activity and their contribution to artistic life in their communities.

If music suggests Lutheran affinities with evangelical piety, architecture recalls the affinities with Roman Catholic worship. In a typical Lutheran church building the altar-table shares prominence with the pulpit, signaling the centrality of the Word of God, both preached and in the sacrament. Since the mid-twentieth century Lutheran congregations have moved toward more frequent communion, though it is still not a weekly event in every place. Both sacraments—the Lord's Supper and baptism—depend upon the conviction that finite things such as water, wine, and bread are capable of conveying infinite things, namely God's gift of forgiveness. This conviction also stands behind the significance of places and buildings. In the nineteenth century, immigrant Lutherans were eager to construct a church building and frequently did so on land donated by a member of the congregation. Today these small, wooden buildings, scattered across the prairies, are joined by newer modernist buildings.

Since the mid-twentieth century the award-winning architect Edward Sovik, the son of Lutheran missionaries in China, has been a major force in reshaping both church buildings and thinking about those buildings.[21] Sovik's notion of church architecture is evident in the approximately 400 projects he has carried out for a variety of Christian communities, where he also taught congregations to read the subtle symbolism in their new space: the simplicity of its forms; its flexibility for multiple activities; and its use of mundane materials such as poured cement floors, brick walls, and wooden chairs. He also explicated his views for professional and churchly audiences in dozens of publications, including *Architecture for Worship*. Sovik's buildings express his understanding of the church as the people of God with a mission to serve both God and neighbor, an understanding in keeping with central teachings of the Reformation with its emphasis upon the priesthood of all believers, all of whom are called by God to use their gifts for the benefit of those around them. The exterior of Sovik's church buildings echo their neighborhoods. The interior often encourages worshippers to see each other by placing rows of chairs perpendicular to each other. Locating a processional cross in the midst of the congregation helps the members recall Jesus, the incarnate one, in their midst. Sovik's notion of the church as "non-church" urges members to practice hospitality toward one another and toward their neighbors. Here a Lutheran architect declares a more universally Christian principle that social scientists recognize in its production of social capital.

Social Services

Beyond congregational hospitality to food-shelves, day-care centers, and 12-step programs, Lutherans are vigorous providers of social services that respond to the full array of human need. The theologian Joseph Sittler once called these efforts the "arm of the Lord." Lutherans understand their work in health care, housing for the elderly, refugee resettlement, services to children, and the like as their response to God's call to serve their neighbors with "daily bread." Luther articulated a broad understanding of daily bread: "everything our bodies need such as food, drink, clothing, . . . home, fields, livestock, . . . an upright spouse, upright children, . . . upright and faithful leaders, . . . good weather, peace, health, decency, . . . good friends, faithful neighbors, and the like."[22]

These things God provides to all people; so too Lutheran social services, though grounded in the Christian gospel and often begun as service to their own communities, are offered to all people. Today, Lutheran efforts frequently receive financial support from government agencies, thus forging partnerships between state and church. Despite debates about these sorts of partnerships, stimulated in part by President George W. Bush's support for faith-based initiatives, the history of Lutheran institutions and agencies reveals that such cooperation, and its tensions, are of long standing. Both the expansion of services beyond Lutheran communities and partnerships with government have the potential to loosen the ties connecting individual Lutherans and their congregations to this work. As in higher education, there are ongoing efforts to resist this loosening and to reestablish a sense of what makes the work of hospitals and general social service agencies identifiably Lutheran.

Is there a Lutheran difference in this arena of public life? In the 1980s Martin E. Marty addressed the question in *Health and Medicine in the Lutheran Tradition: Being Well.* The book launched a series sponsored by Lutheran General Medical Center in Park Ridge, Illinois.[23] Attending to theology rather than telling the stories of institutions or people, Marty highlighted Lutheran emphasis on salvation as being at the heart of well-being and health. This view generates concern for the whole person without denying the physical and makes health a matter of religious as well as medical attention. In the context of education the phrase "whole person" counters overemphasis upon the intellect to the exclusion of the body and spirit; in health care it counters overemphasis upon the body as separate from spirit and a too narrow focus upon individual patients as distinct from their families and communities. This view was pioneered in the 1950s by Lutheran General at its Lutheran Institute for Human Ecology. A similar concern for holistic health informed the parish nursing program devised by the Lutheran clergyman Granger Westberg and launched in 1984 by Lutheran General and six Lutheran congregations.

Fairview Hospital in Minneapolis, like Lutheran General, was founded by Norwegian Americans and has expanded its mission to serve the larger community without regard to religious or ethnic identity.[24] Although Lutherans founded the hospital, the crucial first funding was a gift from an Episcopal layman, who stipulated that the hospital should address the immediate needs of TB patients. In due time, the hospital offered general medical services as well. The history of Fairview's early decades reveals the staff's extraordinary dedication, as well as the remarkable degree to which the hospital was integrated into the Norwegian Lutheran community. This network is evident in the overlap in leadership between Fairview and other institutions, including Augsburg Publishing, Lutheran Brotherhood, and the colleges of the church. Several key leaders belonged to Bethlehem Lutheran in south Minneapolis. Reliance upon individual and organizational memberships for funding and upon volunteers also encouraged social bonding among the hospital's supporters who belonged to congregations throughout the city.

Social connections inside and outside the church were key to the hospital's expansion in the second half of the twentieth century—construction of Fairview Southdale in Edina and cooperative arrangements with other facilities. When Fairview's leaders investigated the possibility of locating a new facility at the growing southern edge of the metropolitan area, widened circles of social interaction made the new venture possible. Informal social contacts led to cooperation with Bruce Dayton, whose family corporation donated 15 acres; that contact facilitated partnership with Senator Hubert H. Humphrey, which led to National Institutes of Health funding.

When the new facility opened in 1965 its services responded to the needs of the young families moving into the area; half of the beds were in obstetrics and pediatrics. By the 1970s Fairview's chief executive, Carl Platou, responded to accelerating demands for service and rising costs in health care by applying a concept from banking: the holding company. To learn how such a scheme might work, he contacted Donald Grangard, a Lutheran layman and chairman of First Bank system. The arrangement allowed smaller regional facilities to draw on Fairview's larger scale and resources, and has helped sustain access to health care outside the Twin Cities. Along the way Fairview has assumed responsibility for the work of Lutheran Deaconess Hospital, St. Mary's (formerly run by the Sisters of St. Joseph), and the University of Minnesota Hospital. This pattern of increased service, enlarged client base, and government funding can weaken connections between an institution and its community so that the institution continues to provide services but does not build relationships. In the final years of the twentieth century Fairview has addressed this by clear articulation of its core values (service, dignity, compassion, and integrity) and with programs to reconnect with congregational members as well as neighbors.

A similar pattern of development is evident in the history of Lutheran Social Service of Iowa (LSS-IA), the largest private human services provider in that state. The agency had its beginnings in the efforts of four immigrant church bodies to care for orphans. By the 1930s the supporters of these scattered homes consolidated their efforts into the Lutheran Social Welfare Society of Iowa, the predecessor of LSS-IA, and began to add other sorts of services. Cooperation across synodical lines in charitable work prior to formal relationships between the church bodies is typical among Lutheran groups. Primarily associated with the

ELCA, LSS-IA has cooperative projects with its LCMS counterpart. Of the original orphanages only the Beloit home continues, now providing psychiatric medical services to children in Ames. Following World War II the Society became involved in refugee settlement in cooperation with national Lutheran efforts. In 1953 it cared for 130 European families. By the 1990s LSS-IA, in partnership with Lutheran Immigrant and Refugee Services (LIRS) and its Roman Catholic counterpart, was resettling about 300 people a year, including unaccompanied refugee minors. The 1997 annual report of LIRS featured the story of a Bosnian family and their Waterloo restaurant, highlighting the cooperation of the national organization, the regional agency, and local people in this major area of Lutheran public work.

Entering the twenty-first century LLS-IA served more than 40,000 clients a year in nearly 100 programs at 32 locations throughout the state, about 25 percent of whom were Lutherans. Over 80 percent of funding came from government sources and less than 15 percent from churches. As at Fairview, efforts were underway to reactivate congregational connections while affirming that "Lutherans believe that God uses both the state and the church as ways of providing resources necessary to bring mercy and justice to people. Most of those resources today come through state and federal taxes, some from the church. As the church and state work together, they complement each other in a way that benefits all people."[25] The work of Lutheran Social Service in other Midwestern states parallels the work in Iowa.[26]

The Evangelical Good Samaritan Society, the largest non-profit, long-term care corporation in the United States, provides another instructive window on the complementary and sometimes conflicted relationship between church and state.[27] It operates nearly 250 homes in 26 states and has national offices in Sioux Falls, South Dakota. The Good Samaritan Society was begun in the 1922 when Pastor August John Hoeger opened a farm home for old people in Arthur, North Dakota and received county funds to pay for the residents' keep. Hoeger's commitment to such work and his approach were nurtured by his parents and informed by German Lutheran mission work. Until his death at over 80 Hoeger articulated the Good Samaritan Society's vision through periods of challenge and change.

He manifested the qualities he wrote about in a college composition: "No man is truly educated until his relation to his fellow men and his desire to serve them fill a large place in his thoughts."[28] In every effort to serve the elderly Hoeger insisted that the whole person be addressed. In the early 1960s he urged local administrators of Good Samaritan homes to make the homes centers of social life for the elderly of the whole community and to provide coordination for outreach services so that both residents and neighbors would be active and connected. These practices became widespread a decade later when state and federal governments recognized their value and provided funding. Hoeger's pioneering efforts were acknowledged by an Award of Honor from the American Association for the Aging in 1966.

With his ear tuned to God's calling and his eye on the needs of the people in the homes, Hoeger was not always attentive to the bank balance, to his board, or to increasing regulations for the operation of such facilities. By the mid-twentieth century government regulations dictated more aspects of the society's work, necessitating new construction rather than renovation of old buildings, stipulating a larger number of single rooms, and rendering homes for 20 residents financially unfeasible. Nonetheless, the Good Samaritan Society entered a period of rapid expansion just as leadership passed to Hoeger's sons. Federal Hill-Burton money helped pay for new buildings. Government regulations became the basis for improved staff training as well as up-dated facilities. Auggie Hoeger, Jr. participated in drafting the original Medicare regulations. Even as it benefited from cooperation with various government agencies, the Good Samaritan Society's legal counsel learned how to defend challenges to its tax-exempt status. In the 1990s Hoeger's grandson, Mark Jerstad, provided mission-focused leadership in the society, in the larger church, and in national associations. In cooperation with Luther Seminary and the University of North Texas he expanded the society's participation in training administrators for its own facilities and other similar institutions.

Throughout its history the society has been adept at articulating its distinctive mission and maintaining its sense of that work as motivated by response to God's call. Currently it is a recognized agency of both ELCA and LCMS. The Good Samaritan Society's commitment to cultivating community among the residents of its homes, among their neighbors, and among its staff expresses well the notion of "human ecology" articulated at Lutheran General Hospital, and is grounded in Lutheran theology while simultaneously producing social capital. Perhaps this tradition of service—motivated by God's grace and responsive to human need—has contributed to the strong commitment to social services that has characterized the upper Midwest. As government funds for such programs diminish, it remains to be seen if Lutheran agencies and their supporters will assume greater responsibility.

Political Life

Lutherans have done works of mercy since the Reformation and are especially active in such efforts when the pietist impulse is strong. Despite Luther's dependence upon and encouragement of civic leaders, his followers have been less vigorous and visible in the political arena. In contrast to radical reformers Luther affirmed continued alliance between church authorities and civic ones for the containment of evil and promotion of good. He urged Christians to use their talents and positions for the well-being of their neighbors in their work and as citizens. Nevertheless, he was vividly aware that neither Christian citizens nor the state could bring about a perfect society or God's reign. That culmination of God's work he left to God's own efforts. Separation of God's own work, specifically to accomplish human salvation and God's work through human hands for earthly good, is the kernel of the doctrine of the two kingdoms that distinguishes the spiritual, right-hand kingdom from the earthly, left-hand kingdom.

This teaching asserts that, in the kingdom on the left, God works through those in authority, and that Christian citizens should obey such authorities. Two-kingdoms thinking undergirds much of Lutheran understanding of proper participation in politics and government, and contributes to the sense of irony about politics that Noll identifies as a Lutheran strength. Two-kingdoms teaching has been used to justify acquiescence to secular authorities even when their actions are unjust, though the German church's cooperation with the Nazis has made Lutherans sensitive to that danger and eager to recall the contrary witness of Dietrich Bonhoeffer and the resistance movement in the equally Lutheran Scandinavian nations.

Lutherans are found on every side of a political or social issue. In the nineteenth century, Lutherans debated among themselves about slavery and abolition on theological and other grounds; early twentieth-century Lutherans were similarly divided regarding prohibition. In congregations that invite prayers from the congregation, worshipers may be asked to join petitions on both sides of the pro-life/pro-choice issue. This lack of unanimous positions is not accidental. It grows from a strong Lutheran conviction that individuals should be guided by scripture and their own conscience in making judgments about matters of morality and citizenship. Such internal variety, while in keeping with Lutheran theology, renders collective action or official statements nearly impossible except in support of the most uncontroversial positions. Characteristically, Lutheran churches, both national bodies and congregations, offer education and opportunities for discussion (i.e., social teaching statements) rather than dictating positions or actions. As a result, even in the states with the highest proportion of Lutherans, there is no talk about the "Lutheran vote," even on moral issues. When observers note a German or Scandinavian political involvement, as in the Nonpartisan League, that group will include many non-Lutherans.

A study of ELCA clergy in the 2000 election illustrates Lutheran attitudes toward political life, though the responding clergy may be more politically liberal than many of their parishioners.[29] The political scientist Daniel Hofrenning found that the clergy reported a mixture of modernist-liberal and orthodox-conservative theological positions; only 10 percent agree that the Bible is inerrant in all matters, and only 23 percent agree that human nature is basically good. While on average these views render the Lutheran clergy moderates, non-Lutheran interpreters might regard some of their positions as contradictory. For example, only 10 percent agreed that all religions are equal, and 63 percent agreed that Jesus is the only way to salvation; nonetheless, 50 percent regard imposition of religion as a violation of civil rights. This combination of responses suggests that the clergy make a distinction between the realm of salvation, which is a matter of religion, and the realm of civic life, which is not. However, a meager 10 percent agree that "Christianity is clear about separating the spiritual and secular realms." Nearly 60 percent regard social justice as at the heart of the Christian gospel and nearly 80 percent think that the "federal government should do more to solve social problems."

In keeping with Lutheran concern that the two kingdoms not be confused and yet that believers be active participants in this world, Hofrenning concludes that "[w]hile [Lutheran clergy] are liberal politically, they resist politicizing their church. They strongly approve of political activity that takes place outside the church, but they are very reticent about politics within their parishes." Many responding clergy supported government-sponsored national health insurance (71 percent) and civil rights for homosexuals (85 percent), but only 20 percent favored a constitutional amendment to prohibit abortion. They approved of personal polit-ical activities such as making a financial contribution (81 percent), participating in a protest march (75 percent), or even committing civil disobedience (57 percent). However, only half as many approved of taking a political stand in the pulpit (38 percent) as approved of taking a moral stand (82 percent). In the most recent pres-idential election 98 percent voted—just over two-thirds for Gore, just under one-third for Bush, and 5 percent for Nader. This corresponds with their reported party preference—about 65 percent Democrats and 23 percent Republicans. Half urged their congregation to register and vote, and 56 percent prayed publicly about a political issue though not necessarily advocating a position.

Hofrenning's data include both more and less than this essay's focus; the clergy are from the entire United States and are only ELCA. In the Midwest, lay Lutherans are members of several churches. Nevertheless, the same theological tradition, with its chastened expectations for political life and encouragement of faithful citizenship, shapes their attitudes about politics. Identifiable Lutheran political engagement is often the work of individuals or groups defined by com-mon convictions rather than congregations or synods. Late in life Ruth Youngdahl Nelson, from a family prominent in Minnesota politics and Lutheran circles, became a vigorous anti-nuclear activist; her personal reputation secured a hear-ing for her views in congregations. Though the church did not endorse those views, members of the national Lutheran Peace Fellowship likely did. Lutherans occupy the other side of the social spectrum as well. Lutherans for Life, an anti-abortion group, offers a typically Lutheran view of faithful political engagement on its Web page. "Christian citizens have the opportunity and responsibility to represent God's will, working for justice and wholistic human care in a number of social and political settings."

Some exceptional congregations take collective action, even in opposition to the church policy. By calling "open and active" homosexuals as their pastors, congregations in the Twin Cities; Ames, Iowa; and Kansas City have protested the ELCA's prohibition. Lutherans Concerned and the Extraordinary Candidacy Project are national organizations in concert with these actions. In May 2003 Edina Community Lutheran in suburban Minneapolis spearheaded a suit brought by three-dozen religious communities (including synagogues and a Buddhist center) to challenge Minnesota's new "conceal and carry" gun law. The suit was filed by David Lillehaug, a congregation member and former U. S. Attorney. Edina Community's efforts reflect the congregation's secure place in the local community and suggest Lutherans' potential for critical participation in upper Midwestern political life. The congregation includes influential, well-placed individuals such as Lillehaug; its commitment to peace-making and community involvement is long and solid; and its voice is listened to by other religious communities. Nonetheless, the congregation's political agreement and willingness to act remain unusual.

Lutherans serve in elected and other public offices in the Midwest more often and more visibly than nationally. Minnesota's 2002 elections illustrate this participation as well as the range of Lutherans' political positions.[30] Both Lutheran members of the U.S. House, Martin Sabo (DFL-ELCA) and Collin Peterson (DFL-ELCA) were reelected, though ELCA member Greg Mikkelson, running on the Green Party ticket, was defeated. (Nationally, 20 Lutherans—11 Democrats and nine Republicans—served in the 107th Congress in 2000.) Of the 40 Lutherans running for the Minnesota state legislature, 13 Republican and four Democratic-Farm-Labor (DFL) candidates won. Four Independence or Green Party candidates were defeated. In at least two races both the Republican and DFL candidates were Lutherans. Familiar winners included incumbent House Speaker Steve Swiggum (IR-ELCA) and Senator John Marty (DFL-ELCA), a protegee of the former Illinois U.S. Senator and Lutheran layman Paul Simon. On slates for governor and lieutenant governor were five Lutheran candidates. Carol Molnau, the Republican candidate for lieutenant governor, was the only winner and the only member of the LCMS. The four losing candidates, including the long-time leader of the state senate, Roger Moe (DFL), and his running mate, Julie Sabo (Martin's daughter), all belong to ELCA congregations. Had Moe or Tim Penny (Indep-ELCA) won, they would have joined outgoing Jesse Ventura and more than a half-dozen Lutherans who have held that office.[31] This impressive group reflects the range of Lutheran political opinion while tilting toward the conservative.

A guide to Christian citizenship provided by the LCMS and posted on the Lutherans for Life web page urges prayer, education, voting, and efforts to influence others, including legislators. Beyond what Lutherans do as individual citizens they participate in church-sponsored advocacy through official offices and groups focused on specific issues. (When used in contrast to *lobbying*, the term *advocacy* emphasizes concern for justice and human welfare rather than support for personal or corporate interests.) In Washington, D.C., the LCMS supports the Office of Government Information; the ELCA, the Lutheran Office for Government Affairs. In 20 states Lutherans support similar offices, some of them ecumenical. Staff members monitor state legislation in order to represent Lutheran concerns and to educate congregations.

Lutheran Immigration and Refugee Services (LIRS) is more focused in its advocacy, concentrating on immigration issues. Its concern for legislation grows out of its primary work: LIRS staff and volunteers in four thousand congregations have helped to settle nearly 16,000 people since the late 1930s. This long and daily experience gives staff and volunteers a deep understanding of the legal and human issues involved and makes testimony and letter-writing an expression of ministry as well as of citizenship.[32]

Bread for the World cultivates the same connection between advocacy and action. Founded by an LCMS pastor, the organization is strong among Midwestern Lutherans; the largest portion of its covenanted congregations are Lutheran. Alongside legislative advocacy, Lutherans are involved in local efforts to address hunger, food shelves, CROP walks, and feeding programs, and they contribute to national and international church programs concerned about hunger. In politics as in social service and education, the Lutheran way is to address the whole person and the whole situation, to link person to principle, and to act simultaneously as citizen and believer.[33]

Conclusion

While Keillor's portrayal of Pastor Inqvist's flock describes some congregations, Midwestern Lutheranism is far more varied; not all are rural, not all are Norwegian, and not all vote Republican. Not all Midwestern Lutherans run things in their towns, but particularly in the upper Midwest they make significant contributions to education, the arts, and human services. As citizens, their influence and visibility are muted by the range of their political positions. The average of the group may be a bit more religiously, socially, and politically conservative than their co-religionists in other regions, but the average obscures the richness of the spectrum represented here. This variety is possible because there are so many Lutherans and they are in close proximity to one another. There is some stratification by theological positions and cultural stance, but few congregations—not even those founded in the midst of disputes—are entirely homogenous.

Although Lutheran numbers are nearly as significant in the upper Midwest as Baptist numbers are in the South, their presence is more subtle. Certainly there are at least as many kinds of Baptists as there are kinds of Lutherans, so the reason for this difference must be found elsewhere. Through World War II most Midwestern Lutherans were recent immigrants or the children of immigrant families; the church and ethnic community defined their primary spheres of activity. Practical need and Lutheran theology encouraged development of schools and service institutions to serve their own people. The overlap among circles of support for these institutions, membership in congregations, and ethnic communities produced strong networks and generated rich social capital.

Those same institutions, now serving a more religiously and ethnically diverse community, provide a large part of the social infrastructure in the upper Midwest. Participation in the work of such institutions and agencies stimulates and informs Lutherans' political activity, by both individuals and groups. While normative Lutheran teaching encourages faithful citizenship, many Lutherans involve themselves in service and cultural endeavors rather than political ones, leaving the government to fulfill its appropriate role in the kingdom on the left. While the movement began as a protest against the treasury of merit, whereby Christians built up spiritual benefits that could be transferred to others, contemporary Midwestern Lutherans are busy building up temporal social capital that contributes to the quality of life in their region.

Now that ethnicity and related status issues are less significant, Lutheran influence may be muted or hidden by theological characteristics central to Lutheranism, the very sort of thing Noll praises. Even Lutherans deeply involved in political life, either in government or in reform efforts, usually have limited expectations for what can be achieved by human effort and regard the church's political role as educational rather than organizational or directive. Alongside this wariness about human efforts is a tendency to make secular rather than religious arguments in the public arena and a consistent lack of uniform policy positions. If matters of basic human need or morality are at issue, Lutheran citizens are more likely to articulate a religious foundation for their positions.

They and their agencies are often willing partners with government in efforts to address human welfare but are careful not to confuse the church's responsibility to proclaim the gospel with provision of daily bread. The church's specific responsibility is clearly defined as preaching the good news and administering the sacraments of baptism and Holy Communion. When these tasks are done well, the members offer themselves and their resources in all arenas of public life in response to the real needs they discern. This motive is recognizably Lutheran, as is the meaning the members attach to their work; but beyond insisting upon concern for the whole person—mind, body, spirit, and relationships—the mode of work is seldom distinguishable from that of others differently motivated.

If Lutherans seem indistinguishable from other Midwesterners, how is it possible to suggest that all Midwesterners, or even all Minnesotans, are Lutheran? Most obviously, many in the upper Midwest are the beneficiaries of Lutheran involvement in education, the arts, and human services. Neither graduating from a Lutheran college, nor attending a choral concert, nor engaging in family counseling makes a person Lutheran, but anyone who receives such education, pleasure, or reconciliation has experienced something of Lutheran concern for serving the neighbor or Lutheran appreciation for the religious value of art. Of course neither education, the arts, nor human wellness is passively received, so even those who do not count themselves as Lutheran may find themselves engaged with Lutherans, or with Lutheran sponsorship, in these activities. When Lutheranism coincided more neatly with ethnic communities, the boundaries of benefit and participation were clearer and less permeable than they are today. As the significance of ethnicity declines, more expansive theological identity can foster greater openness to such participation, though some worry that the cost will be further muting of Lutheran distinctiveness.

Beyond benefiting from Lutheran work or participating in it, others may seem Lutheran because they share typical features of Lutheran orientation in the world. Two aspects of this stance have recurred in this exploration of Lutherans in the Midwest. The first is the way that vocation—the call to serve one's neighbor—motivates Lutheran endeavors in many arenas, by both individuals and groups. This teaching is no guarantee of unwavering niceness as battles in congregations and on agency boards demonstrate. Still, it may inform regional commitments to strong social welfare programs and expectations of generous corporate giving. Second, while vocation encourages engagement, and teaching about the two kingdoms gives government an essential role, Lutherans' deep sense of human sin makes them realistic about the limits and dangers of efforts to perfect, or even improve, the world. Often they concentrate their efforts on helping people rather than promoting principles or changing systems. Such an ironic combination of hope and limited expectation may seep from Lutherans to their fellow citizens. Perhaps an upper Midwestern propensity to legislate good behavior derives especially from the pietist impulse, though there are plenty of religious and other factors that encourage it. This stance of service and wary engagement identifies Lutheran participation in the public arena more than any political or social agenda.

Finally, focusing on Lutherans in the public arena highlights two significant characteristics of their engagement. Lutherans have long been willing to work in partnership with government agencies, in part because they regard the government as a way that God tends to the temporal needs of the world. These partnerships have developed from fee-for-service arrangements to a more complex system. Government money allows expansion of both services and client base; it also brings regulation and can dilute both mission and connections with church members. The potential for loss of clear identity along with loss of generative mission is real. In addition, focus on Lutherans, especially in light of Putnam's work, urges a holistic notion of public life. Public life must include the entire range of human experience—politics and government to be sure, but also education, aesthetic experience, family life, health, and the like. In this regard the truth of Keillor's insight into Midwestern Lutheranism is in his attention to the many and mundane aspects of life more than in the accuracy of any single detail.

Endnotes

1. Eunice Scarf, *Pillars of Salt*, unpublished mss.

2. Dale E. Jones, et al. *Religious Congregations and Membership in the U.S.: 2000* (Nashville: Glenmary Research Center, 2002), loose map.

3. These numbers are from 2000 and include only LCMS and ELCA, ARDA online.

4. For general treatments see: L. DeAne Lagerquist, *The Lutherans* (Mystic, CT: Greenwood Press, 1999); E. Clifford Nelson, ed. *Lutherans in North America* (Philadelphia: Fortress Press, 1975); Christa R. Klein, "Lutheranism," in *Encyclopedia of American Religious Experience: Studies of Traditions and Movements*, 3 vols (NY: Scribner, 1988): 431-50.

5. Ronald F. Thiemann, "What's Faith Got to Do with It?: Lutheran Social Ministry in Transition," *Taking Faith Seriously* (Cambridge: Harvard University Press, 2004): 11-13.

6. Mark Granquist, "Lutherans in the United States, 1930-1960: Searching for the 'Center,'" in Douglas Jacobson and William Vance Trollinger, Jr., eds., *Reforming the Center: American Protestantism, 1900 to the Present* (Grand Rapids, MI: William B. Eerdmans Publishing Company, 1998): 234-51.

7. Gordon Melton, *Encyclopedia of American Religions, 5th edition* (Detroit: Gale, 1996). 8,336,231 is the total of all groups whose memberships are listed, though these are not all 1996 figures.

8. Peter J. Thuesen, "The Logic of Mainline Churchliness: Historical Background since the Reformation," in Robert Wuthnow and John H. Evans, eds., *The Quiet Hand of God; Faith-Based Activism and the Public Role of*

Mainline Protestantism (Berkeley, CA: University of California Press, 2002), 44.

9. Dean Kelly, *Why Conservative Churches are Growing* and Robert Wuthnow, *The Restructuring of American Religion: Society and Faith Since World War II* (Princeton, NJ: Princeton University Press, 1988).

10. Jackson W. Carroll and Wade Clark Roof, "Introduction," *Beyond Establishment: Protestant Identity in a Post-Protestant Age,* (Louisville: Westminster John Knox Press, 1993), 12.

11. Robert Putnam, *Bowling Alone: The Collapse and Revival of American Community*, (NY: Simon & Schuster, 2000), map on p. 293. Very high: MN, ND, SD, NE, IA; high: WI, KS. Putnam discusses the concept of social capital most directly on pages 18-28.

12. John D. Buenkeer, "Wisconsin as Maverick, Model, and Microcosm," and Cullom Davis, "Illinois: Crossroads and Cross Section" in *Heartland: Comparative Histories of the Midwestern States*, ed., James H. Madison (Bloomington: Indiana University Press, 1988); Stephen Dunn, "The Same Cold" in *Different Hours* (New York: W. W. Norton & Company, 2000).

13. See p. 136 of Putnam; Charles T. Mathewes "Reconsidering the Role of Mainline Churches in Public Life, *Theology Today* vol. 58, n. 4 (January 2002): 555. Mathewes responds to Robert Wuthnow and John E. Evans, eds., *The Quiet Hand of God: Faith-based Activism and the Public Role of Mainline Protestantism* (Berkeley: University of California Press, 2002).

14. The three are: Washington Prairie Lutheran in Decorah, Iowa; Trinity Lutheran Church in Freistatt, Missouri; and Mount Olivet Lutheran Church in Minneapolis. *Grant Us Courage: Travels Along the Mainline of American Protestantism* (New York: Oxford University Press, 1996).

15. Mark Noll's phrase from "Ethnic, American, or Lutheran? Dilemmas for a Historic Confession in the New World," *Lutheran Theological Seminary Bulletin* Vol. 71, no. 1 (Winter 1991): 17-38 also published in a slightly revised form as "The Lutheran Difference," *First Things*, Number 20 (February 1992): 31-40.

16. In addition, Valparaiso University, an independent Lutheran institution with strong ties to the LCMS, is located in Indiana, and small schools sponsored by other groups are located in Minnesota and Wisconsin.

17. www.lutherancolleges.org.

18. James Tunstead Burtchaell, *Dying of the Light: The Disengagement of College and Universities from their Christian Churches* (Grand Rapids: Eerdmans, 1998); Richard T. Hughes, ed., *Models for Christian Higher Education* (Grand Rapids: Eerdmans, 1997), Conrad Cherry, Betty A. DeBerg and Amanda Porterfield, *Religion on Campus* (Chapel Hill: University of

North Carolina Press, 2001), Robert Benne, *Quality with Soul* (Grand Rapids: Eerdmans, 2001).

19. Paul E. Neve, *The Contribution of the Lutheran College Choirs to Music in America* SMD Union, NYC, 1967 and J. C. K. Preus, *The History of the Choral Union of the Evangelical Lutheran Church, 1847-1960* (Minneapolis: Augsburg Publishing House, 1961).

20. "Voices of Minnesota" broadcast Sunday, June 9, 2002 on KNOW.

21. Mark A. Torgerson, "An Architect's response to Liturgical Reform: Edward A. Sovik and his 'Non-Church' Design," *Worship* 71, 1 (May 1997), 19-41

22. "Explanation to the Fourth Petition," *A Contemporary Translation of Luther's Small Catechism*, trans., Timothy J. Wenger (Minneapolis: Augsburg Fortress, Publishers, 1994), 41.

23. Martin E. Marty, *Health and Medicine in the Lutheran Tradition: Being Well* (New York: Crossroads, 1983).

24. Hakala Communications, *A Legacy of Service* (Minneapolis: Fairview Press, 1996).

25. George L. Hanusa, *Hope for All Generations: Lutheran Social Service of Iowa —125 Years, 1870-1995* (Minneapolis: Kirk House Publishers, 1996), 109.

26. Adoptions have been less significant for LSS-IA than in some other states where LSS led the way in international adoptions and in open adoption practices.

27. Lynwood E. Oyos, *Following in His Steps: The Evangelical Lutheran Good Samaritan Society, 1922-1997* (Sioux Falls, SD: Ex Machina Publishing Company, 1998).

28. Oyos, 4.

29. Daniel Hofrenning, et al, "The Political Attitudes and Activities of Evangelical Lutheran Church in America (ELCA) Clergy in the Election of 2000," Presented at the Symposium on Religion and Politics, The Henry Institute for the Study of Christianity and Politics, Calvin College, May 3-4, 2002.

30. Robert Ylvisaker, "How Lutheran Candidates Fared in Minnesota's mid-term elections," *Metro Lutheran,* December 2002, 16.

31. These include: Jesse Ventura (Reform); Al Quie (IR); Harold LeVander (R.), Karl Rolvaag (DFL), Elmer Anderson (R.), Luther Youngdahl (R.), and J.A.O. Preus (R.).

32. Richard W. Solberg, *Open Doors: The Story of Lutherans Resettling Refugees* (St. Louis: Concordia Publishing House, 1992).

33. Charles P. Lutz, *Loving Neighbors Far and Near: U. S. Lutherans respond to a Hungry World* (Minneapolis: Augsburg Fortress, Publishing, 1994).

CHAPTER FOUR

A DIFFERENT BREED
OF CATHOLICS

Jay P. Dolan

From Ohio to the Dakotas, the Midwest did not become an integral part of the nation's development until the second half of the nineteenth century, and this was also the time when the Catholic Church came of age in the region. By then, the institutional structure of the Church in the United States was firmly established. Several Church councils, dominated by an East Coast hierarchy, had taken place prior to the Civil War. Through their legislation these councils made the national parish and the parochial school the centerpieces of the immigrant Church. The republican model of Catholicism that was normative in the late eighteenth and early nineteenth centuries was pushed aside in favor of a more monarchical, clerical model that remained the rule well into the twentieth century. The recruitment of clergy and women religious from Europe became a standard practice as well. Not surprisingly, the nascent Church in the Midwest tended to adopt these norms, at least in principle.

The new institutional pattern was a response to the rise of nativism in the 1850s. Based along the East Coast, this Protestant crusade to discredit Catholicism resulted in bitter religious battles that quickly taught Catholics that they were religious outsiders in a Protestant nation. Assuming an island mentality, they turned in on themselves and concentrated on building up a religious and cultural citadel within American society. The Midwest was not without its anti-Catholic bigots, but anti-Catholicism in the Midwest came later, and was more rurally based. The anti-Catholic American Protective Association (APA), which was centered in rural Iowa, gained a sizable following in the Midwest in the 1880s and 1890s. In the 1920s the Ku Klux Klan, headquartered in southern Indiana, made Catholics a favorite target of its heated hostility. Yet, just as anti-Catholicism was different in the Midwest, Catholicism acquired a distinctive character.

A land of small farming communities and wide-open spaces throughout the nineteenth century, the Midwest was mission country, characterized by a lack of regular religious services. A small church was most often the only visible Catholic presence in a town. Lacking large institutional complexes and sizable Catholic populations, Catholicism in the Midwest developed a spirit or style that was not so tied to the hierarchical structure and legalistic mentality of the Church back East. It was more open to adaptation and experimentation, notably in the area of liturgy.

Because of its late start, the Midwest was never the heartland of Catholic America. Even though the Church has been a major player in shaping the public culture of the Midwest, it cannot rival the East Coast Catholic powerhouse. In the Midwest, only 23 percent of the population is Catholic. That is considerably less than the Catholic population in New England (42 percent) and the Middle Atlantic region (37 percent), and somewhat less than the Pacific region (29 percent). Also noteworthy is that from 1990-2002, the Catholic population in this region increased only 5 percent, while the national Catholic population increased 14 percent, almost three times as much.

The Great Lakes region—Illinois, Michigan, Ohio, Wisconsin, and Minnesota—the most heavily Catholic area in the Midwest, at one time comprised the nation's industrial and economic core. Vast numbers of Catholic immigrants settled in the region during the great era of immigration, from 1820-1920. Today, many of their descendents still call the Midwest home. Illinois, with 3.9 million Catholics, and Wisconsin, with 1.7 million Catholics, are the two most Catholic states in the region; in each state Catholics make up almost one-third of the population. The Plains states—Iowa, Nebraska, Kansas, North and South Dakota—are heavily rural; they never attracted large numbers of Catholics.

Illinois has more than twice as many Catholics as the 1.6 million who live in the five Plains states. Illinois is the most urban state in the region, with an urban population of 88 percent, followed by Ohio and Michigan, both of which have an urban population of 77 percent. Not surprisingly, North Dakota and South Dakota are the most rural states in the region, with 44 percent and 48 percent, respectively, of their population living in rural areas.

Indiana is somewhat of an anomaly in the region. The northwest portion of the state, which borders Illinois and Michigan and in times past shared the industrial features of this Great Lakes region, is the most Catholic area of the state. The rest of the state is much more rural and agricultural, with a heavy Baptist and Methodist population. As a result, only 13 percent (776,441) of the state's population is Catholic, making Indiana the least Catholic state in the entire Midwest region.[1]

Throughout the nineteenth and early twentieth centuries the nation's cities were the chosen destination for the millions of unskilled immigrants, large numbers of whom were Catholic. Chicago, Detroit, and Cleveland were the major cities of the Great Lakes region. Linked to one another by railroads and waterways, they formed a huge industrial-urban complex. Like a magnet, they attracted immigrant newcomers searching for work in what they envisioned as the Promised Land.

This heavily urban nature of the Great Lakes states has shaped the Midwest Catholic Church. Rooted in the developing urban-industrial complex of the nineteenth century, Catholicism in the twenty-first century remains a very urban religion. This is most evident in Illinois. The archdiocese of Chicago, which comprises Cook county and a small part of Lake county, numbers 2.4 million Catholics, 63 percent of the state's total Catholic population. Cook county—the Chicago metropolitan area—is overwhelmingly Catholic. Detroit offers another example of the heavily urban nature of the Catholic Church. The Detroit archdiocese, which comprises five counties in the metropolitan region, has a Catholic population of 1.5 million, 75 percent of Michigan's Catholic population. Even in the rural areas of North and South Dakota, Catholics remain a very urban people. In North Dakota, for example, the largest concentrations of Catholics in the state are in the cities of Fargo and Bismarck.[2]

Here Comes Everybody—Ethnic Diversity

James Joyce's reported description of Catholicism—"here comes everybody"—is certainly applicable to the Midwest. In 1900 the Catholic gospel was preached, at least occasionally, in 28 languages. Today the Catholic Mass is celebrated regularly in Chicago in at least 20 languages, and irregularly in as many as 44. But this diversity, characteristic of the Church throughout America, should not be permitted to obscure the unique ethnic roots of Catholicism in the Midwest.

Germans

While Germans settled in many regions of the country, it is to the Midwest that they came in the greatest numbers, intent on settling and farming the land. Perhaps 30 percent of them were Catholic. Today, nearly one in four Midwesterners can claim German ancestry, making them the single largest European ethnic group in the region. Ohio has the largest German-American population (2.8 million), followed closely by Illinois (2.5 million) and Wisconsin (2.3 million). But every state in the Midwest region has a sizable proportion; according to the 2000 census, more than 40 percent of the inhabitants of North and South Dakota are of German descent.

It is the German presence that sets Midwest Catholicism apart. The heartland of German Catholic influence is what historians describe as the "German Triangle"—the area anchored by Cincinnati in the east, St. Louis in the west, and Milwaukee in the north.

Early on, Midwestern bishops recruited German-speaking Benedictine monks to establish monasteries in the region. Emigrating from Switzerland and Germany, the monks ministered to the large numbers of German farmers who had settled in places like southern Indiana, Minnesota, and the Dakotas; as in the early Middle Ages monasteries became the center of local religious life. The rich Benedictine liturgical tradition that the monks brought with them quickly became a marker of Midwest Catholicism, distinguishing it from the plain, stern Irish style of liturgy that was so commonplace in much of Catholic America. The Benedictine Abbey of St. John in Collegeville, Minnesota, eventually became the center of a vibrant liturgical renewal that swept across the Midwest and the rest of the country in the middle of the twentieth century. This could only have developed beyond the pale of East Coast Catholicism which, given its intense institutional structure and the dominance of an Irish style of Catholicism, was less open to innovation.

The powerful influence of German Catholicism in the Midwest weakened with the rise of anti-German sentiments during World War I. Hitler and World War II reinforced this climate of suspicion, persuading most Germans to emphasize their American loyalties rather than their German ancestry. By the mid-twentieth century *das Deutschtum* (German culture, with its language and customs) had disappeared as the Germans became fully American. The "Little Germanys" that for so long had preserved the strong sense of *das Deutschtum* in cities like Chicago, Cincinnati, and Milwaukee vanished with the arrival of African-American migrants from the South. Most Germans moved out of the old immigrant neighborhoods into the surrounding metropolitan region.

Even though Chicago's German ethnic villages are gone, the Germans remain the largest European ethnic group in the city, with 189,618 people claiming German ancestry in 2000. In the surrounding metropolitan Cook county, over 600,000 people (611,008) are of German descent. A similar pattern is present in Cincinnati. The neighborhood of Over the Rhine may no longer be a German enclave, yet there are more than 65,000 people of German ancestry living in Cincinnati (65,659); in the surrounding Hamilton county the Germans are also the largest ethnic group, numbering 258,917. It is striking that as much as experts write about the mobility of the American people, the descendents of the immigrant generation, in this case the Germans, appear not to have moved far from the old immigrant neighborhoods.[3]

While the urban ethnic villages have disappeared, some rural enclaves remain. One striking example is Stearns county in Minnesota, a rural agricultural area situated in the center of the state that has been a citadel of Catholicism since the mid-nineteenth century. Fifty-eight percent of the county's population is of German ancestry, and 86 percent of them are Catholic (66,563). Simply put, this means that one of every two people in Stearns county is a German Catholic. It is hard to imagine a more German Catholic enclave in the entire country.[4]

These people trace their roots back to pioneer settlers of the mid-nineteenth century. Benedictine monks arrived in 1856 from their monastery in LaTrobe, Pennsylvania, at the request of the local bishop who needed their assistance in caring for the increasing number of German immigrants. The monks took responsibility for a number of parishes in the county. In 1866 they built a monastery, St. John's Abbey, in Collegeville. This abbey, together with St. John's University, a college they had founded in 1857, became a vital center for the German Catholic community. Both of these institutions have flourished and remain an important center for the Catholic community of central Minnesota. Today the college has an enrollment of close to 4,000 undergraduates. The abbey has become an internationally recognized center for liturgical studies.

Writing about the county in 1990, the historian Kathleen Conzen noted that "the descendents of German immigrants have not only preserved distinctive rural communities and cultures; they have also retained their commitment to a rural way of life to a greater extent than almost any other ancestry group—particularly Anglo-Americans—among today's rural farm population." In doing so they constructed a world that still "bears their stamp, a stamp that shapes the values and goals that their descendents bring to current public policy debates and thus to the continuous making of American culture far beyond" Stearns county. This distinctiveness can be seen "in everything from the area's aggressive anti-abortion movement to the fiscal caution of its governmental bodies, the high persistence rates of its conservative farmers, the unusually large size of its families and the traces of traditional legalism, clericalism, and devotionalism that still mark its spirituality."[5]

Irish

Though they never rivaled the Germans in terms of population, the Irish of the Midwest did gain considerable clout both in the Church and in politics. Most settled in Illinois, Michigan, and Ohio; as for cities, Chicago was clearly the most famous Irish city in the Midwest. Even though the Irish in New York or Boston outnumbered them, the Chicago Irish put their stamp on the city by "exerting an influence all out of proportion to their numbers."[6]

The Irish clergy ran the Catholic Church in Chicago for much of the nineteenth and twentieth centuries. As their numbers declined and their Irish parishioners moved to the suburbs, the Irish clergy ceased to be the power brokers in the Church. A similar scenario took place in city politics. The Irish took control in the 1930s, building a powerful machine that would rule the city into the 1970s. Richard J. Daley was the major figure in this 40-year reign of power. Elected as mayor in 1955, he ruled the city with a firm hand until his death in 1976. During his time in office the Irish held key city government, judicial, and police and fire department positions. But even before his death it was clear that the Irish control of Chicago politics was changing. This became most evident in 1983, when Harold Washington became the first African American mayor in the city's history. The Daley name returned to prominence when Daley's son, Richard M. Daley, became mayor in 1989. But his success on election day did not depend on the Irish vote. The Irish had long abandoned the city for the suburbs. Daley owed his successful tenure as mayor through four terms, 1989-2003, to a powerful Democratic coalition of African-Americans, Latinos, and an ethnically diverse group of whites.

What has happened in Chicago took place in other Midwest cities as well. In St. Paul, Minnesota, the Irish were a dominant presence through much of the twentieth century. A 1959 study noted that "being Catholic is almost essential for political success in St. Paul...and among the Catholics, the Irish predominate."[7] In 2003 that was no longer true. As in Chicago so in St. Paul, the Irish are no longer in control of the Church or the city.

Latinos

One of the most dramatic changes in recent years has been the immigration of thousands of Latinos to the United States. According to the U.S. Census, the Latino population has grown from 22.4 million in 1990 to 35.3 million in 2000, an increase of 58 percent. This large influx of Latinos has presented a special challenge for the Catholic Church, since the majority of Latinos, about 70 percent, are Catholic. Even though Latino Catholics have been present in the United States since colonial times, the twentieth century, and most especially the last 40 years of the twentieth century, witnessed unparalleled growth in this community. It is estimated that 71 percent of the growth of the Catholic population in the United States from 1960 to 2000 was due to this increase in the Latino population. As a result of this expansion and because of the initiative of both lay and clerical leaders, Latino Catholics have formed a church within a church. In many ways they resemble the German Catholics of the late nineteenth century. Like the Germans, they have their own national gatherings, lobby for their own Latino bishops, have their own parishes where they celebrate their liturgies in a uniquely Latino style, and seek to maintain their Latino heritage.

Recent surveys indicate that they are now the largest minority group in the nation. The favorite destination of these immigrants has been the states of California, Texas, New Mexico, and Arizona. Comparatively speaking, relatively few Latinos have settled in the Midwest. Only about 3 million Latinos have settled in the 11 states that comprise the Midwest region; more Latinos, 4.2 million, live in just one county, Los Angeles, than in the entire Midwest region.

Latinos first arrived in the Midwest in the early twentieth century. As elsewhere, their presence blossomed in the last 40 years of the twentieth century. As a result, Latinos are now the largest minority group in Iowa, Kansas and Nebraska. But it is in Illinois where the largest number of Latinos have settled—1,530,262 as of the 2000 census. The next largest concentration is in Michigan, where 323,877 Latinos lived in 2000. In Illinois the Latino population is concentrated in the Chicago area; Cook county has the fourth largest Latino population in the United States—1,071,740—70 percent of the entire Latino population in Illinois. Chicago, with 753,644 Latinos, has the third largest city population, outdistanced only by New York and Los Angeles. This represents a 38 percent increase since 1990 with the result that today approximately one of every four people who live in Chicago is Latino. [8]

One striking example of the growth of the Latino population in this area is in the Chicago suburb of Cicero. Since 1990 there has been a 40-percent increase in the town's Latino population, with the result that today 77 percent of the community is Latino. This remarkable growth is due primarily to immigration and higher-than-average birth rates. Such growth is expected to continue. In fact, "the Census bureau projects that the Latino population in Illinois will double in size between 1995 and 2025," reaching an estimated 2,275,000. [9]

In the Chicago archdiocese, which comprises Cook and Lake counties, there are 878,000 Latino Catholics; 36 percent of the total Catholic population in the archdiocese. About 10 percent of the parishes in the archdiocese (57) are designated as Latino parishes. On any given Sunday the Catholic Mass is celebrated in 44 different languages in the archdiocese. The language in the vast majority of these liturgies is English, but Spanish is the language of choice in 13 percent of all Sunday Masses. It is worth noting that the next most popular language after English and Spanish is Polish. Five percent of the Sunday Masses in the archdiocese are celebrated in Polish. Such a large number of Polish-language Masses is principally due to the immigration of significant numbers of Polish immigrants in recent years. [10]

Asians

The Chicago archdiocese has an Asian population of 80,000, which is expected to grow by about 10 percent by 2010. A relatively new group within the Midwest Catholic mosaic, Asian Catholics are ethnically a diverse population. Because of such diversity, as well as the lack of a native clergy, they will present a formidable challenge to the Church's pastoral ministry in the years ahead. Presently only one parish and three missions serve this growing population.

African Americans

In the Midwest region there are approximately 5.8 million African Americans, about 16.7 percent of the nation's African-American population. Three states in the region—Illinois, Michigan, and Ohio—account for 79 percent of the region's

African-American population. Nationwide, the number of African-American Catholics is relatively small, an estimated 2 million, or about 3 percent of the total Catholic population. The majority live in the South and Mid-Atlantic regions. In the Midwest, it is safe to say that the bulk of African-American Catholics live in Chicago and Detroit. The Archdiocese of Chicago has an estimated 99,000 African-American Catholics; 4 percent of its total population. Thirty-nine parishes in the archdiocese are designated as African-American parishes.[11]

In Detroit, 82 percent of the population is African American, making Detroit one of the most African-American cities in the nation. About 9 percent of Detroit's African Americans (70,000) are Catholic. As in the Chicago archdiocese, this represents about 4 percent of the total population. Within the archdiocese there are 36 parishes designated as African American.

Native Americans

Catholic missionaries first evangelized the Native Americans in the Midwest region during the seventeenth and eighteenth centuries, but this endeavor came to an end with the British takeover of Canada and the suppression of the Jesuits in France. Then, in the mid-nineteenth century, the apostolate was revived. Many nineteenth-century missions still exist in South Dakota, Minnesota, and Michigan, even though they remain invisible to most Americans in the Midwest.

In the Midwest there are 374,414 Native Americans, representing about 15 percent of the total Native-American population in the United States (2.4 million). South Dakota, Michigan, and Minnesota are the three states in the region with the largest number of Native-Americans. The estimated number of baptized Native American Catholics in the United States is 493,614, about 21 percent of the nation's Native-American population. There are 87,897 Native American Catholics in the Midwest region, 18 percent of the total number of Catholic Native Americans.

There is a vibrant evangelization program at many of the Midwest Catholic missions. Of the 101 parishes in the region designated as serving Native-American communities, 74 of them are located in North Dakota, South Dakota, and Minnesota, where they serve an estimated 15,305 people. Most of these parish communities are quite small.

One of the most dynamic centers of this missionary apostolate is in the Diocese of Rapid City, South Dakota. This diocese includes the Pine Ridge and Rosebud reservations. Catholic priests, brothers, and women religious have ministered to the Lakota Sioux on these reservations since 1886. There are three other reservations in the diocese—Lower Brule, Standing Rock, and Cheyenne River. Catholic parishes are also located in these communities of Lakota Sioux. In the Diocese of Marquette, Michigan, there are six Native-American Catholic missions ministering to the Ottawa and Ojibway, who were first evangelized by

Jesuit missionaries in the seventeenth century at places like St. Ignace and Sault Ste. Marie.

Many Native-American Catholics have moved off the reservations and into the cities, and "being urban dwellers and likely scattered among many neighborhoods, these and many other Native Americans may be invisible to the pastoral eye."[12] Pastoral care of Native Americans continues to be a major challenge for the Catholic Church, and has become even more acute in recent years as the number of clergy has declined.

The Spirit of Reform

Nothing differentiates Midwest Catholicism from Catholicism in other parts of the country more than the number of reform movements that originated there during the twentieth century. The center of this reformist tendency was the Archdiocese of Chicago, where a zest for innovation and experimentation took hold in the late 1930s and 1940s, in many respects anticipating the spirit of reform unleashed by the Second Vatican Council of the early 1960s. A key figure in the early years was Bernard J. Sheil, an auxiliary bishop in Chicago who founded the Catholic Youth Organization (CYO) in the early 1930s. It was not long before the CYO became one of the most successful youth organizations in the country.

Sheil was also an activist on behalf of social justice, working closely with the emerging labor-union movement in the 1930s. He was a key supporter of a young activist, Saul Alinsky, who was attempting to organize the workers in the slaughterhouses on Chicago's South Side. With Sheil's support, as well as the support of other clergy in the neighborhood, Alinsky was able to put together a neighborhood organization, the Back of the Yards Neighborhood Council. By forming a unique partnership that joined together Church, labor union, and community, the council was able to organize the packinghouse workers and bring peace to a neighborhood and industry notorious for its labor unrest. Alinsky's success in Chicago launched his career as a community organizer who, for the next three decades, helped to organize dozens of powerless urban neighborhoods. In the 1950s he would return to Chicago and once again join with the Catholic clergy to help organize other neighborhoods that were struggling with urban blight. These neighborhood organizations that brought church and community together became models for similar organizing efforts in cities across the country.

Another innovative movement that got its start in Chicago and the Midwest was known as Catholic Action. Imported from Europe, it took root in the Midwest, where it sought to evangelize young Catholic workers and students. Known as the YCW (Young Christian Workers) and the YCS (Young Christian Students), these organizations sought to reform society rather than the individual, according to the values of the gospel. Another Catholic Action organization born in Chicago was the Christian Family Movement (CFM). Founded by a husband and wife, Pat and Patty Crowley, it spread across the country and throughout the world during the course of the 1950s and 1960s. CANA was another organization identified with the Midwest in the 1940s and 1950s. With its nerve center in Chicago and under the direction of a charismatic priest, John Egan, it sought to reform society by strengthening the family. CANA quickly became popular with Catholics throughout the country and remains a viable organization whose goal is to strengthen family life.

In the 1950s and 1960s the civil rights movement galvanized the nation. The nation's cities became the main arena for this struggle for full civil rights for all people regardless of their race, creed, or color. The Catholic Church in Chicago, spearheaded by a number of lay men and clergy, took a leading role in this struggle. In January 1963 Chicago's Catholics hosted the first National Conference on Religion and Race, which brought together Catholics, Protestants, and Jews in an unprecedented ecumenical effort to combat racial discrimination in the United States. Once again, Chicago became the epicenter of a movement whose influence would spread well beyond the city.

Urban ministry took on a new urgency in the 1960s as racial unrest and urban blight challenged the churches. In Chicago, Fr. John Egan sought to organize the Catholic clergy working in the inner cities. His organization, The Catholic Committee on Urban Ministry, headquartered at the University of Notre Dame, sought to promote the cause of social justice. Chicago was also the setting for one of the first professional associations of Catholic clergy. Established in 1966, the Association of Chicago Priests not only sought to protect the rights of the clergy, but also became a catalyst for Church reform. It was not long before clergy in other dioceses formed similar associations, using Chicago as their model.

The Midwest, Iowa in particular, was the center of the Catholic rural life movement that flourished in the middle decades of the twentieth century. The Catholic Charismatic Movement was also centered in the Midwest, both at Notre Dame—in South Bend, Indiana—and in Ann Arbor, Michigan. Call to Action, one of the most active reform movements in the Church, has its headquarters in Chicago. Significantly, Catholic lay men and women are the leaders of this organization.

In recent years the energy for reform that was so noticeable in the Midwest in the middle decades of the twentieth century has dissipated. Catholicism has adopted a more rigid character, less open to the spirit of innovation so prevalent in the 1950s and 1960s. In this respect, sameness rather than diversity seems to distinguish the Church in the United States. As a result, Midwest Catholicism is now very similar to its East Coast or Pacific Coast counterpart. There are many reasons for this. In the wake of the Second Vatican Council (1962-65) a zeal for renewal captured the hearts and minds of many Catholics, which fostered a climate in the Church that was open to change and innovation. But this climate began to change by the early 1970s as the enthusiasm generated by the council waned. The activists of the 1950s and 1960s aged, losing some of the spark of their youth. In 1965, a new archbishop, John P. Cody, took control of the Church in Chicago. Unlike his predecessors, Cody was not open to change or innovation. An autocratic monarch, he succeeded in slowly but surely destroying the climate of optimism and hope generated by the Vatican II. Large numbers of clergy in Chicago, many of whom were actively involved in the changes initiated in the 1960s, left the priesthood.

During the presidency of Richard Nixon (1969-1974) a culture of conservatism swept across the nation. This became even more pronounced during the presidency of Ronald Reagan (1981-1989). Politically, Catholic suburbanites joined this shift to conservatism by supporting the Republican Party. In 1978 a new pope, John Paul II, was elected. He has since sought to fashion a culture of authoritarianism and rigid adherence to orthodox Catholic teaching. Such a climate has stifled the spirit of innovation in the Church.

Today's Church hierarchy, the vast majority of whom have been appointed over the past 25 years by John Paul II, are cast in his mold. Rather than encourage independent thinking and creative responses to pastoral issues, they favor an adherence to the past. The declining number of priests and women religious has also diminished the pool of potential innovators.

With the decline of the clergy, the laity have assumed leadership roles at the local parish level. They are the ones who are pushing the Church to become more open to the modern world and, in the words of Pope John XXIII, to bring "herself up to date." This is very noticeable in Chicago, where one of the most visible reform groups, Call to Action, is based. Enjoying a national constituency, this organization has inherited the legacy of Midwestern Catholicism, a spirit open to experimentation and innovation. How successful it and other lay reform movements will be may well shape the future of Catholicism in the United States.

The Catholic Priest—A Tale of Decline and Scandal

"The Roman Catholic Church faces a staggering loss of diocesan priests in the United States as it moves into the 21st century." That was the opening line in a book written in 1993 by Richard A. Schoenherr and Lawrence A. Young, *Full Pews, Empty Altars.*[13]

This study projected a 40-percent loss in the priest population from 1966 to 2005. In the Midwest there was a 16-percent decline in the priest population over the years from 1990 to 2002, somewhat worse than the 13 percent national decline.

During this same period the Midwest Catholic population increased 5 percent. This pattern has been present for many years—as the Catholic population increases, the number of priests declines. In the Archdiocese of Chicago, from 1990-2002, the Catholic population increased 4 percent while the priest population decreased 24 percent. In the Archdiocese of St. Paul-Minneapolis the population increased 22 percent and the number of priests declined 6 percent. Every state in the Midwest but one had fewer priests and more Catholics in 2002 than in 1990. The lone exception was North Dakota; it had 31 more priests in 2002 than in 1990 while its Catholic population declined by 5,649.

Why has there been such a significant decline in the number of priests? Without question, a major factor is the large number of resignations from the priesthood. From 1966 to 1984, 6,938 diocesan priests resigned. It was projected that the rate of resignations would continue, resulting in an additional 2,840 resignations between 1985 and 2004.[14] The principal reason for such resignations, according to numerous studies done over the past 30 years or so, is the high cost of celibacy. As long as the Church maintains its commitment to celibacy as a requirement for the priesthood, priests will continue to resign.

Another key reason for the declining number of priests is the decrease in the number of men studying to become priests. Between 1992 and 2002, the number of seminarians in the United States declined 29 percent. As a result, each year fewer men are ordained as priests. The Archdiocese of Chicago ordained 20 priests in 1990 and 11 in 2002; St. Paul-Minneapolis ordained nine in 1990 and four in 2002. This pattern is fairly consistent throughout the region. As these figures suggest and as several studies indicate, a vocation to the Catholic priesthood is no longer as popular a choice for young men as it was in the 1940s and 1950s, when seminaries were overflowing with record numbers of students.

In addition to the decline in the number of diocesan priests and seminarians, the median age of the clergy is rising each year. In 1999 it was 62. Indicative of this trend, more priests are over 90 years of age than under 30.

Because of this aging and declining priesthood, parishes either had to close or survive without a resident pastor. This was unheard of in the 1950s and 1960s, but the closing of parishes and the emergence of the priestless parish has become commonplace in the Midwest.

A study issued in 2000 reported that 2,334 parishes in the United States did not have a resident priest, a significant and ever-rising number. The Archdiocese of Chicago reported that in 2002, of the 378 parishes in the archdiocese 27 were without a resident priest. In 2004, it is projected that there will most likely be eight more parishes without a priest by the end of the year, though it is very possible that the number could be as many as 35. In the Archdiocese of Dubuque, Iowa, lay people run 100 of 350 parishes. One priest said, "When I was ordained 18 years ago, there were almost 300 of us, and now there are about 120. In five to ten years, they project it will be 75."

As the number of clergy has declined, the number of lay people involved in parish ministry has increased dramatically. They have taken on roles previously reserved for the priest, such as ministers of the Eucharist at Mass, readers of the scriptures, and directors of worship. By 1999 as many as 29,146 lay people and religious were working as paid parish ministers in the nation's Catholic parishes. The vast majority of them (82 percent) were women. Such a development has been described as "a virtual revolution in pastoral ministry."[16] One such woman-led parish is located in Saginaw, Michigan, where Sister Honora Remes is the woman pastor of St. Mary's Cathedral. She "does everything a pastor does except say Mass and administer the sacraments. She hires the staff, manages the finances and budget, provides counseling and advice to parishioners, oversees the liturgies and supervises the religious, social, and educational programs."[17] Such an arrangement, where the priest is "a special guest star, a visiting shaman who does his routine and is gone," has become common throughout the Midwest, most especially in the more rural areas of the Great Plains states.

Recently, the reputation of the Catholic priesthood has been severely tarnished because of the revelations of widespread sexual abuse of children by Catholic priests. This issue first gained notoriety in Louisiana in the 1980s with the conviction of Rev. Gilbert Gauthe, who was sentenced to 20 years in prison for molesting more than 100 boys. Hardly an isolated instance, similar accusations of sex abuse by priests came to light in Texas, Minnesota, New Mexico, and Massachusetts. For the first time in their history, American Catholics had to acknowledge the scandalous and criminal behavior of abusive priests.

In January 2002 came the revelation that for years the leadership of the Archdiocese of Boston had been covering up the criminal behavior of abusive priests who preyed upon innocent children. These priests were quietly reassigned, millions of dollars of hush money was paid to their victims, and the Boston faithful were kept in the dark about these abusive priests, many of whom continued to minister in parishes where they still had contact with young children. This scandal left Catholics shocked and angry.

Reporters from the *Boston Globe* broke the story. They continued their investigation for several months and each new revelation of the abusive behavior of priests only increased the people's feeling of betrayal. By the end of the year 94 priests had been accused, 27 of whom had been removed or suspended from the ministry. Eventually, because of his complicity in the cover-up of abusive priests, the cardinal archbishop of Boston, Bernard Law, was forced to resign.

But what happened in Boston was not an isolated phenomenon. Across the entire nation victims began to come forth and level accusations against abusive priests. In Florida the bishop of the Palm Beach diocese was forced to resign after admitting he sexually abused a seminarian more than 25 years earlier. A bishop in Kentucky also resigned after accusations of sexual abuse. The cardinal archbishop of Los Angeles, Roger Mahoney, was accused of covering up numerous instances of sexual abuse by priests. The scandal appeared to know no boundaries. Boston was but the epicenter of a scandal that rocked the Church from Maine to California. A *New York Times* study, reported on January 12, 2003, found that in the United States as many as 1,205 priests were accused of sexual abuse in 2002; of these 432 have resigned, retired or been removed from ministry. The Midwest was scarcely immune.

In 2002, 308 priests in the Midwest region were accused of sexual abuse. The largest numbers were in the major dioceses of Chicago (30), Cleveland (33), and Detroit (26).[18] In Cleveland, a priest accused of molesting a girl committed suicide. The archbishop of Cleveland, Anthony Pila, and his auxiliary, A. James Quinn, were both accused of obstruction of justice and forced to testify before a grand jury, which decided not to indict the bishops. The prosecutor for Cuyhoga County told Cleveland's *Plain Dealer* that 145 priests in the Cleveland archdiocese had been accused of sexual abuse, but only a handful would come to trial because of the statute of limitations. Four priests in the Cincinnati archdiocese have been suspended because of charges of sexual abuse. In addition, the *Cincinnati Enquirer* reported that the local prosecutor accused the archdiocese of Cincinnati of "withholding documents" that were supposed to have been turned over as part of an investigation into sexual abuse allegations.

Milwaukee was the scene of one of the most improbable and shocking revelations. Rembert Weakland, the well-known and highly respected archbishop of Milwaukee, publicly acknowledged that he paid $450,000 to a man who claimed he had been sexually abused by Weakland. The archbishop resigned shortly thereafter. More shocking news came from the rural, monastic environment of Collegeville, Minnesota, when it was revealed that as many as 13 monks at the Benedictine Abbey of St. John were suspended and put on restriction by the abbey after credible evidence of sexual misconduct involving 24 victims. Among the accused was the monk who, in 1971, was elected as the seventh abbot of St. John's, the largest Benedictine institution in the world.

The list of accusations appeared to be endless. Some of these may well be bogus. Too many, however, are well founded. Such scandalous behavior has done immense harm to the Church. In terms of public opinion, the Church has reached its nadir. Never before, even in the days of rabid anti-Catholicism, when the Ku Klux Klan was riding high in popularity, has the Church's prestige descended to such a low ebb. Because of the complicity of numerous bishops in covering up the charges of sexual abuse by priests, their prestige and authority as moral and spiritual leaders have diminished considerably. The Catholic hierarchy has been challenged to become more open and honest in how it deals with this scandal. How it responds may well determine what future the Church has in this country.

Education—The Parochial School, Vouchers, and the Fighting Irish

The national scandal of sexually abusive priests has commanded so much media attention since 2001 that the press has largely ignored the good the Church has done and continues to do. As understandable as this is, it does diminish the attention the Church's good work deserves. One area deserving recognition is education. The Catholic Church has the second-largest elementary school system in the country, behind only the public schools. Like its public counterpart, the Catholic educational enterprise has helped shape an educated populace, which is the foundation of a free, democratic society. In providing such an education it has also stressed the necessity of a moral and religious perspective as a foundation stone for building a just society. Equally significant, it has stressed the need for a society where community welfare balances individual needs. These values, intrinsic to the Catholic educational enterprise, have helped shape the public life of the nation in general and the Midwest in particular.

The concept of a private parochial school transformed the American educational enterprise. It may be argued that, in terms of shaping public policy, this is the area where Catholics have had the most decisive influence. Catholics were the first to challenge the nineteenth-century idea of the public school, a free education for all children. Because Protestant culture and religion shaped the early public school education, Catholics were reluctant to have their children attend such schools. Not only did they establish their own parochial schools, but they also sought to gain public funds to support these schools. Catholics waged this battle throughout the nineteenth and twentieth centuries, precipitating debate over the issue of public funds for private schools that has continued to the present day.

At the beginning of the twenty-first century, the Catholic parochial school remains very much alive. In the Midwest in 2002, there were 2,255 Catholic elementary schools, educating 596,998 children, close to one-third of the nation's parochial schools. Even though this is a major commitment on the part of the Church in the Midwest, still only one in three parishes has a school. In Ohio, close to half the state's parishes support a parochial school. Illinois, Wisconsin, and Indiana also have a sizable elementary-school population. The Church in the Dakotas, however, is able to support very few parochial schools; only 10 percent of its parishes have such a school. Such a disparity underscores the vast differences in this region. Those states that border the Great Lakes are the heartland of Midwestern Catholicism, whereas the Plains states resemble Mission territory. A similar pattern is evident in secondary parochial schooling. There are only four Catholic high schools in North and South Dakota combined, while Ohio has 79; Illinois is close behind with 76 schools. The entire region supports 355 secondary schools.

This snapshot of Catholic education can be very misleading. Hidden behind this data is the chilling reality of a shrinking educational enterprise. Since the

1960s the number of Catholic schools has been in decline. The reasons for this are complex; a declining birth rate, doubts about the value of a parochial-school education, aging physical plants, a declining number of women religious teachers, and the necessary increase in the number of lay teachers, who need to be paid a living wage, all lead to large increases in the financial cost per pupil of operating an elementary or secondary school. As a result, between 1964 and 1984, 40 percent of the nation's Catholic high schools and 27 percent of its elementary schools closed their doors. This trend has continued into the twenty-first century.

In 1990 Catholics supported 7,395 parochial schools; by 2002 this number had declined to 6,886. In the Midwest a similar decline has taken place; since 1992 the number of Catholic elementary schools in the region declined from 2,465 declined to 2,255. The archdiocese of Chicago, which has the largest Catholic school system in the country, is typical of this shift. In 1965 Chicago supported 429 parochial elementary schools; by 2001 the number had declined 39 percent to 261. The same was true of secondary schools, whose numbers declined from 95 in 1965 to 43 in 2001. As in other dioceses, the Chicago archdiocese recorded a decline in the Catholic school population in every year since 1965. This decline has moderated in recent years. In fact, in some regions enrollment is up to a modest degree. According to a *New York Times* report in 2000 "more than 40 percent of all Catholic elementary and secondary schools have waiting lists for admission."

A key transformation in the educational enterprise has been the disappearance of the women religious teacher. Books and plays have lampooned the strict nun who ruled the classroom with an iron fist. This may have been true in the 1940s and 50s, but in 2002 that image is as out-of-date as the dinosaur. The teaching sister is a vanishing breed, principally because of the catastrophic decline in the numbers of women religious. Since 1966 the number of women religious nationally has declined 58 percent, from 181,421 to 75,500 in 2002, and many among them are retired from active ministry.

In 1960 three out of every four teachers in the parochial schools were women religious. The Catholic sister, in her medieval-looking religious garb, was an icon that represented everything the parochial school stood for—religion, discipline, tradition, education. Over the course of the next few decades this icon disappeared. By 2000 only 7 percent of the teachers in the nation's Catholic schools were sisters; the other 93 percent were lay men and women.

The financial implications of this shift in personnel have been significant. In years past, the financial survival of parish schools was never an issue. The sisters who taught in these schools were free labor in many respects; some would even say slave labor! With the arrival of lay teachers, salaries had to become more competitive, although Catholic school teachers tend to earn less than their public-school counterparts. This raised the cost of operating the schools, and as a result tuition rose substantially. A Catholic education was no longer a bargain, especially in comparison with a free, public-school education. Increased labor costs and the refusal of parents to pay substantial tuition fees forced many schools to close; they were simply too much of a drain on the parish budget. In addition, as the landscape of urban America changed, many Catholics moved from cities to suburbs, depopulating urban Catholic neighborhoods. In fact, it was in these inner-city neighborhoods where the worst of the decline in the Catholic school population took place.

Because of the financial demands associated with operating and maintaining an elementary school, Catholics have once again looked to the public sector for financial assistance. In recent years such assistance has become more feasible with the introduction of tuition vouchers. The voucher system "provides parents with a portion of the public educational funding allotted for their child...and allows them to use these funds to attend the school of their choice." [19] In 1990 "the Wisconsin state legislature authorized the first state funded urban school voucher initiative."[20] This law allowed Milwaukee children from low-income families to attend private schools, both religious and non-religious, using state vouchers. Such a radical change in the state's educational policy caused a fire storm of controversy. It was not long before the law was challenged in the courts. In 1998 the Wisconsin Supreme Court decided in a 4-2 decision that a school-voucher program that included religious schools was constitutional. By 2002 enrollment in Milwaukee's voucher program exceeded 10,000 students in about 100 schools, nearly 40 of which are Catholic schools.

A similar program began in Cleveland in 1995. Opponents to this voucher program also challenged it in the courts. As in Wisconsin, the main objection was that public money should not be used in religious schools. In 2002 the U.S. Supreme Court, in a 5-4 decision, upheld the constitutionality of the Cleveland program. The three Catholic members of the court voted with the majority.

Inner-city Catholic schools have benefited greatly from these school-choice programs. Many of these schools, which faced declining enrollments before the voucher programs were enacted, now have waiting lists. One such school is Messmer High School, located near a freeway in one of Milwaukee's poorest neighborhoods. Like other inner-city parochial schools, many of its students—about 80 percent of its 400 students—are not Catholic. As *The New York Times* reported in August 2000, "More than half are there because of the voucher program." In Cleveland it is much the same. At St. Francis, an elementary school founded in 1887 to serve German immigrants, the enrollment is 97 percent African American and 98 percent non-Catholic. Three out of four students are living at or below the poverty level. The voucher program has been essential for these children and has kept the school open. In 2003 there were 155 students on vouchers out of a school population of 250. As the assistant principal told the

National Catholic Reporter in March 2003, the voucher program "has changed the mission of who we serve. We now serve the poor."

Although the voucher program was initially promoted by civil rights groups and conservative Republicans, Catholics have become strong supporters of this version of school choice. At the national level the Catholic Educational Association and the United States Catholic Conference of Bishops have given strong support to the voucher concept. At the state level the Catholic Church, through its state Catholic conferences, has become an active advocate of voucher programs. The Wisconsin Catholic Conference, a lobbying organization, monitors the activity of the state legislature. Not surprisingly, it is an avid supporter of the Milwaukee voucher program and issues press releases to that effect whenever the opportunity arises.

Surveys indicate that as many as 60 percent of Americans support vouchers. These same surveys show that as many as 72 percent of Catholics, together with a wide majority of born-again Christians, are "especially supportive of vouchers."[21]

Religion clearly seems to have an influential role in shaping people's attitude toward vouchers. The National Survey of Religion and Politics, conducted by John Green and his colleagues at the Bliss Institute at the University of Akron, reached a similar conclusion. Better than half of those who described themselves as high-commitment Catholics (those who attend church at least once a week) favor school vouchers, and close to one-third oppose them. Only 39 percent of self-described low-commitment (less than weekly attendance) Catholics favor school vouchers, while 44 percent oppose them. Among Midwest Catholics the percentage of those supporting and opposing vouchers are almost identical to the national figures. Black Protestants and Hispanic Christians, those groups most likely to benefit from the voucher programs, match Catholics in terms of support for school vouchers.

The success of school-voucher programs has clearly reshaped the educational landscape in the United States. Though these programs still have many powerful opponents, the U.S. Supreme Court decision in 2002 suggests that school vouchers will become a permanent fixture in American society. The Catholic Church and its school system has not only profited from this program, but it also remains a major supporter of this program.

Catholic colleges have long been beneficiaries of public funding. Such funding, most often in the form of research grants, has enabled many colleges to achieve a degree of excellence unimagined in the pioneer days of the nineteenth century. These schools represent the capstone of the Catholic educational system.

The most authoritative source lists 212 Catholic colleges in the United States, about 40 percent of all church-related colleges in the country. Sixty-eight of the nation's Catholic colleges are located in the Midwest. Traditionally, Catholic colleges were mainly located in the cities, where the bulk of the Catholic population lived. These colleges—DePaul and Loyola in Chicago, University of Detroit, Xavier in Cincinnati, Marquette in Milwaukee, John Carroll in Cleveland, and Creighton in Omaha—educated scores of professionals—lawyers, doctors, accountants, teachers, and businessmen—who lived and worked in these cities. Many of the political power brokers in these cities were educated in Catholic colleges. The most notable perhaps was Mayor Richard Daley of Chicago, who was a graduate of DePaul University. His son, Richard M. Daley, the current mayor of Chicago, is also a DePaul graduate.

The University of Notre Dame, located in South Bend, Indiana, is clearly the most well known and most highly ranked Catholic college in the Midwest and perhaps even in the country. Its impact on public affairs in the nation can be measured by the participation of its graduates in the political arena. Condoleezza Rice, President George W. Bush's National Security Advisor, is a Notre Dame graduate, as is Richard Allen, who served in the same capacity for President Ronald Reagan. Peter King, a noted New York Congressman, and Bruce Babbitt, Secretary of the Interior in the Clinton administration, are also alumni. Many others have held elected offices at the state and local level.

"Notre Dame," in the words of its most well-known president, Theodore Hesburgh, "is where the Church does its thinking." This boast is well founded, since the university has become a major center for the study of religion and American life. One reason for this is the close relationship the University has established with the Lilly Foundation. Located in Indianapolis, this foundation has been a major supporter of research related to the study of religion. The Cushwa Center for the Study of American Catholicism, founded in 1975, was one of the first Notre Dame enterprises to benefit from Lilly Foundation largesse. Through its newsletter, publications, seminars, research grants, and conferences, the Cushwa Center has established itself as the leading center in the country for the study of American Catholicism.

As a national center for liturgical studies, Notre Dame has annually sponsored gatherings where Catholics from across the country discuss various aspects of the liturgy. It was also a major center for the Charismatic movement, which was quite popular in the 1970s and 80s. The Institute for Latino Studies, recently established at Notre Dame, has emerged as a major research center. The Kroc Institute for International Peace Studies has become a key resource in helping Church leaders understand issues of peace and justice as they pertain to American society. The university has also sponsored debates on such controversial public issues as abortion, the death penalty, and war. These discussions have influenced policy makers within the Church as they seek to articulate their response to such critical issues.

Without a doubt Notre Dame is best known for its football team. The ghosts of Knute Rockne, "the Gipper," and Frank Leahy still haunt the stadium. In the 1920s, 1930s and 1940s Catholics across the country took pride in the Fighting Irish when they defeated such powerhouses as Southern California, Southern Methodist, or Army. These fans became known as the subway alumni—men and some women who never had the opportunity to attend Notre Dame, but became loyal supporters of the school and its football team. Immigrant Catholics took pride in Notre Dame's accomplishments on the gridiron. Even those who were not Catholic learned to root for the Fighting Irish. Such recognition has continued to the present day.

Catholics and Protestants alike look upon Notre Dame as the embodiment of the Catholic success story. Catholics especially take pride in its achievements, both in athletics and in the classroom. Indeed, they visit the campus by the thousands every year. In fact, Notre Dame is one of the most popular tourist sites in Indiana, second only to the Indianapolis Speedway. For many people it is more than a university; it is a shrine where they can personally experience an appreciation of the Catholic story as they walk around the huge campus.

The Quest for a Good Society

In the course of the twentieth century, Catholic Church leaders increasingly began to articulate moral and political positions they believed would benefit the welfare of American society. This concern for the public square took on a renewed vigor as a result of the Second Vatican Council. As one observer noted, the council "moved the Church into far greater participation in social and political affairs. The council stressed that the Church as an institution and Catholics in general had a positive obligation to involve themselves in the problems of the world."[22]

The council document, *Pastoral Constitution on the Church in the Modern World*, provided Catholics with a theological rationale for a public Catholicism. It not only recognized the importance of culture shaping religion, but it also underscored the need for religion to transform culture.

One major initiative in the post-Vatican-II era was the establishment of episcopal conferences. These conferences have allowed the bishops of a particular nation to exercise their pastoral office jointly for the welfare of their respective countries. In the United States, this resulted in the formation of what is now known as the United States Conference of Catholic Bishops. This conference has been very active in issuing statements and lobbying on a wide range of issues, many of which relate to social justice. Between 1966 and 1988 the American hierarchy issued 188 official statements and letters, more than half of which addressed issues of social justice. Such activity persuaded one commentator to write that "through the unprecedented activism of the National Conference of Catholic Bishops during the 1980s, American Catholic bishops assumed a position as chief religious commentators on American politics."[23]

One of the most important pastoral letters was the 1983 letter on nuclear war, *The Challenge of Peace: God's Promise and Our Response*. One commentator claimed that it was the "most significant event in the American Catholic Church, and perhaps in the international church, since the Second Vatican Council."[24] The driving force behind this letter was the Archbishop of Chicago, Joseph Bernardin. Appointed archbishop of the most prestigious diocese in the Midwest in 1982, Bernardin quickly established himself as the recognized leader of the American hierarchy. Known as a moderate, he envisioned himself as a major actor in the public arena, seeking to influence public policy through lobbying Congress as well as the White House and the Illinois State House. In a series of lectures he crafted what he described as a "consistent ethic of life," urging Americans to protect human life in the womb as well as in the face of nuclear war. He soon "extended his consistent ethic beyond abortion and war" to such life issues as capital punishment and poverty.[25]

Another key pastoral letter in the 1980s addressed the state of the national economy. Published in 1986, after two years of consultation, *Economic Justice for All* was able to draw on a rich tradition of Catholic social teaching. One commentator described it as the "most detailed, systematic, and thorough application of Catholic social thought to a concrete, particular economy."[26] The principal architect of this pastoral letter was another Midwesterner, Archbishop Rembert Weakland of Milwaukee. A Benedictine monk, he was elected the Abbot Primate of the Benedictine Order in 1967 at the age of 40. Ten years later the Pope appointed him as the archbishop of Milwaukee. He soon became identified with the more liberal wing of American Catholicism. Other dioceses even began to copy some of his "innovative policies" such as "placing women in senior positions, streamlining the bureaucracy, assuring pensions for lay employees and higher pay for teachers, establishing a program for spritual renewal for parishes, and mandating that each parish have a lay council."[27] With Bernardin's death in 1996 and Weakland's resignation in 2002, Midwest Catholicism lost two charismatic leaders. No one has been able to replace either of them in terms of national prestige.

As active as Church leaders are at the federal level through the United States Catholic Conference of Bishops, it is at the state level where the Church is having a most significant influence. Every state in the Midwest has a Catholic conference that serves as the official voice of the Church on matters of public policy. Though very little has been written about these conferences, they are often influential, representing the Church as lobbyists in the state legislatures and keeping track of proposed legislation.

In Minnesota, the conference tracks legislation dealing with issues as diverse as special education, so-called partial-birth abortion, increasing the minimum wage, prescription drug rebates, gun control, and the death penalty.

The Michigan conference outlines its public policy initiatives in the following way:

> Through the Michigan Catholic Conference, the official Catholic position on public policy matters is presented with one voice to the legislative and executive branches of government at both the state and federal level. ... Guided by the biblical imperative for a commitment to justice, MCC advocates on such wide ranging matters as education, health care, economics, assisted suicide, capital punishment, abortion, immigration, and the environment. Issues are viewed in light of their effect on the well-being of all persons, the significance of their impact on public policy, and their implications for the Catholic community.[28]

In North Dakota, each year the conference publishes a report card on its achievements and its defeats. In 2003 the conference director listed the two best bills passed in the legislature: to ensure conscience protection for adoption agencies and a ban on human cloning.

North Dakota's concern about the conscience clause highlights an issue of public policy that worries Catholic Church leaders. The conscience clause grants to Catholic institutions such as hospitals or social service agencies that receive federal or state funding an exemption from providing contraceptive and sterilization services that are contrary to Catholic ethical teaching. The conscience clause is not without opponents, however. Such organizations as Planned Parenthood oppose such a situation in which a Catholic hospital, receiving public funds, does not provide a full range of reproductive services because of the conscience-clause exemption.

The chief beneficiary of conscience exemptions are hospitals. The Midwest has 238 Catholic hospitals, which serve over 31 million patients annually. A huge enterprise, these hospitals depend on state and federal support through the Medicare and Medicaid programs. If these hospitals were to lose public funding, many would be forced to close. For this reason Catholic lobbyists at both the federal and state level are vigilant in protecting this exemption.

Human life issues are paramount with state Catholic conferences. Taking their cue from the national conference of bishops, they focus on issues that both respect the dignity of the human person and serve the common good. For the most part, their agenda does reflect the opinion of most Catholics. The one area where the official Church position differs considerably from the people in the pew is sexual ethics. The Catholic laity is much more liberal on these issues. Abortion is a good example of this divergence of opinion.

All state conferences take a strong anti-abortion stance trying to halt any legislation that would enhance the status of abortion. Yet the Catholic laity are divided on this issue. One recent poll found that two-thirds of Catholics believe abortion should be legal. If the woman's life was in danger, the percentage of Catholics approving abortion climbs to 83 percent. If the reason for the abortion is the likelihood of a birth defect, the rate of approval declines to 51 percent. Such differences of opinion based on different situations suggest that Catholic lay attitudes about abortion are quite nuanced. But official Church position on this issue does not allow for any such fine tuning. It has adopted a firm anti-abortion, pro-life stance. In doing so it has aligned itself with organizations in American society who seek to overturn the 1973 Supreme Court decision legalizing abortion. Indeed, it is not an exaggeration to say that the Catholic hierarchy is in the forefront of this movement to change the legal status of abortion in the United States.[29] Nevertheless, a significant number of people in the pews refuse to support the bishops in this regard.

Another issue of human life is the death penalty. Along with Pope John Paul II, the Catholic hierarchy has taken a strong anti-death-penalty stance. State conferences in the Midwest have also taken strong stances against the death penalty. The personal journey of the Catholic sister Helen Prejean, chronicled in her book, *Dead Man Walking*, has linked Catholicism with opposition to the death penalty. Such opposition has led to an increase in Catholic support for the abolition of the death penalty. Nonetheless, the majority of Catholics (62 percent), like most Americans, still favor the death penalty.[30] Once again, individual Catholics differ from the Church's official stance on an issue of pubic policy. The same can be said about opposition to the war in Iraq. The Catholic Church leadership, both John Paul II and the United States Catholic Conference of Bishops, opposed the American act of war against Iraq. But the majority of Catholics, like most Americans, supported President Bush's decision to invade Iraq.

This difference of opinion between the Church leadership and the people in the pews on such issues as abortion and the death penalty raises the question of just how effective the Church is in shaping the public policy of American society. If it cannot persuade its own members on such key issues, how can it be expected to persuade the rest of the American public who are not Catholic? Nonetheless, its prophetic voice is still an important force in the public square.

The Church is also actively lobbying on behalf of the poor. In this area there is much more agreement between the hierarchy and the Catholic laity. At the state level every state conference in the Midwest seeks to encourage legislation that will benefit the poor. According to one national survey, the majority of Catholics, 63 percent, believe that "society has a responsibility for helping poor people get out of poverty." Another poll found that three of four Catholics believed that more money should be provided for health care for poor children. Even more telling was the poll that indicated that 58 percent of Catholics believed charitable efforts toward helping the poor was essential to their faith. This element of faith was second only to the belief that God is present in the sacraments.[31] All of those data suggests that Catholics "have a more communitarian ethic that emphasizes solidarity, interdependence, and the common good rather than the individualism, independence, and self-help characteristic of the Protestant ethic."[32] This attitude has supported the efforts of Church leaders at both the national and state level to shape public policy.

The Catholic effort to influence public policy does not end at the state level. Every diocese has its own departments that follow the lead of the state conferences on issues of concern. An office of Catholic Charities operates in every diocese. Such offices monitor legislation at the state and local level that affects the welfare of the underprivileged. Some dioceses sponsor offices of peace and justice. They too work on behalf of social justice. As the Chicago archdiocese office of peace and justice puts it, they promote "advocacy efforts to assist the poor and vulnerable in the Chicago area. Through education and advocacy, parishioners are encouraged to take informed action to influence pubic policy in line with the Catholic Conference of Illinois, and the U.S. Catholic Conference."[33] Thus, at all levels—national, state, regional, and local—Catholics are linked together to form a powerful political lobby that seeks to shape public policy.

In spite of its late start Catholicism in the Midwest has caught up with the Church in the Northeast in terms of prestige and significance. Even though Catholics in the different regions of the country may have many similarities in terms of belief, worship, devotional practices, and attitudes toward social policy, Catholicism in the Midwest maintains a certain distinctiveness. This is due to its historical tradition, its location in the rural heartland of the nation, its very diverse ethnic heritage, and an openness to innovation. Given the vastness of the nation and its diverse geographical and cultural regions, this tension between uniformity and regional diversity will likely always remain a hallmark of Catholicism in the United States.

Endnotes

1. The population data for this section was taken from the *U.S. Catholic Directory 2002* and from *North American Religion Atlas*.

2. The data for this section was from *Census 2000* in addition to the *U.S. Catholic Directory 2002*.

3. This data on Germans was taken from the *Census 2000*.

4. This data is from *Census 2000* and Dale E. Jones et al, *Religious Congregations and Membership 2000* (Glenmary Research Center: Nashville, 2002).

5. Kathleen Neils Conzen, *Making Their Own America* (New York:Berg, 1990), 5, 33, 2.

6. Michael Glazier (ed.), *The Encyclopedia of the Irish in America* (Notre Dame: University of Notre Dame Press, 1999), 141.

7. Mary Lethert Wingerd, *Claiming the City: Politics, Faith and the Power of Place in St. Paul* (Ithaca: Cornell University Press, 2001), 266.

8. See Gaston Espinosa, Virgilio Elizondo, and Jesse Miranda, *Hispanic Churches in American Public Life: Summary of Findings* (Notre Dame: Institute for Latino Studies, 2003) and U.S. Census for data on Latinos.

9. *Bordering the Mainstream: A Needs Assessment of Latinos in Berwyn and Cicero, Illinois, January 2002* (Notre Dame: Institute for Latino Studies).

10. This data is from the Web site of the Archdiocese of Chicago, www.archdiocese-chgo.org.

11. See Web sites for the Archdiocese of Chicago and Archdiocese of Detroit, www.aodonline.org.

12. *Native American Catholics at The Millennium* (Washington, D.C.: U.S. Conference of Catholic Bishops, 2002), 8.

13. Richard A. Schoenherr and Lawrence A. Young, *Full Pews and Empty Altars* (Madison: University of Wisconsin Press, 1993), xvii.

14. Ibid., 208.

15. "Corpus Christi and the priest shortage," *Churchwatch-Call to Action*, August 2003, 7.

16. Jay P. Dolan, *In Search of an American Catholicism; A History of Religion and Culture in Tension* (New York: Oxford University Press, 2002), 230.

17. Ibid., 231.

18. "Trail of Pain in Church Crisis Leads to Nearly Every Diocese," *New York Times*, January 12, 2003, 1 and 20-21 for statistics on priests accused of sexual albuse.

19. *National Catholic Reporter*, March 21, 2003, 29.

20. William G. Howell and Paul E. Peterson, *The Education Gap:Vouchers and Urban Schools* (Washington, D.C.: The Brookings Institution Press, 2002), 30.

21. Terry M. Moe, *Schools, Vouchers and the American Public* (Washington, D.C.: Brookings Institution Press, 2001), 213, where he discusses religion and support for vouchers, and 254 for the quote.

22. Mary Hanna, "Bishops as Political Leaders," 75-86 in Charles Dunn (ed.) *Religion in American Politics* (Washington,D.C.: Congressional Quarterly Press, 1989), 76.

23. Richard Gelm, *Politics and Religious Authority:American Catholics Since the Second Vatican Council* (Westport: Greenwood Press 1994), 90; thanks to David Yamane for sharing this and the Hanna reference with me from his work on Catholic state conferences.

24. Quoted in Dolan, *In Search of an American Catholicism*, 200.

25. John T. McGreevy, *Catholicism and American Freedom* (New York: W. W. Norton and Company, 2003), 285.

26. Jose Casanova, *Public Religions in the Modern World* (Chicago: University of Chicago Press, 1994), 191.

27. Paul Wilkes, "The Education of an Archbishop," *The New Yorker*, July 15, 1991, 49.

28. Web site of Michigan Catholic Conference, www.micatholicconference.org/home/home.html

29. Data on attitude toward abortion was taken from Mary E. Bendyna and Paul M. Perl, *Political Preferences of American Catholics at the Time of Election 2000* (Washington, D.C.: Center for Applied Research in the Apostolate, 2000), 30-32.

30. Ibid.

31. Ibid., 34 and William V. D'Antonio. James Davidson, Dean Hoge, and Katherine Meyer *American Catholics* (Walnut Creek, CA: AltaMira Press,2001), 96 and 49.

32 Bendyna and Perl, *Political Preferences*, 34.

33 Web site of the Dept. of Peace and Justice for the Archdiocese of Chicago, www.archchicago.org/departments/peace_and_justice/peace_and_justice.shtm

CHAPTER FIVE

RELIGION AND RECENT IMMIGRANTS: NEW FERMENT IN AMERICAN CIVIC LIFE

Raymond Brady Williams

Chicago's World's Parliament of Religion in 1893 attracted representatives of what appeared then as exotic religions from around the world. Swami Vivekananda intrigued Americans with his graceful presentation of the spiritual wisdom of the East. Mr. Gandhi presented Jain non-violence. The Turkish village had a mosque from which the call to prayer echoed across the Midway Plaisance. In lecture halls Buddhist, Muslim, Hindu, and Zoroastrian scholars, and others from around the world, joined Jews and Christians in presenting their beliefs and explaining their religious practices. A veritable religious Olympics! Then they went home.

A century later representatives of 250 religious groups—Hindu, Buddhist, Muslim, Zoroastrian, Confucian, Taoist, African, Native American, and scores of others—met in Chicago for a second World's Parliament of Religion. Then they went home: to the Chicago suburbs, to Detroit, the Twin Cities, and other towns and cities across the Midwest. The world's religions have come and made themselves at home in the American heartland, with profound results on American religion. They reopen and intensify the negotiation about the religious foundations of American civic life. The nature of this negotiation and experience of recent immigrants is not distinctly different in the Midwest from that in other regions. Hence, the context of the heartland provides a case study that sheds light on the major religious and social issues in other regions and the nation as a whole.

The negotiations of earlier immigrants, sometimes embittered and violent, moved American civic order from a Protestant establishment to a Protestant, Catholic, and Jewish synthesis with Enlightenment principles represented in the mottos of "In God We Trust" on coins and "one nation under God" in the Pledge of Allegiance. Two major civic leaders of the early 1960s enunciated these principles powerfully. John F. Kennedy defended his right to nomination as a Roman Catholic for President of the United States in a speech to the Greater Houston Ministerial Association (September 12, 1960) by appealing to that synthesis. Martin Luther King's "I have a dream" speech for the March on Washington (August 28, 1963) may have been the last time a religious leader has reached a national audience with a clarion call based on the rich combination of Judeo-Christian and Enlightenment ideals that had provided a foundation for American civic life for at least one generation. The new social realities—including the diminishing power of the Judeo-Christian synthesis in American life and the presence of many religious and intellectual traditions that have no clear place in the earlier synthesis—engender a reformulation, a revision, or perhaps a negotiation of a new synthesis.

The most important factor in shaping American Christianity and the future of American religion is the changing pattern of immigration that through the centuries selected people from different countries with a variety of religious affiliations. The *Harvard Encyclopedia of American Ethnic Groups* traces the immigration history that shaped American religion and civic life through five periods: Colonial Period, 1609-1775, when the Crown encouraged emigration from the British Isles; the Open Door Era, 1776-1881, when immigration, largely of Protestant Christians from the British Isles and northern and western Europe, was encouraged by various states; the Era of Regulation, 1882-1916, when the federal government took control of immigration and Roman Catholics and Jews from central and southern Europe entered in larger numbers; the Era of Restriction, 1917-1964; and the Era of Liberalization, 1965 to the present, when doors of immigration were reopened.[1]

The Era of Restriction, 1917-1964, could be called "The Period of the Lull." It was a peculiar period of American history when restrictive laws, the Great Depression, World War II, and other special circumstances caused many fewer people to immigrate to the United States. Indeed, in some years during the lull, more people left the United States than entered as immigrants. Restrictive legislation excluded Asians and others in order to prevent changes in the ethnic composition of American society that might come from a new infusion of immigrants. The average annual immigration for the period from 1931 to 1945 was under 50,000. The McCarran-Walter Act of 1952 assured that more than 85 percent of the annual quota served people from northern and western Europe. Most countries had quotas of only 100 people per year. This lull has profound effects on developments in American culture and religion. Successive generations of immigrant families passed through a common experience of Americanization undisturbed by the arrival of new immigrants on the scene. The growth and influence of the ecumenical movement among Protestants, the homogenization of ethnic groups, the shape of American general education, and the general placidity of the 1950s could be attributed, in part, to the lull in immigration. Second- and third-generation Americans were learning to get along, after a fashion, in what Will Herberg called "the triple melting-pot."

The Immigration and Nationality Act of 1965 fundamentally changed patterns of immigration. It abolished the national-origins quota system, eliminating national origin, race, or ancestry as a basis for immigration, established a seven-category preference system for family reunification and those with special occupational skills needed in the United States, and greatly increased the annual quota for immigrants. The phrase "brain drain" became the description for the immigrants selected by the preference system. They were not "your tired, your poor, / Your huddled masses, yearning to breathe free..." of Emma Lazarus's description of the earlier immigrants. These were doctors, engineers, professors, scientists, and technicians, along with their families. Those arriving under employment preferences were among the best educated, most professionally advanced, and most successful of any immigrant group. Two groups of people entered the United States outside these categories, refugees and undocumented aliens.

Migration patterns and networks are different for each of these immigrant groups. Most legislative or administrative adjustments in the categories of immigrants have ripple effects, intended and unintended, on the demography and networks of religious groups in the United States, as do economic and political events that increase the flow of refugees and illegals.

Many recent immigrants are part of the "brain drain" from their respective homelands and have moved quickly into middle- and upper-middle-class status. That should not mask the reality that some struggle in positions for which they are overqualified and others, who are refugees or come for family reunification, are poorly prepared to compete in the job market. Nevertheless, they contribute religions, ethnic identities, and national groups from Asia, Africa, Latin America, and the Middle East that were not part of the previous negotiation of religious identities and civic discourse. They bring with them all the religions of the world and spread them across America.

They bring to negotiations in the American context a diverse array of expectations regarding religion and the civic political order. Many Hindus and Buddhists follow the example of Swami Vivekananda in criticizing the individualism and materialism of American society and prescribing a cure of Eastern spiritualism. Many Muslims and Christians join evangelical Christians in criticizing various forms of immorality and decadence, especially perceived in American youth culture portrayed in the media. All have made religious accommodations with the modern nation-state, with a variety of results regarding the role of religion in the state, the relation of religious leaders and politics, the basis and nature of civil liberties and individual rights, and the processes of adjudication of individual and communal differences.

The Midwest has become home and fertile soil for most of the religious migrations that have peopled America. The profile of religious affiliation of recent immigrants in the Midwest is only marginally distinct from those in other regions of the country (see Philip Barlow's chapter on demography). Most of the religions of the world, including their ethnic and regional variations, are present in the Midwest, and religious affiliation influences personal and group identities and civic negotiations. The National Conference for Community and Justice gathered data from religious communities and estimated the numbers for religious communities in metropolitan Chicago: Muslim (400,000), Buddhist (150,000), Hindu (80,000), Sikh (6,000), Jain (5,000), and Zoroastrian (700). The numbers in the American Religious Identification Survey (ARIS) suggest smaller populations: Muslim (269,694), Buddhist (135,297), and Hindu (78,175). (The most up-to-date listing and description of religious organizations in Midwestern states are found on the Harvard Pluralism Project Web site: http://www.pluralism.org/resources/map/index.php.)

The Midwest is a religious heartland where all previous immigrants have established their religions in fairly stable and representative forms. As Barlow details, several Christian communions have headquarters in the Midwest or on its borders, including several Lutheran bodies, the United Church of Christ, Disciples, Nazarenes, Brethren, Church of the Brethren, Church of God, and the Presbyterian Church (USA). The main campus of the Reform Jewish seminary, Hebrew Union College, is in Cincinnati. The newer forms of religion also established national centers in the Midwest: Islamic Society of North America in Plainfield, Indiana; Tibetan Buddhists in Bloomington, Indiana; Kananya Indian Christians in Chicago; Nation of Islam in Chicago; Bahá'í in Wilmette, Illinois; and a non-territorial Korean Presbyterian Presbytery, formed from Chicago. More important is the fact that all of the religions are present in Midwestern urban areas where the important negotiations are taking place daily about the future of American religion and civic order.

All religion, like politics, is local, but it is also national and transnational. The story of each religious group in the Midwest is local, so there are hundreds of stories of families and groups that give them place and character. Transnational networks and push/pull forces that generate emigration and settlement shape each religious group. It is necessary in the case of each of hundreds of religious groups to learn why they left home as refugees, asylum seekers, migrant professionals, or family members. The patchwork of religious groups throughout the Midwest is the result of such movements. Each is distinct in detail, but not different in character from co-religionists in other regions of the country.

The stories are fascinating.

The 340 Muslim families in Cedar Rapids, Iowa, point with pride to the fact that their Syrian and Lebanese ancestors established the first mosque in the country in 1929 and dedicated the first independently owned Islamic cemetery in 1949. Other refugees from Lebanon and Syria, both Muslims and Christians, moved to Dearborn, Michigan, to work in Ford assembly plants and nearby to Toledo, Ohio, to start businesses. Iraqi Christians and Shi'a Muslims joined them in the 1990s as refugees fleeing persecution by Saddam Hussein following the Gulf War. President Bush visited that community for an important speech at the beginning of the second war in Iraq.

Many Buddhist and Christian Korean women entered the United States as brides of American servicemen stationed in Korea. They have been able to sponsor family members under the family reunification provisions of the 1965 law. Young students and professionals from Korea joined them in churches and temples.

Christian resettlement agencies created networks for placing Somali Muslims and Hmong refugees in the Twin Cities; some 20,000 to 30,000 Somali Muslims now reside there. The first Shi'a Muslim family in the Twin Cities was resettled from Uganda in 1972 by a Christian relief agency.

Christians from South India and the Philippines were prominent among the nurses recruited in the 1970s for Cook County Hospital in Chicago and other urban public hospitals. Doctors from South and East Asia, trained in Western medicine and proficient in English, were in great demand in American urban public hospitals and in small towns in the 1970s and 1980s.

Engineers and scientists joined companies and universities throughout the Midwest. Many who came under family reunification provisions became entrepreneurs in hotels, motels, and franchise outlets. They quickly generated considerable wealth that funded religious institutions, charities, and major building projects. The stories are local; the cumulative impact is national and transnational.

It is necessary to distinguish between the population centers of recent immigrants scattered across the Midwest, especially in Illinois, Ohio, Michigan, Minnesota, Wisconsin, Indiana, and Iowa, and the location of major temples, *gurdwaras*, and churches that are located primarily in the major urban areas of Chicago, Minneapolis, Cleveland, and Detroit. Buddhists, Hindus, Sikhs, Jains, Christians, and others from across the Midwest travel to the major centers for family rituals and communal festivals. Mosques tend to be more residentially based, but Muslims isolated in small cities and towns travel to cities for Friday prayers or Id celebrations. Imams, priests, and religious specialists travel out from the urban centers to visit homes and conduct rituals. Three of

17 Hindu temples in metropolitan Chicago serve Swaminarayan Hindus from Gujarat in India. The temples illustrate the pattern by drawing devotees from across the Midwest, and the largest of the three, in Bartlett, which is the largest Hindu temple outside of India, houses two sadhus who give guidance to temples in Cleveland, Columbus, Detroit, St. Louis, Minneapolis, and Kansas City, and centers in Akron, Ohio; Centralia, Illinois; Cincinnati and Dayton in Ohio; Indianapolis; Louisville; Munster, Indiana; Rockford, Illinois; Rolla, Missouri; Wichita, Kansas; and in nearby temples in Pittsburgh and Paducah, Kentucky. The growth of religious infrastructures across the Midwest has been rapid and effective.

The numerical impact on religious affiliation of recent immigrants should not be overestimated. The number of adherents of religions other than Christianity in the United States is relatively small, perhaps 5 percent of the current population. Philip Jenkins notes that one of the reasons is that a significant portion of recent immigrants from Africa, Asia, and Latin America are Christian before they emigrate and others become Christian after they arrive.[2] Estimates are that half of the immigrants from Korea are Christian prior to arrival, and another quarter has become Christian. Still, because of the significance of religion in American culture, the appearance of forms of religion previously absent or invisible has an impact out of proportion to current numbers. Even recent Christian immigrants from places like Korea, India, and Ethiopia bring new beliefs and practices that affect American Christianity. They also have to adjust to the new religious, cultural, and political context. The United States is at the same time the most religiously diverse nation in history and the most Christian. The Midwest represents both realities.

The thesis of this chapter is that these recent immigrants and their religious groups, many new to the United States, reopen the negotiation regarding the religious and moral foundations of civic life in the Midwest, just as they do in the nation as a whole. A majority of recent immigrants report that they are more religious in the United States than they were prior to emigration. One reason is that religion functions to provide a transcendent basis for personal and group identity through the transitions of emigration, which helps make this country of immigrants so religious. In general, recent immigrants do not establish separate religious and ethnic groups in order to isolate themselves from American society. Rather, they form such groups to socialize their children and, at the same time, to negotiate their entry into American society from a position of relative strength. The negotiation will determine what "one nation under God" and "In God We Trust" will mean in the future.

Scholars characterized the adaptation of earlier immigrants as a model of assimilation. Indeed, the homogenization that took place during the lull of immigration did appear to be a form of assimilation. Many factors cause the experience of recent immigrants to be much more complex, in part because there are so many with such diverse cultural and religious backgrounds. Nevertheless, each immigrant group is adapting to the new religious and cultural situation in the United States, and each is negotiating the terms of its participation in civic life. Much of this negotiation takes place out of the public eye in families and religious groups that determine the reaction to societal values and practices. These surface when differences and misunderstandings within and between groups must be adjudicated in the work of local journalists, court reporters, school administrators, governmental bureaucrats, and interfaith religious associations. Those deciding or reporting on isolated, local events need to be aware that those events are part of a continuous, comprehensive negotiation of identity and social location within a larger context of meaning.

Negotiations internal to families and religious organizations cover virtually all of life and those between religious and social organizations cover most of civic life. Here we focus on the following issues:

1. marriage, family and gender relations;
2. social ethics and public morality;
3. institution building;
4. language and religion; and
5. transnationalism and citizenship.

The major mediating agencies, other than religious organizations, are schools, prisons, government agencies, health care system, and ecumenical/interfaith councils.

Marriage, Family, and Gender Relations

Many recent immigrants assert that a major contribution they will make to American society is the value and strength of families. Indeed, the first Hindu, Islamic, Sikh, Parsi, or Buddhist ceremony other Americans witness is generally a wedding in the family of a co-worker or neighbor. At one Hindu wedding the Brahmin priest chanted the ceremony in Sanskrit and provided brief translations into English for the guests. At one point, regarding traditional wifely duties, he added the aside, "But now you are an American and you will do whatever you want." Well, it is not that simple.

The extended families of many recent immigrants expect to be involved in the selection and approval of the prospective bride or groom in arranged marriages and in psychological and financial undergirding of the married couple. Indeed, some ceremonies mark the union of families as much as the union of individuals. Arranged marriage within pre-existing marriage networks is common. Parents have distinct preferences regarding marriage partners that extend in various circular configurations of preference for religious affiliation, ethnicity, language, national origin, color, race, and occupation. Some Pakistani groups have a traditional preference for cross-cousin patrilateral marriage. Muslim law requires women to marry other Muslims and men to marry monotheists, preferably Muslims but including Christians and Jews. Knanaya Indian Orthodox and Catholic Christians form a single endogamous group that prohibits marriage to outsiders. The authority of the family to arrange marriage is attenuated in the United States. Hence, recent immigrants refer to semi-arranged marriage in which the couple meet and express common interest and the parents negotiate the marriage and gift arrangements. The phrase "love marriage" is used for those for which the couple decides, often in defiance of their parents' preferences. The religious ceremonies are occasions for gathering of extended transnational families and are the culmination of extended negotiations within family, ethnic, and religious groups regarding the meaning of family in America.

The function of group or family identity and family decisions in relation to individual identity and personal decisions about marriage and many other matters creates significant generational tensions among immigrant families. These are identified, discussed, and negotiated in the context of religious groups where issues of public/private, personal/corporate, and individual/communal relate to basic religious worldview and commitment. Dating, especially for daughters, is a point of conflict, and a number of levels of misunderstanding exist. The primary social idiom for many immigrant parents is family, and much of their social interaction takes place within family and with fictive family members recruited within the ethnic group. The primary social idiom in the children's social context is friendship, primarily among peers at school. Parents view dating as a threat to a good marriage and secure family. Senior prom nights are often preceded by angry discussions and are occasions of parental terror.

Young people view dating as a stage in friendship, expecting that their spouse might eventually be "my best friend," a concept from a different idiom. Because many immigrant parents rarely interact socially in the homes of their children's friends or other acquaintances, they often have a distorted view of American family life and values that are based on what they view in movies or on television. Hence, they fear the negative influences of American society in the form of decadence, crass materialism, drug and alcohol abuse, rampant sexuality, and neglect of family virtues. Harsh criticism of American immorality and youth culture is common in immigrant churches, mosques, temples, and *gurdwaras*. "You love your friends more than you love your parents," is often heard in angry exchanges. The children feel that parents operate on a double misperception of what society is currently like in the place from which they migrated and of what their children's social context is like. The parents fear that they have gained the whole world of professional and material benefits at the risk of losing their children.

The Hindu priest at the wedding mentioned earlier provided a glimpse into the changing gender relations within immigrant families. Emigration always changes gender roles and status. Indeed, some women and couples emigrated for that reason and welcome new dynamics within families. For others the changes are more difficult. In some instances, familiar support structures of extended families and cheap labor for household chores are absent in the United States, requiring both men and women to take on additional responsibilities. Female Indian and Filipino Christian nurses gained permanent resident status and higher incomes than their spouses, dramatically changing gender roles in families and churches. More nurses are currently being recruited for urban hospitals. A discussion continues in most immigrant religious groups regarding the degree to which various gender roles and expectations are part of religious orthopraxis or simply traditional custom. The religious and cultural context is varied and complex, even within a single religion such as Islam, Christianity, or Hinduism. These issues rise to public view when they raise legal issues of social ethics and public morality.

Social Ethics and Public Morality

Free exercise of religion is an essential part of American jurisprudence, but the boundaries are somewhat blurred between the free exercise of religion and legal requirements or social norms. Many immigrants come from countries, such as Saudi Arabia or northern Nigeria, where different sets of religiously authorized norms are enshrined in national legal systems. Others come from countries, such as India, where religious minorities preserve rights to administer religiously based personal and communal laws. In such cases, some aspects of the legal system and public policy are determined by interpretations of Shariah, Dharmashastras, or the equivalents of Canon Law. Renegotiation of personal and communal laws and norms is part of the immigration experience.

Women's rights among immigrant groups appear regularly in news reports and public discussions. A common presumption in the courts, at least until recently, is that in cases of divorce young children remain under the care of their mothers. According to some interpretations of Islamic law, the children legally belong to the father and his family. Other areas of conflict are the rights of a woman at the time of divorce and the control of a woman over the dowry and other gifts presented by her family at the time of marriage. These also involve inheritance rights for wives, daughters, and other family members. Some religious groups have specialists who adjudicate disputes in these matters when the issues are extraneous to current American laws and practices. Occasionally these issues surface in the courts and in public-policy debates. The issues of the nature of marriage as a religious sacrament or a secular contract, and the rights of all parties, are so complex and malleable that some legal scholars suggest adoption of a communal law option in state laws. Then parties could determine prior to marriage what form of personal and communal law would be applicable to their agreement. That might change fundamentally the individual basis of the legal system and empower religious courts to act as alternatives to state courts where most family and communal laws are administered. Hence, these negotiations take place in the courts and legislatures of all 50 states.

Other accommodations are necessary in business and banking practices. For example, the Koran contains a prohibition of usury, which is variously interpreted by schools of Shariah. Because all the schools of Sunni and Shi'a law are represented among Muslim immigrants, various banking and investment arrangements are necessary to enable immigrants to participate in financial networks without violating religious obligations and prohibitions.

Immigrants tend to keep their heads down and avoid public conflicts over contentious issues of public policy. Two issues on which some of the religious groups have very strong inclinations are abortion and sexual orientation. Discussion of these issues is common in immigrant religious groups, which tend to be more conservative on social issues than liberal Protestants. Negotiation of these issues requires detailed interpretations of the various religions' sacred texts and traditions. For example, the issues of prenatal ultrasound screening or amniocentesis, and the abortion of female fetuses, are hotly debated. Gay and lesbian groups face resistance when they seek to march in Indian Independence Day Parades in Chicago and other cities. Recent immigrants generally avoid public conflicts about such issues while they are working them out internally because they fear that as minorities they will attract unnecessary negative reactions.

Institution Building

Post-1965 immigrants organized religious meetings in homes, apartment community rooms, rented halls, and church basements throughout the Midwest long before the majority population realized they had arrived. They were drawn together by two powerful functions of religion in immigrants' lives:

1. Religion serves to ground personal and group identity in transcendent realities in the midst of wrenching transitions, enabling immigrants to affirm their past, resist overwhelming societal pressures, and shape their futures. Because religion has functioned in this manner throughout the immigration history of the United States, it is the most religious of the Western industrialized countries.

2. Religious organizations serve as powerful agents in the socialization of immigrants' children. In fact, the growth of religious organizations and the purchase and construction of new buildings coincide with immigrants' children reaching an

age at which they begin to be socialized outside the home in schools and neigh-borhoods. A number of mosques and the Islamic Society of North America in Plainfield, Indiana, developed out of the Muslim Students Association because the student association had space on university campuses for religious and social meetings. Some students remember the early days when they baby-sat small chil-dren for recent immigrants during meetings. When the children began school, the parents established separate mosques and institutions to serve their needs.

The new organizations have to meet requirements of various governmental and social agencies. In order to obtain essential tax-exempt status, the religious organizations have to conform to stipulated organizational structures (e.g., stated officers, board of trustees, by-laws, and budgets). They need to state the number of individual members, even in instances where members are calculated as fami-ly units and not individuals, as in Mar Thoma and other Malayalee congregations, or where formal affiliation of membership is not expected or recorded, as among Swaminarayan Hindus or some Islamic groups. Leaders of the organizations have to adapt to appropriate legal and social procedures for essential ceremonies such as weddings and funereal rituals. Some recent immigrants come from areas that operate on a lunar religious calendar, and they find it necessary to adapt their reli-gious calendars to a system of expectations based on a solar calendar and Christian and public holidays.

Some post-colonial interpretations note that many ethnic and religious groups in colonial contexts adapted to fit the categories of anthropologists and govern-ment bureaucrats who described groups according to arbitrary categories. A sim-ilar process is necessary for recent immigrant groups, who tend to conform to expected categories. For example, some sociological analyses of American reli-gions elaborate categories of church, sect, and denomination. Those categories are foreign to the previous experience of recent immigrants. Nonetheless, pres-sure exists to shape the religious organizations and affiliations of newer groups into the categories used for earlier groups. Hence, Syro-Malabar Catholics are treated as ethnic Catholics, like Irish or Italian, rather than as an ancient oriental rite in communion with Rome. Shiite Muslims are seen, and perhaps come to see themselves, as a denomination of Islam.

Numerical comparisons of religious groups are fraught with difficulty and laden with political significance. "More Muslims than Episcopalians" or "More Muslims than Jews" or "over a million Hindus" are common claims. Because the United States government has been prohibited since 1957 from keeping records of citizens by religion, the numbers bandied about are notoriously unreliable. Some religious groups keep records by individuals, others by families. Still oth-ers have no records other than mailing lists. Still, the assigned numbers establish status and political leverage and hence are much disputed. The current estimates of Muslims in the United States range from 1.5 million to 10 million. It is unclear whether the statistics refer to those practicing a particular religion or those with regional or ethnic ties to a religious tradition. Id dinners at the White House at the end of the month of fasting for Muslims in the month of Ramadan or Hindu prayers at political gatherings are political responses to the increasing significance of these and other new religious communities.

Most of the religious groups of recent immigrants were organized and are now led by what Christians would call lay people. Few religious specialists, except Christian pastors married to nurses, accompanied the early brain-drain immigrants. Hence, the recruitment and training of religious specialists is an acute need. In the early days, lay people learned basic rituals, songs, and texts in order to lead ceremonies and teach their children and others. When formal temples, mosques, and *gurdwaras* were built, some groups imported religious specialists from their home regions, persons trained in the sacred rituals and at home with the ethnic language and customs. This occasionally creates confusion and difficulties in obtaining visas and other documentation because training of specialists in other religions—for example, through years of apprenticeship with parents or even a charismatic call—does not result in the academic records needed for legal residence in the United States. Some groups rely on religious specialists who travel to the United States in the summer months to perform rituals, initiate new followers, and teach. Christian groups rely on some American seminaries to educate and certify immigrants as pastors.

Currently no other religious group serving recent immigrants has an accredited or effective educational or training institution for their religious specialists in the United States. A few, such as Swaminarayan Hindus, have recruited young men to "renounce the world" and return to India for training as sadhus. They have returned following training well prepared to lead large temples and organizations in Chicago and Cleveland, and to visit followers in other cities. That avoids the problems that some priests, pastors, and other religious specialists and their families from abroad have in adapting to American culture and social expectations. A major challenge for the future is the recruitment and training of a new group of religious specialists for American Hinduism, American Buddhism, American Islam, and American forms of other religions.

Most of these religious groups have a presence in the virtual reality of the Internet. Some of the Hindu Web sites provide digital darshan or worship of deities by providing digital images from temples in both India and the United States. Many of the religious texts and discourses appear online. Indeed, students and others can learn a great deal about the religions and their local organizations through the Internet. What can be shown on computers and how the materials are organized and related in cyberspace may eventually have significant impact on both the presentation of the religion by insiders and understanding of the religion by outsiders. The religious wisdom of the world is migrating to the United States and appearing in the homes and offices in shapes and configurations created in cyberspace.

Language and Religion

Emigration requires for all but a handful of recent immigrants a change in language, which is one of a number of symbol systems for which plausibility structures cease to exist in their new homeland. The sights and sounds of a Babel of languages are present in the neighborhoods, in schools and business, in religious meetings, and even in homes. Several religions have specific languages of sacred texts and rituals. Sanskrit, Arabic, and Syriac are sacred languages for Hindus, Muslims, and Eastern Christians, even though few adherents can read, speak, or understand them. Regional ethnic languages, such a Gujarati, Hindi, Swahili, or Malayalam, take on the aura of sacrality when their main use outside the home is in religious gatherings. Experience of earlier immigrant groups is that the second generation loses its ability to read and write in the ethnic language and that the third generation develops only minimal facility in their ancestors' language. Nevertheless, some groups make Herculean efforts to teach their children sacred or ethnic languages. Temples, mosques, *gurdwaras*, churches, and other religious institutions organize language classes for their children, along with other classes in symbolic arts such as dance, music, and drama. The current situation requires multilingual priests and leaders who can communicate with all constituencies. If current levels of immigration continue, future leaders will also have to have facility in several languages.

The Roman Catholic Mass is celebrated in 44 languages in the Chicago archdiocese. The mosque on North Broadway in Chicago is home to adherents who speak almost as many languages, even though Arabic is the common language for prayer. No single language other than English, except Spanish, is dominant in religious ceremonies in the Midwest. Nevertheless, the language use of new immigrants in relation to successive generations is a major dynamic in future social and religious negotiation by recent immigrants.

Transnationalism and Citizenship

"Transnationalism" is a designation of the experience of recent immigrants of maintaining many associations that span several societies and develop identities and maintain communications with social networks that connect them with two or more societies simultaneously.[3] Latino Catholics in Chicago maintain close contacts with families and Madonna shrines in Mexico. Hindus return to Tirupati in South India to worship the same deity as they worship in the Venkateswara

Temple in Aurora. The primary factors creating the new transnational reality are instantaneous communication and rapid mobility. Emigration of relatives and associates to other countries establishes networks in many parts of the world. Immigrants are inherently insecure, and uncertainties in the global economy and politics force them to cultivate options in more than one setting. One way to do this is to use the wealth, social ties, and status gained in one location to develop status and social capital in another. One result is the necessity of remapping the social and religious fields of recent immigrants.

It is common to refer to globalization and to the global character of the religious groups. It is better to refer to the transnational networks because each religious group holds fast to multiple strands of a network stretching from Midwestern cities, configurations unique to that religious and ethnic group reaching many countries. For example, Swaminarayan Hindus in Chicago maintain close contacts with Gujaratis across North America, Britain, East Africa, Australasia, and India that are firmly rooted in the Indian State of Gujarat. Sikhs in Palatine, Illinois, have similar networks that are rooted in the Punjab. Buddhists maintain associations reaching out in different directions in Asia. American Muslims maintain a crazy quilt of regional and family associations around the world, and one of the challenges is to keep the strands untangled as they maintain associations with their linguistic and regional groups and, at the same time, the universal Muslim focus on Mecca. So, it is important to trace the particular transnational networks of each religious group because they have a significant influence on experience and adaptation, both at home and abroad.

Religious groups established by recent immigrants in the Midwest are affected by developments abroad and also affect the religious institutions in the countries from which they emigrated. Leadership transfer is important. Temples, mosques, and churches in Chicago, Detroit, Minneapolis, and other cities recruit leaders from other countries. Religious leaders from many countries regularly trace transnational networks to visit their American followers, usually in the summers when travel in the United States is relatively easy and national gatherings common. Religious leaders are part of a larger migration of cultural, artistic and political celebrities across the Midwest every summer. The impact of such leadership transfer travels both ways as the leaders help shape religious adaptations in the United States and as they carry back home insights and resources derived from American adherents.

Transnational transfer of funds by religious groups is receiving a great deal of attention because of questions about funding of transnational political and quasi-military organizations. Transfers by religious groups have been common in support of institutional growth and relief activities. It is virtually impossible for reporters or researchers to determine the exact amounts or directions of these transfers. New ideas travel across these networks as well. It is important to trace the impact that American Hinduism, American Islam, American Buddhism, and other religions will have on those religions outside the United States.

Transnational experiences and identities of recent immigrants call into question previous understandings of citizenship and ethnicity. Dual citizenship is recognition of the significance of the transnational networks described above and illustrates the increasing facility that recent immigrants have to manipulate multiple identities in the process of negotiating a secure, advantageous, and comfortable social location. The hyphen in Asian-American, for example, may not signify, as it may have in the past, a previous home and allegiance of citizenship followed by a new home and citizenship, but concurrent national or ethnic identities and allegiances. A recent immigrant shapes identities as an Indian, or Kenyan, or American Gujarati Muslim Ismaili physician, and each of those identity components is malleable and carries a wide array of associations. Dual citizenship in the new transnational context raises the question of what citizenship connotes and how one socializes or educates recent immigrants for citizenship.

Recent immigrants create new ethnicities—new as part of their identities and also new to American culture. The process of immigration, especially that governed by regulations of the modern nation state, selects particular groups and places them in novel associations in the United States. For example, groups of Muslims in Chicago mosques represent a constellation of evolving ethnicities different from those experienced by any of the participants prior to migration and more diverse than anywhere outside of Mecca during the Hajj. Hindu worshippers and even Hindu deities that would be separated in India by region, language, ethnicity, perhaps caste, and doctrine, live together in the 17 Hindu temples in Chicago. So, recent immigrants are recreating ethnicity, and the relation of religion to ethnicity is one of the major issues being worked out in current negotiations involving complex transnational networks.

These networks have foreign policy implications because recent immigrants are in immediate contact with social and political groups in other countries. The recent immigrants, some of whom hold dual citizenship, support and vote for political groups and causes in their birth countries. In some instances religious groups in the United States maintain close relations with political groups; for example, the Vishwa Hindu Parishad supports the Bharatiya Janata Party in India. Politicians and governmental officials travel frequently to gain political support for their parties and to encourage economic investment in their countries by nonresident citizens. They regularly visit temples, mosques, churches, *gurdwaras*, and other religious centers in the Midwest. It may be the case that the relations of these governments to the United States will be influenced by developments among recent immigrants. It is certainly the case that American politicians are aware of the foreign policy significance of recent immigrants. President Bush's visit to Dearborn, Michigan, the home of the largest Christian and Muslim Iraqi population outside of Iraq, in the midst of the Iraq War of 2003 is evidence of their foreign policy significance.

Recent immigrants also have an increasing role in national policy decisions. Astute local politicians in major cities were the first to recognize the presence of new groups of immigrants. Aldermen in Chicago visited religious gatherings and helped facilitate religious festivals and processions because their grandfathers and mentors had been the ones serving the same functions for the Irish, German, Italian, and other earlier immigrants. That grassroots work in the wards built the political party base in earlier decades. Ward politics is more complicated now because many recent immigrants are dispersed across the wealthier urban areas, are not congregated in ghettos, and are affiliated with a wide array of social and religious groups. Moreover, a competition is underway to attract the allegiance of recent immigrants, in part because it is uncertain what party and/or politicians they will support. Therefore, religious festivals are significant venues for politicians. The chairman of the Illinois Republican Party joked with a large Hindu audience at the Swaminarayan temple in Bartlett that he was pleased to see so many carved elephant heads in the building, which in that context are symbols of the Hindu deity Ganesh. Governor Rod Blagojevich campaigned among Asian Indians at the same temple and returned to a gathering on Devon Street, renamed Mahatma Gandhi Marg, to thank Asian Indians for their support.

Discussions of homeland security following the attacks on the World Trade Center in New York and the Pentagon relate directly to recent immigrants and their religions. Religious organizations and schools have come under intense scrutiny and suspicion at the same time the groups are negotiating internally and externally what the relation is and will be among religious, ethnic, and national identities. Issues of civil rights and freedom of religion, so central to the socialization and "Americanization" of earlier immigrants, are front and center in the current negotiations. "Americanization" in this sense does not mean assimilation so much as it means how recent immigrants negotiate how they will participate in the structures of American society, political, economic, religious, professional, and social.

Decisions about these matters are intensely personal and are often made in light of fundamental moral and ethical commitments based on religious commitments. Most humans have constructed, adapted, and preserved their basic societal values and mores as part of their religious systems. Religion functions for recent immigrants, as it has for other Americans, as the arena in which they recreate and adapt from previous commitments and experiences those beliefs and prac-

tices that will best serve them in the new setting. Most fine-tuning of these decisions takes place in private, in local religious gatherings or within family gatherings. Occasionally issues surface in public settings in which the services of public agencies and institutions play a role in negotiating between recent immigrant
groups and the majority society, between sacred and secular commitments, and
between religious organizations and governmental agencies. Since the September
11 terrorist attacks, some recent immigrants have become suspicious of American
domestic and foreign policy. They affirm freedoms that are based on
Enlightenment principles while simultaneously disassociating those from the earlier Judeo-Christian synthesis and criticizing the Jewish and Christian communities. That may complicate inter-religious dialogue and cooperation. It is not possible to predict all the "hot button issues" of the future, but most of them will surface in important mediating institutions: schools, prisons, governmental agencies,
the health care system, and ecumenical/interfaith councils.

Mediating Agencies

Schools

The public-school system has been the major mediating agency for generations of immigrants and their families. Schools socialized and, as some would
say, Americanized, successive generations of immigrant families in the particular
language, history, politics, and mores of American society. That process is poten-
tially more powerful and homogenizing now than in previous generations
because of the power of the media to erase regional and even ethnic distinctions.
At the same time, powerful intellectual and political forces oppose the homogenizing power of public instruction. What is taught, how it is taught, and the
expected behavior of those taught and those teaching are all points of tension and
conflict. English textbooks adopted for sophomore world literature classes
approved by Indiana's Department of Education include sample texts from world
religions. Even though Midwestern school systems do not dominate the textbook
market to the degree that California and Texas do, the results are that textbook
adoptions are an important part of the negotiation. Thus, public schools are primary loci of competing claims and practices that generally appear in brief local
news items.

These tensions surface immediately regarding provision for aspects of personal and communal custom based in religious law and observance. Local school
boards and administrators deal with questions regarding religiously mandated
garb, dietary practices, standards of modesty, and religious symbols. Muslim girls
in Shaker Heights, Ohio, negotiated permission to wear head covering during athletic contexts. Sikh boys request permission to wear turbans and carry ceremoni-
al knives under their clothing at school in Mentor, Ohio, as part of their religious

duty. Muslims request provision of halal food in school cafeterias. Muslim boys and girls request exemption from taking physical education classes because of rules of modesty. Students of many religions request permission for release time for prayers and holidays for special festivals. *Zelman v. Simmons-Harris*, decided 5-4 by the U. S. Supreme Court in June 2002, arose from a Cleveland suit and permits parents to receive tuition vouchers from the government in order to send their children to nonpublic schools, religious or otherwise. Recent immigrants were not party to the suit, but the implications of that decision for Muslim, Buddhist, and Hindu schools are enormous. Issues raised by religious schools will undoubtedly work their way through the courts.

Colleges and universities, both private and public, generally have more freedom regarding religion than public secondary schools. The function of religion courses dealing with religions of Asia, Africa, and Latin America has evolved with the arrival of the recent immigrants. Courses first offered to teach students in a Judeo-Christian culture about religions in other cultures in response to internationalization of American interests and responsibilities have come to function in many institutions to teach children of immigrants about the religions of their families. Development officers in higher education awoke to the significant financial resources and religious commitments of recent immigrants and raised endowments to support chairs and programs in the various religions. Indiana University appointed a scholar of Hinduism to its newly established Tagore chair, which was endowed by immigrants. Youngstown State University raised funds from Muslims for an endowed chair in Islamic studies. Adherents of the religions are establishing new universities, such as the American Islamic College in Chicago, as did earlier immigrant groups.

Prisons

Many of the issues related to public schools are duplicated in the prison system because in both schools and prisons a public agency takes charge of individuals for periods of time. Hence, the issues of personal and religious law and observance regarding garb, diet, modesty, religious symbols, and religious observances are being negotiated in the prison system. Muslim chaplains are being certified in many prisons, and provisions are being made for regular prayers, especially the Friday prayers. Muslim women prisoners obtained permission to wear head covering in court in Columbus, Ohio. These are results of detailed and sometimes contentious negotiations between prison authorities, prisoners, and religious leaders. Muslims have a national program and have been particularly effective in propagating Islam in prisons. The focus results, in part, from Malcolm X's conversion experience while in prison and the effectiveness of the Nation of Islam in converting African Americans in prison.

Governmental Agencies

Legal protection of freedom of religion and the non-establishment provision in the Constitution limit the role of governmental agencies in religious matters. Nevertheless, the government establishes policies and procedures that affect religious organizations along with other social groups. For instance:

- Religious groups find it advantageous to gain recognition as tax-exempt organizations as soon as they form. They must, therefore, conform to organizational requirements, policies, procedures, and reporting standards established by the Internal Revenue Service.
- The Immigration and Naturalization Service determines who may enter the United States to be religious leaders for recent immigrants and under what conditions they may stay as temporary visitors or permanent residents.
- Transfer of funds to other countries comes under scrutiny of the Treasury Department, which is paying close attention to religious groups as part of the campaign against terrorism. Some religious organizations feel that they are being singled out for special discrimination.
- The Islamic Society of North America in Plainfield, Indiana, provides some specialized training for the Federal Bureau of Investigation.
- Local zoning boards and building inspectors control many aspects of locating or building structures to house new religious organizations. Some religious leaders believe these local officials are the primary agents of discrimination against unwanted religions. In some locations it can be very difficult for groups to build new temples, mosques, *gurdwaras*, or centers. For that reason, groups often purchase buildings previously used for religious services because it is more difficult for neighbors and local boards to deny zoning, parking, and building permits.

Traditional religious practices that recent immigrants bring with them often are at variance with local codes, so they face the question of whether to adjust the practice or fight the codes. Muslims in Cedar Rapids, Iowa, faced local opposition to their plans for a Muslim Youth Camp of America (MYCA) on a site on Coralville Lake. Traditional Hindu weddings require a fire sacrifice in the wedding hall, into which the priest and the couple place oil, grains, and other sacrifices. Fire codes in most cities and towns prohibit such open fires in public buildings and halls. Creative adaptation occurs, in one ceremony replacing the open fire with a candle. Santeria rituals originating in Africa and transmitted through the Caribbean require animal sacrifices prohibited in some urban areas. Likewise, some groups perform rites of passage on young girls that include clitoridectomy that are judged by some local authorities as abusive. All of these matters have to be adjudicated in terms of traditional practices and expectations of recent immigrants, and the customary behaviors of the majority society.

Negotiations between recent immigrants and the majority population reach the courts when the mediating agencies fail to adjudicate differences. Most of the issues surface in state courts, and only when some constitutional issue is raised are they transferred to federal jurisdiction. The result is that the formal negotiations of difference appear in state courts, and it is difficult to trace the national and transnational effects of these regional disputes or negotiations.

Political parties are quasi-governmental agencies because their policies and candidates shape the legislative and executive actions that determine the social context for the adaptation of recent immigrants. Recent immigrants and their families have complex agendas for political action, among which religious matters have a relatively restricted place. Nonetheless, politicians congregate at major religious festivals and appoint staff people who maintain contacts with ethnic and religious groups. Leaders of religious groups realize that they must influence the political process in order to negotiate from greater strength their role and place in American society.

Health Care

Many immigrants of the brain drain are doctors, nurses, pharmacists, and medical technicians, and obtained their green cards because they were trained in modern, Western science and medicine. In some ways these were the most secularized of the recent immigrants. Nevertheless, illness and healing have diverse cultural and religious meanings around the world and among recent immigrants. The theological and religious contexts for interpreting illness and healing influence selection of the physician and the process of therapy. Some immigrants rely on traditional ways of treating illness, often in conjunction with Western medicine. Some Hindus rely on traditional ayurvedic medicines, both preventive based on diet and yoga exercises as well as traditional pharmaceutical cures. In fact, some discoveries have been made through study of these herbs and medicines. The religious leaders often assume chaplain roles and demeanor similar to Protestant ministers just as Jewish rabbis did in previous generations. Many temples, mosques, and other religious centers offer health clinics and other medical assistance to members, especially to those without health insurance. Thus, they supplement the work of several social welfare agencies.

The religious and moral codes invest people with responsibilities for the care of children, siblings, cousin-brothers and sisters, and parents. Some recent immigrants are scandalized by what they interpret as abandonment of parents into nursing homes. The extended family should respect and continue to care for the elderly as they remember being the case in India, China, or Africa. Now, however, as elderly parents arrive for family reunification and early immigrants retire, the care of the elderly under the changed conditions of American society becomes a major challenge. Some religious organizations are planning and raising funds for retirement homes and nursing homes for the community.

Great sensitivity is required when ultimate decisions about life and death are being made because these have deep religious significance for most recent immigrants and their families. Most major decisions in many devout families are corporate rather than individual. So, family conferences are often necessary before life-and-death decisions can be made, and these may include religious leaders. For example, some Swaminarayan Hindus consult their guru in India regarding any decisions about life-support systems. Providing last rites for the dead is one of the first challenges facing the immigrants because death waits for no group to develop support structures. Hence, hospitals have to learn quickly and adapt to different requirements for last rites. The immigrants also have to adjust quickly. Muslims need consecrated ground for burial. Hindus generally cremate the corpse on the same day, with the eldest son charged to light the funeral pyre. Parsis in India leave the corpse exposed to the elements and birds in Towers of Silence. Each group adapts to new requirements for certification of death and treatment of the remains. Hospitals and mortuaries develop new procedures for accommodating last rites. These negotiations continue as the communities face new health challenges and adapt to governmental requirements and social customs.

Ecumenical/Interfaith Councils

Ecumenical councils of churches and local ministerial associations were active and relatively influential in the middle of the twentieth century. Establishment of the Federal Council of Churches in 1908 and the National Council of Churches in 1950 led to formation of many local councils. They provided opportunities for negotiation among various religious groups and were themselves evidence of a developing Judeo-Christian synthesis by religious groups before and after the lull in immigration. They began as distinctly Protestant and represented the Protestant establishment. Gradually and regionally Roman Catholic and Orthodox Christian priests and Jewish rabbis became active in the councils and associations. These ecumenical/interfaith religious leaders were heard on the radio, quoted in newspapers and journals, and appeared on screen in the early days of television. They were apostles of the Judeo-Christian synthesis and of civic religion.

The second half of the century saw a diminution of power and influence of ecumenical/interfaith organizations that accompanied the weakening of mainline

Protestant churches and the Protestant establishment. Religions of recent immigrants are not localized in urban residential settings, so it is more difficult for local associations to take account of their presence. The arrival of other religions in the post-1965 period coincided with the rise of conservative and fundamentalist forms of religion. Conservative religious leaders form new allegiances and dominate religious publishing for the public and the electronic media. So, recent immigrants engage in religious negotiations in a rapidly changing and more conservative context.

Interfaith associations are developing in urban areas in response to the recognition that religions other than Judaism and Christianity are strong and growing in the United States. Devout followers of many religions in the United States recognize the need, and some even rejoice in the opportunity, to develop new forms of religious accommodation and unite in efforts to solve some social and ethical problems in American life. The movement received considerable impetus from the tragedy of terrorist attacks on the World Trade Center and the Pentagon, and the resulting conflicts in Afghanistan and Iraq. The Islamic Center in Columbus, Ohio, was one of several mosques that were desecrated. Local religious leaders, churches, and synagogues provided meeting places and support for those displaced from their worship and school facilities.

It is too early to predict the future for these interfaith initiatives and their success in providing context for negotiation of religious differences in the future. They could be the successors of earlier ecumenical initiatives in working toward a new synthesis of religious and moral bases for American civic life. Jews, Christians, and Muslims have the most adherents, although the exact counts are much disputed. References to Abrahamic religions and social and governmental recognition of Islamic celebrations and leaders suggest that the negotiations among these three religions will be the most immediate. However, even within those three religious traditions great diversity exists among recent immigrants that must be adjudicated. One hopes that such initiatives will facilitate civil relations among diverse religious and ethnic groups in a manner that will preserve religious freedom and civic order.

Conclusion

Throughout the history of the United States immigration has profoundly shaped American religion. Each change in immigration policy or procedure affects religious life, often in unanticipated ways. Immigrants bring religions with them, transform them in their new home, and use them to establish new personal and group identities in America. That is one reason the United States is among the most religious countries in the world and why religion is such an important part of the foundation for American civic life and social order.

The post-1965 immigration brings different religions from various cultural settings that will influence the development of religions in the United States in ways not yet determined. This diversity adds new voices in the ongoing debates about the secular and religious concepts that undergird civil religion. Even though the adherents of religions other than Christianity remain a relatively small cohort in the Midwest, they will have an impact greater than their numbers because doctrines of religious freedom, a free marketplace of religious and other ideologies, and the separation of church and state, variously interpreted by different groups, require that provisions be made for minority ideologies and religions. The next few decades will be an important period of negotiation among different religions about the future identities of recent immigrants and the religious commitments of civic life.

Two factors will shape immigration and the future of religion in the United States.

First, the current responses to the terrorist attacks in New York and Washington have been negative in attacks on mosques and families of recent immigrants and positive in outpourings of sympathy and support of Muslims and others. Those events increased public awareness of the presence of other religions and curiosity about their beliefs and practices. Americans have become accustomed to the role of religion in a relatively secularized society. The aftermath of the terrorist attacks and engagement with the Taliban and its supporters have highlighted the political role of religion in societies not influenced by Enlightenment principles. The transnational networks and their influence in international affairs were exposed. It is unclear what the long-term effects of these events and the increased awareness will be on the American psyche and inter-religious relations.

Second, the immigration door has been opened, closed, and swinging half open at various times in American history. Each revision of immigration policy has significant impact, and the closing of the door and the resulting lull in immigration was one of the most important factors shaping American religious life in the twentieth century. The door is currently relatively open and non-discriminatory, so new immigrants arrive in the Midwest regularly. It is uncertain, however, what adjustments will be made in the future. Some reports suggest that large numbers of Muslims have left the United States for Canada since September 11, 2001. The most important factor in shaping religion in the region and in the nation in the twenty-first century is: who is permitted to come, how many, from where, and perhaps most important, who wants to come and stay.

Endnotes

1. Stephan Thernstom. *Harvard Encyclopedia of American Ethnic Groups.* Cambridge: Belknap Press, 1980.

2. Philip Jenkins. *The Next Christendom, the Coming Global Christianity.* New York: Oxford University Press, 2002, 104.

3. Nina Glick Schiller, et al. *Towards a Transnational Perspective on Migration.* New York: New York Academy of Science, 1992.

CHAPTER SIX

RELIGION IN THE
CITY ON THE MAKE

Elfriede Wedam and Lowell W. Livezey

In the 1950s, Nelson Algren reminded Chicagoans their city was a hustling town. In Algren's tough assessment, the likes of Jane Addams and Dwight L. Moody had not reduced Chicago's capacity for being "an infidel's capital six days a week." Yet Algren could not shake St. Columbanus' cross on 71st Street from his childhood memory. Because, as he grudgingly acknowledged beneath the lines of his 1951 prose poem, *Chicago, City on the Make*, it's the tension between warmth of heart and freezing greed that holds its capacity for being a praying town as well. In this chapter, religion and its congregations are explored as diverse and complex places that, interlinked with the economic, geographic, and political aspects of the city, built Chicago.

Chicago is the largest urban center in the Midwest; together with New York and Los Angeles, it is one of America's global cities. Scale and speed describe the increase in the population and development of a cultural and political economy that Chicago built in less than 100 years. From a forbidding marshland that even the Miami Indians refused to settle on in the early nineteenth century, by 1930 Chicago had become an industrial powerhouse of over 3 million. It had the natural advantage of a serviceable harbor on Lake Michigan, which was positioned close to the navigable, westward-flowing Illinois River—a short "portage" soon to be connected by canal—that gave Chicago strategic advantage over other cities on the Great Lakes. Chicago also had the social assets of intense effort put out by workers, investors, and civic boosters, in Algren's term, "the hustlers and the squares." Midwest farmers, together with immigrant-European and black in-migrant factory workers, created an industrial city; their children and new global immigrants have created a postindustrial city. The legendary Democratic political machine retains core control, but includes a broader representation of Chicagoans who are better positioned to argue for local needs. The geographic spread of the region is still marked by racial and income inequality, but the strong presence of nonprofit organizations, especially the congregations and religiously based community groups, fight to improve the quality of life in less privileged areas. Up until now, what was known about religion in the Midwest is largely religion in the context of settling farmlands and building industrial cities. But this chapter focuses on religion in Chicago in the new context of technological change, global demographic shifts, cultural transformation, and political realignment.

There is perhaps no other American city that would so purely exemplify the large, modern, industrial city that is undergoing transformation to the global, post-industrial, post-modern city of the future. Moreover, since these changes also affect smaller cities and towns throughout the region, this chapter provides in bold relief many of the realities local religious organizations across the Midwest cope with, as well as some of the strategies by which they respond (Map 6.1). Finally, because the American population continues to become more urbanized—the 2000 U.S. Census showed that nearly 80 percent live in urbanized areas—understanding religion in a future-oriented urban area is highly instructive for grasping American religion in general.

Religious institutions are active agents in the restructuring of the Chicago region, even as the many structures of the region alter the face of religion itself. In order to examine this interaction, we will discuss religion in terms of four dimensions of urban space. Religious congregations interact with each of these dimensions and produce different responses, both in the formation of the congregation and for the remaking of the urban environment.

1. To begin, *centrality* is an intrinsic dimension of urban space. Central places—cities themselves, and city centers—draw people and resources from their surrounding communities and provide opportunities for new discoveries and new meanings to be channeled outward again. Chicago's Central Business District, or "Loop" (named for the loop made by rapid transit trains as they enter and leave the area), represents the classic city center. By contrast, the "edge city" of Naperville, 30 miles to the west in DuPage county, is one of several new centers of employment, commerce, and culture located on the fringe of the Chicago metropolitan area that, like the Loop, draw people and resources. The Loop and Naperville, therefore, represent classic and new forms of centrality, respectively, and each supports large religious congregations (Maps 6.2 and 6.3 on pages 162 and 163). Moreover, the centers compete with each other, and the addition of the new centers—Naperville, but also others like Northbrook and Schaumburg—alters the structural dynamics of the metropolitan region.

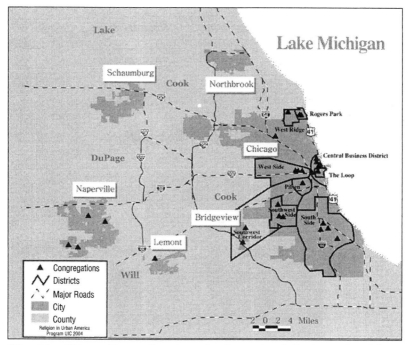

Map 6.1: *Chicago Metropolitan Area showing regional districts and outlying edge cities.*

2. Urban space includes the dimension of *local place*, or "placeness," and to varying degrees is made up of particular places that provide a meaningful reality for residents. Historically, the neighborhood has been the primary source of a sense of place for urban people, supporting individual identity, a sense of community, a sense of past and future, and a sense of being at home.[1] Neighborhoods are peripheral in relationship to the Loop and other centers like Naperville. They depend on people and resources internal to the area, and these resources most often direct opportunities internally as well. The neighborhoods of Chicago's Southwest Corridor illustrate some of the kinds of places—these are deeply Catholic, for example—that direct themselves and their resources internally. The Southwest Side has long competed with the Loop for control of its own resources and space, and its residents are now drawn away not only by the Loop but by edge cities like Naperville where they seek jobs, shopping, culture, political influence—and religion.

3. Another dimension of urban space is *political culture*, which both shapes and is shaped by the economy, and which underpins the livelihoods and fortunes of

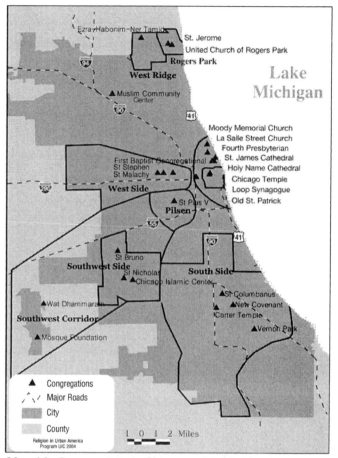

Map 6.2: *Congregations in Chicago and Bridgeview.*

people living and worshipping in the metropolitan region. This dimension is illustrated by the impact of deindustrialization on areas populated by blacks in Chicago and is often seen through the activities of black churches. Black Chicago has a prominent role in city and county government, and black congregations have been effective partners in coalitions that elected a black Chicago mayor and a black U.S. senator. Yet as heavy industry declined, it was the black population of the South and West Sides that was hardest hit and that benefited least from access to new economic opportunities in a restructured city.

4. A fourth dimension, *diversity*—racial, ethnic, class, and religious—is a persistent aspect of urban space. But in Chicago, as in the nation as a whole, the

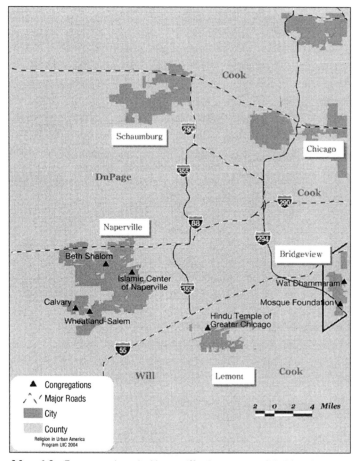

Map 6.3: *Congregations in Naperville, Lemont, and Bridgeview.*

nature of diversity and the way it functions socially and politically, are rapid-ly changing. The religiously rooted racial and ethnic enclaves of the Rogers Park and West Ridge neighborhoods on the city's North Side provide lenses through which to examine both persistence and change, and how religion plays a role in each. These last two themes help decipher the metropolitan region's racial dimension as it struggles to achieve a viable pluralism and eco-nomic equality.

In the areas of Chicago that form the settings for discussions of each of these dimensions, religious congregations have adapted to the new urban conditions and also resisted and reshaped those conditions. Their resistance comes in part

from their membership in a set of structures that operate with an alternative institutional logic.[2] That is, congregations are embedded in religious structures—
denominations, seminaries, judicatories, and pan-religious groups such as the
National and World Councils of Churches or the Parliament of the World's
Religions, which is located in Chicago. This world of religious organizations
operates according to transcendental principles in the pursuit of religious truth
and the moral values that emerge to guide everyday behavior. While religious
organizations compete with each other for naming the "right" construction of
reality, it hardly needs saying that they are often in deep conflict with secular constructions. Furthermore, in the competition to create religious voices, congregations and religiously based special-purpose groups are increasingly more effective actors relative to denominational bodies.

Chicago is a product of its changing economies and demographies, to be sure,
and the styles of life and neighborhood they support. As one of Algren's grizzled
characters asserts, "A church and a W.C.T.U. never growed a big town yet."
Perhaps size is the special domain of the capitalist economy. But this chapter
demonstrates that religion as a public, cultural, and moral force competes vigorously with political and economic power in shaping the *kind* of place Chicago is.

Chicago's Religious Demographics

Since the titanic immigrations from Eastern and Southern Europe at the turn
of the twentieth century, Chicago's religious landscape has been heavily Catholic.
In Cook county, which includes the city and a swath of heavily populated north-
ern suburbs, data from the North American Religion Atlas (NARA) show that
Catholics are 40 percent of the total population. Using NARA's county-level data,
Chicago's Catholic predominance compares to Cleveland (35 percent), another
large industrial city, but is unlike smaller cities such as Detroit (23 percent),
Milwaukee (28 percent), Indianapolis (13 percent), Minneapolis (23 percent), and
Cincinnati (27 percent), where independent, historically African-American, and
mainline Protestantism predominate. All three American global cities—New
York, Los Angeles, and Chicago—contain approximately the same proportion of
Catholic residents, from 37 to 40 percent. Chicago's (Cook county) Jewish population, 4.4 percent, while considerably smaller than New York county's 20 percent (half of all American Jews live in the Northeast), is a significant presence in
Chicago, where the U.S. Census reports that the white population is now 31.3
percent. African Americans are overwhelmingly Protestant, and increasingly
Pentecostal. Chicago's 2000 black population is 36.4 percent, and black churches are an important political as well as religious dimension of Chicago's public
life. Immigrants from Mexico and other Central and South American countries
are predominantly Catholic, yet are also converting to Pentecostalism in signifi-

cant numbers. The Latino population is growing rapidly in Chicago, now 26 percent and, because the black population has been slowly but steadily declining, is expected to become the largest ethnic group in Chicago by 2020.

Religiously unaffiliated or uncounted residents make up a large percentage in each of the cities compared, but the heaviest Catholic cities, Chicago and Cleveland, have the lowest proportion of unaffiliated, 27 percent and 24 percent, respectively. The highest is Indianapolis, 43 percent; followed by Milwaukee, Cincinnati, Minneapolis, and Detroit at 37, 37, 36, and 34 percent respectively.

Since the fundamental revisions of U.S. immigration laws in 1965, many newly built religious structures are Hindu, Buddhist, and Jain temples, Sikh *gurdwaras*, and Islamic mosques, founded by recently immigrated professional and technical workers. Many of these workers have taken jobs in the "information economy," high tech industries that migrated from the city to the suburbs or were started in one of the technology corridors along I88 westward or I90 to the northwest. (DuPage county to the west of Cook now imports the second highest number of workers, next only to Cook.)[3] Metropolitan Chicago is home to more than 24 Hindu temples, five Sikh *gurdwaras*, one Jain temple, 33 immigrant Buddhist temples, and 50 immigrant mosques, located in both the city and suburbs.

The Archdiocese of Chicago (Cook and Lake counties) has 402 parishes and missions for a Catholic population of 2.6 million. The Diocese of Joliet, which includes DuPage county in addition to six mostly rural counties, has 133 parishes and missions for a Catholic population of 630,000 that makes up 37 percent of the total population residing in those counties. Worshipping in one's own language continues to be crucial to the adjustment process for immigrants. Parishes of the Chicago archdiocese say Mass in 20 languages; 120 churches use a Spanish liturgy, 46 use Polish, and others use Vietnamese, Laotian, Croatian, Mandarin, and Cantonese, among others. There are about 60 Orthodox Christian churches in the metro region, which are historically ethnically based, including more recent Ethiopian churches.

Protestant churches number about 3,500; their much smaller average size—about 75 as reported in the National Congregations Survey—as well as independent polity accounts for their larger number of structures. The metro region contains 148 synagogues for a Jewish population of about 250,000, two-thirds of whom live in suburbs.

Religion and Urban Centrality: From Single Center to Multipolar

Chicago's Loop and the edge city of Naperville on the western horizon represent, respectively, the old urban center and the new "postmodern" pattern of multiple, competing centers of metropolitan dominance. The Loop is home to the political, economic, and cultural powers that dominate Chicago and its hinterland, and in certain fields—architecture and commodities markets, for example—its leadership is unquestioned in the national and global arenas. The Loop continues its centralizing functions for the metropolitan region, but is now in tension with other, smaller poles such as Naperville.

As a recipient of the restructuring economy, Naperville has become one important pole within the metropolitan region as well as globally. Among the fastest-growing U. S. towns during the 1990s, Naperville's population tripled in 10 years as high-tech industries attracted professional and technical workers nationally and globally (its population is now 10 percent Asian), as well as from within the Chicago area. Reflecting the new global reality, Naperville's economic significance tends to supersede other dimensions of human life, but its attraction also rests heavily on its reputation for local security and freedom from street crime and overt drug trade, and on the availability of low-density, privately gated, residences. The small village of Protestant and Catholic farmers thus became a city that is the center of a metropolitan sub-region, and is home to new religious institutions, including the Islamic Center of Naperville; Congregation Beth Shalom, the only synagogue in western DuPage county; and a Pentecostal megachurch, all of which draw members and adherents from a large part of the Chicago region, as illustrated in Map 6.3. In addition, the Hindu Temple of Greater Chicago in neighboring Lemont adds to the centripetal force of the area by attracting thousands of Indian immigrants from throughout the Chicago region and the Midwest.

Centrality is an urban dimension that puts in bold relief a particular meaning of place. But places are different from one another in part because they exist in a hierarchy of centrality where the core draws to itself the attention, preference, desirability, and energy of activities from other regions or areas around it, but the peripheral areas are more self-contained and limited by the elements generally already there. Several of Chicago's downtown churches—First United Methodist Chicago Temple, Moody Church, Old St. Patrick Catholic Church, and Fourth Presbyterian Church, the two cathedrals (St. James Episcopal and Holy Name Catholic), and the Loop Synagogue—symbolize urban centrality in its religious dimension. They stand for the importance of the city as a whole and, to varying degrees, take responsibility for it. All of these congregations have large, metrowide commuting memberships who tend to have a cosmopolitan outlook, identify with a diverse span of interests, and participate in multiple networks of opportunity and influence.

Religion and the Loop

The Loop congregations were founded with Chicago itself, except for Moody Memorial Church, whose founding coincided with the industrial consolidation of the city at the turn of the twentieth century (shown on Map 6.2). They remained in or near their original locations and adjusted to the residential migration from the center of the city by attracting metropolitan-wide membership. Today some are adding local members as downtown populations increase. They all contribute, in different ways, to the power of the Loop as the preeminent center for the Chicago region.

First United Methodist Church, founded in 1833, stands tall over the Richard J. Daley Plaza, looking across at Daley Center, the City/County Building, the State of Illinois Building, and the corporate headquarters that line the other sides of Chicago's central public square. Chicago was typical of nineteenth-century Midwestern cities that built Protestant churches on the central public square, representing their active presence in commercial and public life. The first Catholic church, St. Mary's, was built between the square and Lake Michigan at about the same time, and the first synagogue, Kehilath Anshe Maariv, was dedicated three blocks south of the square four years later.

As Daniel Bluestone argues in *Constructing Chicago*, the late-nineteenth century withdrawal of churches to residential areas represented a retreat of religious authority before Mammon as well as an effort by the political and business elite to create a stronger division between public and private life. First United Methodist Church refused to exchange the commercial value of its location for members' advantage. Rather, in 1926 it invested in that location by constructing a 26-story neo-gothic building (named The Chicago Temple) that includes income-producing commercial space as well as a sanctuary, educational and social rooms, a parsonage—and a "sky chapel" that is far higher than any of the public buildings.

First United Methodist's relationship to the city was led by a succession of strong pastors who recognized the unique opportunity—and responsibility— inherent in this religious presence on the public square. The centerpiece of this relationship—the contest over what is public and what is central—has always been the presence of a worshiping community in a place that is otherwise commercial, governmental, and secular. The 1,000 or more people who come from throughout the metro area on Sunday morning (illustrated in the broad distribution of member households shown on Map 6.4) when the bustle of business and the hustle of politics are at their lowest ebb, announce the importance of a countervailing moral order in the public square. But the difference that countervailing order might make depends in part on who it is that makes the trek to the center, as well as on what connection the congregation might have with those who are present during the "regular business hours."

In the years since the civil rights era, Chicago Temple has been home to an increasingly diverse worshiping community, but this did not happen without effort, and the change is far from complete. Historically, First United Methodist Church shared the white, socially elite characteristics of other Loop institutions—

the Art Institute, the Chicago Symphony, State Street department stores—which asserted the dominant cultural identity for Chicago as a whole. And it remains an elite institution and cultural force—a site for the annual Chicago Humanities Festival, for example, and a member of its board. But its current identity is tied to a more complex cultural mission. The racial diversity of the members and friends who travel to its central location for worship is a clue to the cultural diversity it seeks to make legitimate and normative for the city as a whole. Part of this is in the cultural practices of the church itself—the chancel choir and the Skinner pipe organ have to share the sacred space of the sanctuary with the Gospel choir, the piano, and drums. Part of it is the cultural events the church sponsors—the street art in its gallery and the Asian-American theater troupe in residence there. But all this comes into direct political play when the pastor walks across the street to meet with the mayor or joins with other liberal Protestants to challenge the governor of Illinois on the racially explosive issues of police violence, affordable housing, gaming sites in the city, and neighborhood stability. The church can speak for a diverse city and region, and on behalf of diverse people's interests, in part because it represents some of the diversity of the region, and because it does so at the city's—and the region's—center.

Among the least envied spots in the Loop area when Algren was writing was the western border that opened to the flophouses and bars along West Madison Avenue's old skid row. Yet a Catholic parish stood there, resisting the flames of the Great Fire long before the expressway was built at its feet, cutting it off from the immigrant neighborhood it had served for 100 years. Old St. Patrick's Catholic Church, established in 1857, benefited from the changes of urban restructuring and religious denominational change, but not without first undergoing a trough in its parish life, with the parish rolls reduced to four! But in the mid-1980s, the west side of the Loop began to rise from urban decay as the business sector expanded. With looser definitions of parish boundaries permitted by the Second Vatican Council, the church reached out to the young, professional workers leaving the Loop at the end of each day with short-term activities that appealed to their transitional states and interests—relationships and jobs. Mission activities to the Near West Side, and increasingly beyond, attracted many young adults seeking an outlet for service to others. Long before the church reached its current membership of 2,500 families, over 500 people participated in some form of community outreach. Noteworthy is the substantial investment the church has made in a number of nontraditional programs such as CARA, an intensive week-long job-skill preparation in white-collar rather than low-end service or vocational jobs.

Old St. Pat's symbols of inclusivity, the Celtic cross, and the naming of its most active lay center as "Crossroads," represent a historic identity that is true to the universalism of American religion. But these symbols also express a contra-

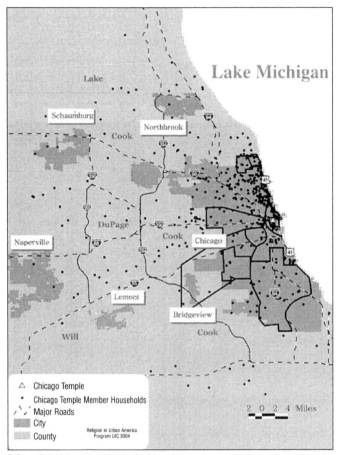

Map 6.4: *Member Households of First United Methodist Church –
Chicago Temple.*

diction between their centrality and the particular character of congregations that
brings like-minded souls together. The Celtic artistry and prominence in the sanctuary of the church's namesake, St. Patrick, gives them an identity rooted in the
events of Irish history, especially the immediate precursor for large-scale Irish
immigration, the Potato Famine of 1848-50, whose survivors founded the church.
As a result, the church gathers together a homogeneous rather than a heterogeneous population despite pluralist intentions.

 Nonetheless, a Catholic church that draws from across the entire metropolitan region in competition with local parishes is a new form of urban Catholicity.

Old St. Patrick's does not claim to speak for the city in the manner of Chicago Temple—it defers to Holy Name Cathedral and to the cardinal archbishop in that regard. Nor does it attempt to replace the role of local parishes. Rather, it proclaims a public, Catholic, pastoral presence at the heart of the city, available to the city as a whole, a presence on whose organizational, intellectual, and spiritual resources other Catholic churches and lay Catholics should draw.

Religion in Naperville: A New Center in the Region

Calvary Church in Naperville brings together several trajectories of urban restructuring that help explain an important growth religion, Christian Pentecostalism (Map 6.3). Calvary was founded in 1967 and grew along with Naperville. Calvary's two multi-function campuses lie over 150 acres along two busy highways. The church now supports a large and successful parochial school, regular Christian entertainment for high school students and adults, a Christian bookstore, and many services to the poor, homeless, and imprisoned. With a weekly attendance of 3,000, the church holds dozens of religious-education programs for adults and children, organized by age and lifestyle groups rather than families. The multiple divisions for adults include a newlyweds fellowship, a singles ministry for the 24- to 30-year olds, a singles fellowship for 30-somethings, single-parent fellowship, seniors fellowship for those 55 and over, a women's ministry, and a men's ministry. To understand the comprehensive and complex outreach of megachurches, one needs to know the variety of lifestyle support groups Calvary sponsors: 12-step and other substance abuse/chemical dependency programs, AIDS/cancer, dysfunctional families, eating disorders, survivors of sexual abuse, parents of children who have been sexually abused, bereavement, physically challenged, and gambling. The divorce-recovery program is especially popular. Forty-one home fellowship programs meet in Naperville and 13 surrounding towns and suburbs.

Like other growing evangelical churches, Calvary's staff runs the church with a corporate operating style and task orientation, and the members participate much as customers, selecting from the rich menu of ideas and services offered, and sharing the good news of the church and its message with their friends and relatives. In fact, most participants and supporters of the church are not members—which would require a greater commitment than they are willing to make. But the church welcomes them at whatever level. Moreover, it offers one-stop shopping—eating McMuffins at Calvary's planned food court makes more time available for both prayer and committee activities on church grounds. All this generates a strong centripetal pull, creating a church community that may shape family norms and values much like the parish model previously did and still does in parts of the city. And the community is racially inclusive—as diverse as

Chicago Temple, and more so than Old St. Pat's. But, like the Loop churches, it also lures families from their local communities, and this may attenuate their relationships with neighbors.

The congregations of Naperville are, of course, a varied lot. Some of the mainline Protestant churches, like Wheatland Salem United Methodist, only a mile or so from Calvary, are also growing and prosperous, but much more local and therefore more homogeneous. Catholic parishes, many of them recently founded as the population multiplied, also encourage neighborhood-scale participation. These congregations do not mirror or contribute to the centripetal power of Naperville; rather they maintain smaller-scale places within the new center. On the other hand, the only synagogue, Beth Shalom, serves a widely scattered Jewish population, and the only mosque, the Islamic Center of Naperville, draws participants from well beyond Naperville itself. They contribute, therefore, to the growth of Naperville's centrality.

Religion Establishing Its Own Center

Lemont, Illinois, is roughly equidistant from Chicago and Naperville. High on a bluff in this village-turned-ambivalent-suburb is an imposing structure of classic Indian architecture—the Hindu Temple of Greater Chicago (Map 6.3). Hindu Temple has a symbiotic relationship with the sprawling metropolis, but is rather different from that of congregations in Naperville and the Loop. Founders of the Temple chose an unincorporated Lemont site, not only for easy expressway access but also for its seclusion from thickly populated residential and commercial areas. Whereas Calvary is one of many factors involved in the emergence of Naperville as a new urban center on the margins of the Chicago metropolitan area, Lemont has no pretense or possibility of becoming such a center. Hindu Temple exemplifies yet another kind of centrality, one that draws adherents to its temple as the center of religious life and practice for Hindu people who live throughout, and even beyond, the metropolitan region.

The enormous, though delicately carved, *gopuram* rising above the entrance to the Temple is evident along the quarter-mile drive winding from Lemont Road to the temple parking lot and prepares the visitor to expect a facility and an institution of considerable moment. The large size of the main hall, with its capacity of 1,000 or more people, has to be taken together with the fact that it houses shrines not only to Rama, a god of near-universal appeal, but also to many gods who are favored locally in different parts of India. Moreover, a smaller temple, connected to the Rama Temple by a large educational and social center, houses shrines honoring the deities Ganesha, Shiva, and Durga. The fact that so many deities are present and revered by the eight temple priests and by lay devotees alike partly explains the metro-wide appeal of Hindu Temple.

By creating an "ecumenical" Hindu organization, one in which many deities are worshiped and in which worship is practiced in many languages, incorporating diverse traditions and cultural forms, Hindu Temple is fostering ethnic diversity within the Indian-American population. From the perspective of the wider American society, the Temple is simultaneously helping to create a common Indian identity and culture. But the Hindu pluralism of the Temple mitigates the tendency to lose Indian differences in the process of becoming Indian Americans. Thus, one large "ecumenical" temple serves as a center of religious life and practice for a large portion of Chicago's Indian Hindus without obliterating their ethnic distinctions.

Religion and the Art of Local Control

The unbroken train of immigrant settlement that begins in Chinatown, just south of the Loop, and extends through the Lower West Side, Bridgeport, the Back of the Yards, and into the Marquette Park and Gage Park neighborhoods before running up against Midway Airport is made up of classic neighborhoods, those that still nourish a sense of place. This swath of Chicago geography is called the "Southwest Corridor" and runs from the center, culminating in several neighborhoods collectively known as the Southwest Side (Map 6.2). The nearest of these neighborhoods were entry ports for Eastern Europeans, Irish, German, and Italian immigrants arriving between 1880 and 1924, and more recently Mexicans and others from Central and South America, and Arabs. These are blue-collar neighborhoods with modest housing stock that have retained Chicago's most consistent working-class culture. The Lower West Side, locally known as Pilsen for its original Bohemian immigrants, and the Southwest Side, provide windows on working-class immigrants; the Americanization process among Hispanics, Europeans, and Arabs; and the interaction between race/ethnicity and neighborhood community. Religious congregations participate in all of these processes, helping the neighborhoods defend and reconstruct a sense of place.

The Barrio in the City

Pilsen is now a predominately working-class Mexican neighborhood, although a small number of East Europeans and Italians remain and an enclave of African Americans has formed at the southern boundary. While Pilsen continues to be a port of entry for workers in the lower service economy, many of whom are undocumented, it is also the neighborhood of choice for a section of the Latino intelligentsia. Pilsen's proximity to the Loop and the expanding University of Illinois at Chicago campus, together with its affordable rental housing and new, higher-scale construction, is attracting a number of students and young white professionals.

St. Pius V Catholic Church is one of Pilsen's major anchors and a visible participant in neighborhood life. Of the eight parishes in Pilsen, it was the first to offer the Catholic Mass in Spanish. Through its teachings and programs, St. Pius helps incorporate new immigrants into a competitive, often hostile environment, translate their immigrant experience and identity into functioning tools for navigating the American context, and construct an ethnic identity that binds them with their home countries. Being at St. Pius is like being in Mexico, some parishioners say, with its many vivid symbols and features of Latin social culture, language, and music.

But it is also not only Mexico, because the progressive politics and sophisticated theology of St. Pius pastoral and lay leaders offers parishioners a way to integrate spirituality and ethnicity with social justice so as to empower the congregation and build community in the new world. The parish has developed Christian base communities adapted from the liberation theology model of Latin America, which in turn produce members for activist block groups and for neighborhood-wide faith-based organizing. Indeed, one of the strongest groups in Chicago is the Pilsen Resurrection Project (formerly the Interfaith Community Organization), an independent organization authentically controlled by the Pilsen congregations, especially the Catholic parishes. They focus on developing the human social capacities of members in a context of strong neighborhood and community ties that build the "kingdom of God on earth" and work toward a critique of the liberal capitalist model in an effort to transcend it politically. This is a tall order, but one that is taken seriously by the Pilsen pastors and leaders, and is woven into the more complex cultural process of creating and sustaining a shared sense of place.

Transformation of a "Defended Neighborhood"

The Southwest Side today is a mix of older Eastern European and recent immigrants including Mexicans, Poles, and a small number of Arabs, as well as a small but growing number of African Americans, particularly along its eastern border with heavily impoverished and black West Englewood. Marquette Park itself has been a classic "defended neighborhood," an area where most of the residents shared an ethnic heritage and a working-class culture, and whose close interpersonal relationships were reinforced by religion and family. The Chicago School sociologists, Robert Park and Ernest Burgess, called these "natural communities," which created social stability through cultural and intergenerational ties forged in the stockyards and steel mills and in parochial school and church institutions (Catholic Youth Organization, Holy Name and Vincent DePaul Societies, Daughters of Isabella and Knights of Columbus, among others). In many cases, the succeeding generation of Catholics did not move out to a "better" neighborhood; they built a new house on the next block. Yet with racial tipping, white flight, and financial disinvestment in adjacent West Englewood in the 1960s and 1970s, change was in the offing and appeared ominous—evoking, initially, fierce resistance made infamous when Martin Luther King, Jr. was hit by a brick.

Today the Southwest Side is pluralistic, and this is due in no small measure to clergy and lay leaders' efforts to shape the moral culture of parishes and the consciences of parishioners. St. Nicholas of Tolentine, adjacent to Marquette Park, and other Southwest Side parishes continue to draw primarily from within their territorial boundaries (note the street-by-street pattern of member households represented by the dots on Map 6.5, some of which merge into white lines due to the density of the membership), and they have used the principles and tradition of the territorial parish as a framework for welcoming people of color. St. Nick's has been a mixed-ethnicity parish since its founding in 1909, when "mixed" meant Irish, German, and Polish, with a few Italians and Lithuanians.

Since the mid-1990s this parish, like adjacent portions of Marquette Park, has had a Hispanic majority, and its school enrollment has declined along with its white population. Many Hispanics also see St. Nick's as a stopping point along the road to outlying suburbs, so it is not clear that Hispanics will re-establish the place-based community the parish once knew. Since the 1970s, well-paid manufacturing jobs on which most of the community depended have drained away, and many of the once-pristine dwellings with tiny, immaculate yards are in foreclosure. In short, the neighborhood is under the stress of deindustrialization, deconcentration, and the globalization of the economy and the culture.

Such changes stimulated two kinds of responses by St. Nick's and the other Southwest Side parishes. First, the Southwest Catholic Cluster Project formulated a theology of place, "Christians and their Neighborhood," that drew on their common tradition, yet confronted the defensive and inward perspective of parish members. Their theological statement reads, "For a Christian (and for others), a neighborhood is not merely a social phenomenon or shared geography, but a community. And the particular God that Christians worship and love is revealed, not so much in private, but in communities." The authors argue that this theology of neighborhoods links individuals to society and this link is an expression of the Catholic principle of subsidiarity, addressing control at the best level for practical action. Acting on the subsidiarity principle helps to humanize the city by endowing participants with moral responsibility and giving them both the freedom and power to act.

The practical consequences of this theology are twofold. First, it aims not to focus on preventing people from leaving but fully on incorporating newcomers instead. Second, it means eschewing personal prejudices and fears that have dogged them in past racial conflicts and have arisen anew in today's globalized context, but also acknowledging legitimate and serious neighborhood fears such as economic insecurity, gangs, drugs, crime, and graffiti. This approach acknowledges "self-interest in the context of the interests of others" as a moral and practical foundation for viable community and parish life.

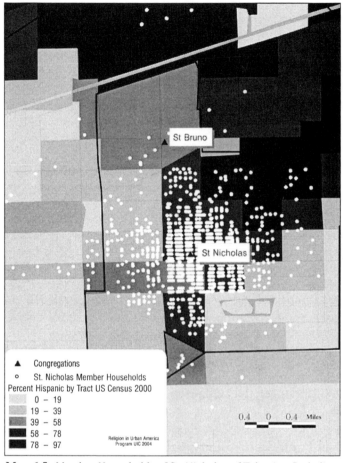

Map 6.5: *Member Households of St. Nicholas of Tolentine Catholic Parish in Chicago's Southwest Side.*

In 1995 they transformed the Catholic Cluster Project into a multi-faith—though Catholic-led—interracial community organization, the Southwest Organizing Project (SWOP). It joined the churches and other nonprofits already working in the Southwest Side—such as the Greater Southwest Development Corporation, the Southwest Youth Collaborative, and the Southwest Women Working Together—to create and retain manufacturing jobs, to provide preventive services for youth and women, to hold politicians accountable, and to resist predatory lending practices, which have become a scourge of blue-collar communities. SWOP, along with the churches, works to build relationships between older and newer immigrants to create a new "climate of desire" for the neighbor-hood—and to fight the "climate of fear" that the neighborhood "is going down." Despite the continuing Catholic identity of the area, many residents tell stories about no longer knowing people on their blocks, feeling fearful when seeing abandoned homes and hearing rumors of increased crime (often exaggerated), and seeking new homes in outlying areas. So SWOP and its partners are in an uphill battle to maintain the security that place-based communities, with their interwoven nature of social relationships and their stability across time, provide. They have decided that if they "let the market prevail"—just looking at housing losses—they will not have a neighborhood left.

SWOP's effectiveness depends on micro-level work by the parishes. St. Nick's, for example, prods members to see each other in a new light, creating new, shared, sacred space across the boundaries of culture and class. A proposal for door-to-door visits unsettled the Parish Pastoral Council members, so they agreed to hold block meetings instead. Less controversial and less risky, the parish holds anniversary events that continue to bring back hundreds of former parishioners, reminding them how their parents' roots in the parish have intrinsic, continuing, and not merely nostalgic value. They hold intercultural events from Mexican and Polish traditions to reveal cultural similarities rather than differences; this culmi-nated in a show of force organized by SWOP in which parish members kept vigil at the mosque on 63rd Street after the tragic events of September 11, 2001. While parishes continue to be the principal anchors of the neighborhood, they now ben-efit from the participation of institutions that were previously unwilling to enter public life, such as the Sisters of St. Casimir, who run Holy Cross Hospital and Maria High School, and five local public elementary schools.

The Southwest Side's Muslim community begins in Marquette Park along West 63rd Street, continues to West 87th Street, and ends, for now, in Southwest suburban Bridgeview (Map 6.2). While a small concentration remains around the Chicago Islamic Center on 63rd Street at Kedzie Avenue, considerable migration to the Mosque Foundation at 92nd and Harlem Avenue in Bridgeview has occurred. Today the mosque's leadership reports that two-thirds of its participants live locally around Bridgeview—compared with one-third a decade ago. These participants are responding to the centripetal power of an Arabic Islamic commu-nity around the Mosque Foundation, which has a membership of about 400 and more than 2,000 active participants. Two worship spaces, two schools, a youth center, and considerable parking space constitute an Islamic center headed by professional clergy and paid staff. The two schools, one for girls and the other for both genders, have drawn more families close by, but the Arabic language and Middle Eastern heritage have played an important part as well. These Muslims are following a parish-like model, building solidarity in a local place on the basis of multi-institutional services, ethnic identity, and close residential proximity. Their innovative adaptation of the parish model emerges from the American voluntary context in which religious communities grow from the ground up with a congregational polity (owned and controlled by the members), rather than an episcopal polity (owned and controlled by a bishop or diocese). As a result, they have developed a sense of place and a morally informed community in suburban Bridgeview and its environs.

Religion, Race, and Political Culture

The residential areas of black Chicago, still highly segregated, comprise most of the South and West Sides. While these areas include the greatest concentrations of poverty in the metropolitan region, a large section of the South Side is historically middle-class. Both the South and West Sides included steel mills, the stockyards, and other major employers in heavy industry. These areas have therefore been hit hardest by the loss of industries that offered unskilled and semi-skilled jobs for southern blacks fleeing destitute sharecropping lives during the Great Migration. But as the sociologist William Julius Wilson has shown, most African Americans entered the industrial economy later than European immigrants, many not until the 1940s when the mighty smokestack industries were at their peak. As the steel mills and stockyards disappeared throughout the 1950s and 1960s, the geographic advantage that black workers had during the industrial era was brief and abandoned them first. As a result, South Side residents today have the longest travel times to work of the entire Chicago labor force.[4]

A similar fate befell West Side workers as nearby manufacturers and retail merchandisers (International Harvester, Sunbeam, and Sears Roebuck) also left.

Religion plays a political, cultural, and communal role for African-American Chicagoans. As the geographer Wilbur Zelinsky has shown, Chicago's black population, 26 percent of Cook county, has about 46 percent of the county's congregations. National survey data from the National Congregations Study confirmed that black churches are smaller on average than churches as a whole (median membership of 65 compared to 75 for all congregations in the United States).[5] Considerable research has also pointed out that black people report higher rates of church attendance than the population as a whole. There is a small black Catholic population, about 100,000 in the Archdiocese of Chicago, which constitutes only 4 percent of the total Catholic population, but there is no black Catholic enclave comparable to the Hispanic Catholic Pilsen. The largest Catholic parochial school on the South Side, St. Columbanus, is located near the Dan Ryan expressway, which makes it accessible to black families in much of the South Side. The black churches resist the destructive impact of deindustrialization and historic discrimination by shoring up the self-identity of African Americans, participating in the distinctive black voice within Chicago and Illinois politics, and forming and leading community organizations that promote and defend the interests of particular black neighborhoods.

Gentrification and Culture on the South Side

Gentrification has occurred in parts of the original "Black Belt," that narrow strip of land along State Street from south of the Loop to about 47th Street (Map 6.2). The southern portion of the Black Belt, which served as the cultural center of black Chicago, was known as "Bronzeville," an appellation that is now being reclaimed. The economic resurrection is also evident in the mid-South area surrounding racially mixed Hyde Park and the University of Chicago. Further south, neighborhoods like Chatham, sometimes called "the bastion of the black middle class," have remained comfortable neighborhoods of choice, challenged but not destroyed by the loss of industry.

In these relatively secure areas, churches are involved in a process of ethnicizing race. That is, they are developing a black identity that is voluntarily constructed, offers diverse rather than monolithic interpretations of race, and becomes socially desirable in contrast to the residual "non-white" category, challenging what Algren called "a soft and protean awareness of white superiority everywhere, in everything." Carter Temple CME Church, which moved south in 1969 from then-desolate Bronzeville, and Trinity United Church of Christ still further south, founded about the same time, are among several black churches that participate in the new construction of black identity. These churches infuse their Christian rituals and practices with elements of African culture and contribute to the development of Afrocentric Christian theologies. Symbols and practices associated with Africa abound in the churches—rites of passage based on African traditions, rituals venerating elders and ancestors, use of the *African Heritage Bible*, representations of biblical characters with African features, and a shared discourse reflecting identity as rooted in African history. Whether these cultural changes can alter the residential segregation and economic discrimination that have long characterized metropolitan Chicago remains an open question, but that does not diminish the appeal of practicing faith in ways that fundamentally reconstruct the identity of black people.

But black churches are by no means limited to the politics of identity and ethnicization. Their political influence has been widely recognized by scholars (William Grimshaw's *Bitter Fruit* and Frederick Harris' *Something Within*, come to mind), and by politicians (the Richard J. Daley "machine" depended on the "black sub-machine" from the outset). But the nature of that influence is complex, and its directions multiple. In 1963, black clergy were deeply divided over whether to support the first school boycott, how and to what extent to participate in the school desegregation movement for the next three years, whether to invite Dr. King to Chicago, and whether to join in the open housing marches. On the South Side, the political alignments were affected by the overflow of the Black Belt to the areas south of Bronzeville; that is, into the previously all-white, middle-class areas of Hyde Park, Woodlawn, Greater Grand Crossing, Chatham, and Avalon Park. As Grimshaw shows, middle-class blacks, churches, and pastors who moved south became more politically independent and activist. Indeed, the pastors most active in the effort to enlist Dr. King's participation in the Chicago Freedom Movement were in churches located in areas into which blacks had only recently moved, and where they were developing what Harris and others have called an "oppositional civic culture."

Churches and pastors active in the Chicago Freedom Movement have since been the setting of challenging actions in conventional politics. It was in one of these churches, the Vernon Park Church of God, at 91st Street and Stony Island Avenue, that Congressman Ralph Metcalfe prayed through the night with Pastor Claude Wyatt before announcing his historic 1975 break with the "Regular Democratic Organization" (i.e., the Daley machine). And it was the Reverend Stephen Thurston, pastor of New Covenant Missionary Baptist Church, at 77th Street and Cottage Grove Avenue (whose father had been president of Southern Christian Leadership Conference's Chicago Chapter in the 1960s), who not only supported Harold Washington—the first black elected mayor of Chicago—in opposition to the "regular Democrats," but also organized a move to publicize and discredit pastors who allowed Washington's opponents access to their pulpits.

The churches that supported Washington for mayor, and later Carol Mosely Braun for U. S. Senate, varied widely in their theologies and denominational affiliations, and they were not limited to South Side or middle-class churches. But churches like Vernon Park and New Covenant do seem to have nurtured a particularistic black identity, in which Christian faith was ennobling, empowering, and legitimating for engagement in civic purposes in tension with the prevailing political order. And the neighborhoods that changed from all white to all black, but remained mostly middle-class, seem to have had a disproportionate concentration of these churches. As a result, we can say they contributed to the development of their neighborhoods as places with shared identity and a measure of autonomy from— and thus, occasionally, opposition to—the central authority of city and county politics and of the Regular Democratic Organization based in Chicago's Loop.

Faith-Based Organizing on the Near West Side

The Near West Side neighborhood that houses the notorious and partially rebuilt Henry Horner Homes is about a stone's throw from the United Center, home of the Chicago Bulls. The neighborhood is black and poor, but the church members are mostly middle-class people who commute in. One is hard pressed to find impoverished neighborhood residents in any of the nearby churches, despite regular outreach programs by several. Indeed, unspoken class boundaries are important barriers to the churching of the poor, whose persistent social isolation includes disproportionately low religious affiliation and participation. Only one of seven congregations in the proximate neighborhood had members from Henry Horner Homes (the setting of Alex Kotlowitz's *There Are No Children Here*), and that was a small Pentecostal church, which no longer exists. Two other large Protestant churches, First Baptist Congregational and St. Stephen AME, as well as the closest Catholic church, St. Malachy, have a commuting membership with the majority coming from the West Side of the city and nearby suburbs (Map 6.2).

In the mid-1980s, First Baptist Congregational, St. Stephen's, and St. Malachy could see clearly that economic development in the Near West Side might be a mixed blessing to the people of the area. The challenge came in the form of proposed sports stadiums, which would bring jobs and investment to their neighborhood but—left to market forces and what one minister called "the white power structure"—would displace the residents and replace them with upscale homeowners. Together with other churches and secular leaders, they created the Interfaith Organizing Project, which led the successful fight to prevent the Chicago Bears from building a football stadium, and then drove a hard bargain with the owners of the Bulls, negotiating terms that incorporated neighborhood interests for building the United Center. Since then, much corollary change has occurred.

The high rises that were once Henry Horner have been replaced by a small number of townhouses for selected low-income residents; a new library named after a longtime resident organizer has been finished; new private homes are being remodeled or built; and the church-community partnership that fueled the changes has dissolved. But both the churches and the Near West Side Community Development Corporation are actively working to reestablish a viable working-class neighborhood for traditional black residents as well as newcomers. Because of the area's proximity to the Loop, with good public transit as well as highway access, young white professionals are beginning to eye the neighborhood's advantageous property values, which worries some of the area's black leaders, secular and religious.

First Baptist Congregational Church, the anchor of the IOP in its heyday, is a signature church of the West Side whose members commute from as far as west suburban Batavia. At the height of white flight from center city areas in 1970, a growing, all-black Baptist church purchased the grand, limestone Gothic edifice from a dwindling all-white United Church of Christ congregation. The black congregation chose to affiliate with both denominations, creating a racially inclusive religious identity that secures support from both the mostly white UCC and the

Baptists, and allows the church to draw on diverse theological resources to shape a new identity. For example, contrary to Baptist policy, First Baptist Congregational ordains women, but unlike the more liberal UCC, they do not affirm homosexuality or use inclusive gender language. The church has 40 ordained ministers, mostly volunteer, allowing it to develop broad-based organizational leadership, pursuing what the church calls a holistic ministry for both its members and those outside.

Much as the churches of the Loop evangelize and extend social services to the nearby Cabrini Green public housing projects, First Baptist Congregational asserts its religious authority by holding religious education classes in Henry Horner. Volunteers from the church bring children whose mothers are incarcerated in one of the outlying correctional facilities for weekly visits. But also like the downtown churches, the people served through such ministries do not join the churches (with the partial exception of Moody Church). The decline of the middle- and working-class black population living on the West Side has affected the church's ability to focus locally. Nonetheless, the church brought other resources to bear in the IOP fight with the Chicago athletic teams, namely a constituency that came out for shows of force, articulate leadership, and an outlet for their sense of Christian responsibility.

Religion and the Patterns of Diversity

More than in any other community areas, new immigrants in Rogers Park and West Ridge are found side by side with immigrants from previous waves. These far-North-Side neighborhoods, bordering on suburban Evanston and Skokie, contain all the major religious and ethnic groups found in the Chicago metropolitan area, giving the area the condensed feel of the whole (Map 6.2). Some rental housing is still available, and public and highway transit to the Loop support an "open" as well as "transient" neighborhood atmosphere. Employment centers are nearby, including Loyola and Northwestern universities and the edge city of Northbrook, providing both service-sector and white-collar jobs.

Different parts of Rogers Park and West Ridge are institutional epicenters for religio-ethnic groups. Honorary street names are associated with sections of Devon Avenue, beginning on the western end in Jewish West Ridge with Golda Meir Boulevard; to the east is Ghandi Marg, for Hindus; and parts are Mohammad Ali Jinnah Way, for Muslims. These epicenters support, and are supported by, major suburban "outposts" including strong Jewish communities in Skokie, Northbrook, and Buffalo Grove, Hindus in southwestern and northwestern suburbs, Muslims in southwestern Palos Hills, northern Morton Grove and Skokie. Population demographics reveal a mixed white and black population as well. Rogers Park is one of only four of Chicago's 77 community areas that has not undergone major shifts in its black, white, and Hispanic population balance in the last decade.[6] West Ridge has gained most of the area's Asian influx; it is now almost one-quarter Asian (compared to 4.3 percent in the city overall), half white, and the rest Hispanic and black.

St. Jerome Catholic Church in Rogers Park tells a story of diversity that probes changes underlying stabilities at the surface. Ten years ago, St. Jerome was about one-third European American white, one-half diverse Latino, and the remaining one-sixth Haitian black. Today it has become more Hispanic, less Haitian, and less old European white, but more global with Bosnian and Somalian immigrants joining the polyglot of Latin American, South Asian, Filipino, African-American, Vietnamese, and recent Baltic and Irish newcomers. Over 3,000 worshippers attend Catholic Mass in Spanish each weekend and about 300 are present for the English Mass. A couple dozen people attend the French Mass twice monthly, down from about 100 in the mid-1990s, since a number of Haitians switched to Pentecostal churches recently and others were pushed out of Rogers Park for economic reasons. These last two changes touch other groups as well. The global rise in Hispanic Pentecostalism is evident in Rogers Park; less than a block from St. Jerome, more than 1,000 Pentecostals worship at Iglesia de Cristo. Yet, many affordable rentals among this group are being lost to condo conversions as well.

The pastors of St. Jerome have used liturgy to enable their linguistically diverse parishioners, who would otherwise remain ethnically and racially separate, to share their common religious heritage, thereby enhancing relationships that could build common social identities. As in other multicultural parishes, these liturgies are less popular than the leaders hope. Furthermore, intracultural differences, as among the various nationalities of Central and South America, create boundaries even if they are less clearly visible. Celebrating the common feast of Our Lady of Guadalupe revealed different nationalistic interpretations of the event at St. Jerome that spilled out in an intense parish meeting, threatening a split in the parish populations. Eventually the groups remained together—once their separate cultural spaces were acknowledged. This contrasts with earlier immigrant parishes, in which cultural conflict as often as not resulted in one group leaving to form another parish. One north-side Chicago neighborhood in the early twentieth century had five Polish parishes in one-half square mile. Today, both church authority and economic reality point to attempting to be the church together.

In contrast to the Catholic parishes' geographic persistence, Congregation Ezra Habonim Ner Tamid in West Ridge has been mobile and undergone considerable change in its 65-year history. Its story is of geography enabling different religious practices. Founded by Holocaust survivors and others who fled Nazi

Germany, Ezra Habonim Ner Tamid, a member of the Conservative movement within Judaism, underwent a series of mergers and splits; its last change showed a particularly poignant face. Having lost members to suburbanization and death, by 1997 Ezra Habonim could no longer afford to maintain its synagogue in West Ridge. Unable to agree jointly on a new destination, or an effective strategy for attracting younger Jews living on Chicago's North Side, the congregation's remaining assets were split in a legal settlement. Half the members chose to join a congregation in suburban Niles Township while the other half merged with one of the last remaining non-Orthodox synagogues in West Ridge.

Just as at St. Jerome, members of Ezra Habonim had internally diverse religious practices that stemmed from ethnic and generational differences. Unlike the Catholic communal tradition, Jewish custom also values individual choice, so that conflicts lead more easily to fission. The older German and Austrian founding immigrants brought an assimilated European ritual that included such practices as choir and organ music rather than a cappella chanting, performance by a cantor rather than participatory singing, and more formal sermons. The younger American members came of age in the 1960s and 1970s, when the Conservative movement began readapting Orthodox practices to regain religious distinctiveness. In the decision to separate, the group preferring the more assimilated worship styles chose suburban affiliation, while those adhering to traditional practices remained in the Jewish center.

A traditionally observant Jewish life requires a geographic concentration of Jewish people and Jewish institutions. West Ridge contains a concentration of mostly Orthodox shuls (synagogues), Jewish day schools, Jewish social service agencies, institutions for advanced Jewish studies, housing for Jewish elderly, and Jewish recreational and cultural services including grocery stores that offer the full array of Kosher food for everyday observance. The central agencies for Jewish law and custom, the Associated Talmud Torah and the Chicago Rabbinical Council, are also located there. The Jews in West Ridge have a far higher level of religious affiliation and observance, and are much more likely to be Orthodox, than the overall Jewish population of metropolitan Chicago. But not all Jews prefer to live in a dense Jewish community, opting instead for communities where their Jewishness is less apparent. By their own accounts, the Jews in West Ridge "struggle to be Jewish." Hence West Ridge provides the material and symbolic ingredients that resist forms of Americanization that erode the distinctiveness and identity of the Jewish community. And Congregation Ezra Habonim Ner Tamid cast its lot with the Jewish center rather than the dispersed population in religiously pluralist suburbs. Yet while the success of the struggle to be Jewish seems to depend on the critical mass of Jews and Jewish institutions, it does not require a homogeneous population or a monopoly over territory.

St. Jerome and Ezra Habonim Ner Tamid, for all their differences, contribute to the stable diversity of Chicago's North Side in a remarkably similar way. Through their religious practices, they create social spaces in which people's ethnic and religious identities can be expressed in mutually reinforcing ways that do not require geographic monopoly and do not depend on conflict with others.

Conclusion: The Contest Continues

No single theme can pull together the variety of ways religious action and ideas interact with the organizations, neighborhoods, and broader sectors of the metropolitan region. The four dimensions of urban space discussed in this chapter frame some of the most important ways religion takes its place among the forces affecting Chicago's economy, demographic distribution, configurations of power, and thus its forms of community life.

Dynamic congregations in Chicago's Loop reflect and help preserve the centrality of industrial cities by drawing resources to it, yet also redistributing them outward again. The congregations of Naperville have developed a different kind of centrality, one that competes with the Loop by providing employment, residential, religious, and cultural possibilities in a physically more secure and private suburban context. At the same time, Naperville's large congregations minister to the job insecurity and family stresses of the mobile, competitive, economically driven population, and help to give this very new urban center a moral and cultural core rather than exclusively a quickly constructed citadel of employment and consumption. In yet another way, religion is its own center for Asian Hindus, where location is secondary to ease of access.

In contrast, the Southwest Corridor, from inner-city Pilsen to suburban Bridgeview, preserves the kind of place-based local community life that made Chicago "the city of neighborhoods." But this has not been possible simply by the defense of parishes or the reassertion of Catholic values, despite formerly Catholic strongholds having remained predominantly Catholic even after decades of suburbanization. Given the centrifugal forces exercised by new employment and commercial centers like Naperville, neighborhoods could only be sustained with the building of politically effective faith-based community organizations. Moreover, new Muslim immigrants found that their culture could best be preserved and adapted by creating a parish-like concentration in a sparsely populated area near the city, much as Catholic immigrants from Europe had done a century earlier.

Chicago's all-black "Second Ghetto" of the South and West Sides has suffered the most devastating impact of deindustrialization since the 1950s. Despite the simultaneous impact of the delegalization of housing discrimination and the rise of the civil rights movement, blacks benefited least from the development of an information-age economy. Black churches could not stem the tide, although they mitigated its impact. Many of them constituted themselves as communities of identity, sometimes with the aid of Afrocentric theology and rituals, which substitute for the loss of the communal character of their neighborhoods. Others added an independent, self-initiated thrust to the historic role of black churches in Chicago politics, a change still evident in city and county government. Still others, seeing the "white power structure" (i.e., the Loop) encroaching on their devastated neighborhood, organized themselves to secure a portion of the benefit and a portion of the power.

Finally, the whole world, its manifold cultures and religions, is represented in the four-square-mile area of Rogers Park and West Ridge in the northern extremity of the city and immediately adjacent suburbs. This area is hospitable to low-wage workers, including recent immigrants, drawn to America by the burgeoning knowledge industries associated with universities like nearby Northwestern and Loyola. These residents live side by side with professional and technical workers from many of the same employers, although in distinct enclaves. While religious organizations did not prevent the socio-economic inequality of the new global economy, they did help make it possible for low-wage immigrants and long-standing American Protestants, Catholics, and Jews to live peacefully in close proximity and to benefit from each other's cultures. This, in turn, helped to prevent the suburban exodus or "white flight" that traditionally results from a rapid influx of people of color to a predominantly white neighborhood.

Changes in all these dimensions of urban space are met and altered by people and organizations as they regenerate local attachments, local identity, and the power of place. But religious organizations are not always rebuilding place-based communities. They often look internally to the needs of members, which in turn may lead them to construct new forms of community among commuting members, perhaps based on cultural affinities. Wherever their focus, religious organizations continue to be, as they historically have been, uniquely tuned to their members' experience of the disruptive impact of urban change. It's useful to bear in mind that Nelson Algren's study of Chicago was not favored by Chicagoans because, in his assessment, "it cut too close to the bone" of economic, political, and racialist perfidy. Algren also didn't flinch from accosting "clergymen wielding two-by-fours nailed in the shape of crosses." But reporting the urban scene today in all its dimensions might help probe what Algren had in mind as he tried to get closer to what's inside Chicago's "rusty heart."

Endnotes

1. Anthony M. Orum, and Xiangming Chen. *The World of Cities: Places in Comparative and Historical Perspective.* Malden, MA: Blackwell, 2003.

2. Roger Friedland and Robert R. Alford, "Bringing Society Back in: Symbols, Practices, and Institutional Contradictions," in Walter W. Powell and Paul J. DiMaggio (eds.) *The New Institutionalism in Organizational Analysis* (Chicago: U of Chicago Press) 1991, 232, 248.

3. Siim Soot, Joseph DiJohn, and Ed Christopher, "Chicago-Area Commuting Patterns Emerging Trends" Urban Transportation Center, University of Illinois at Chicago, 28 March 2003, 8.

4. Soot, DiJohn, and Christopher, ibid.

5. Chaves, Mark. 1998. "National Congregations Study." Data File and Codebook. Tucson, Arizona: University of Arizona, Department of Sociology.

6. James Lewis, Michael Maly, Paul Kleppner and Ruth Anne Tobias, "Race and Residence in the Chicago Metropolitan Area, 1980-2000" softbound manuscript, 84.

Acknowledgement: We are grateful to Tim Moreland for his assistance in producing the maps.

CHAPTER SEVEN

RELIGION AND PLACE IN THE MIDWEST: URBAN, RURAL, AND SUBURBAN FORMS OF RELIGIOUS EXPRESSION

Rhys H. Williams

The task of writing something definitive on "urban/suburban/rural" religion is quite daunting, made all the more so by trying to focus on a region as underdefined as "the Midwest." However, both of these tasks are part of a larger theme concerned with writing about "religion and place." Place has two dimensions, a physical reality and a symbolic meaning. These are related, but distinct.

Physical reality has a number of different implications, the most obvious being geographic. Mountains, rivers, rainfall, the length of the growing season, and other features of the natural environment have shaped settlement patterns, the development of particular ways of life, and religious observations. More importantly for this essay, the physical reality of place also has a social meaning—whom one sees every day on the streets, the density of life, the time one travels to work or school, and the laws and political system one must negotiate. These are "facts of life" that one is not free to avoid, even if one does one's best to ignore them.

Physical reality also matters for social life because it becomes symbolically meaningful. The symbolic meanings are just as important as the physical reality. Symbolic meanings involve the stories about the place, its history, its people, whether the others one encounters in daily life are "like us" or "different," and the relationship between the place and the sacred. As the sociologist Nancy Eiesland has observed, "Localities matter because they are the sites of shared history and of relations of interdependence. . . ."[1] Understanding contemporary religion and place involves considering the important intersections between physical place and symbolic location. This essay offers some thoughts, as well as some empirical observations, about a triangle of concepts—the Midwest as a region, religion as a sphere of human activity, and urban-suburban-rural locations as physical and symbolic places.

The concepts and realities of urban, suburban, and rural involve locating religion in particular places and understanding how those places help produce the religion that is practiced there. The distinction among urban, suburban, and rural is fundamentally based on differences in the density of the populations that live in particular locations; by definition, urban places are the most densely settled, and rural places the least. Density matters; humans behave differently in large groups, and social encounters are more frequent and varied in densely settled places. But the social and cultural meanings of urban, suburban, and rural go well beyond the physical reality of population density. Those concepts designate particular "types" of places that have cultural, racial, and moral meanings, and even affect personal identity.

Similarly, religion in the Midwest is a product of a particular region that has particular geographic and demographic features. But more than that, the importance of the Midwest is connected to the history and meanings, as well as the physical reality, of the place. Both constructions of place—that is, the "Midwest" as a region, and urban-suburban-rural as types of locations—have shaped and continue to influence particular styles and forms of religion.

Midwestern America in History and Culture

The Midwest is particularly interesting in terms of the connection between physical reality and symbolic meaning.[2] In some important ways, those two dimensions of understanding the Midwest are in conflict. The symbolic images that resonate with the idea of the Midwest are in some respects not accurate reflections of the history and sociology of the region. For example, the states that comprise the Midwest do not have much of a "pre-U.S." European history—they were never settled colonies. Not only do they lack the cultural history of connection to the birth of American independence, but the modern European-based civilizations that emerged in the Midwest, the "America" that emerged in the region, had no European precursors to deal with. For another example, the Midwest, as a regional identity, is somewhat recent, and has been historically malleable.

For example, the Ohio River and Mississippi River valleys were once "The West." Cincinnati is still known as the "Queen City of the West," an appellation common in the city by 1820 (first appearing in print on May 4, 1819, in a newspaper article by a B. Cooke) and later reaffirmed in a poem by Henry Wadsworth Longfellow. As "The West," the region began to absorb the American myths of mobility, opportunity, and adventure that characterized the frontier in Frederick

Jackson Turner's famous thesis. While many people settled in the region, thousands passed through, in search of opportunity further on—a classic American tale. And yet, the Midwest region is currently imagined as a great location of cultural and social stability within the United States.

There is another example of tension between physical reality and symbolic meaning in the history of the Midwest's economic development. That growth was fueled by immigration and transportation, and the region became the backbone of the development of an industrial capitalist America. It became the home of some of the great industrial cities that built America's economic growth—as the examples of Chicago, Cincinnati, Cleveland, Detroit, Flint, Ft. Wayne, Milwaukee, and Toledo all attest. Further, these factory cities were places of neighborhoods full of immigrants, first German, and then Italian, Greek, Slavic, Polish, and other "second wave" ethnic immigrants from southern and eastern Europe. Still later, after the United States shut down immigration in the 1920s and southern states imposed a Jim Crow apartheid racial system, these cities absorbed hundreds of thousands of African Americans leaving the South during the Great Migration to northern industry and northern ghettos. The regional identity of a distinct "Midwest" did not really develop until after the Civil War—concurrently with the rise of industrial America.

And yet, Midwestern mythology, often associated with the phrase "the Heartland," portrays the Midwest as a place of bucolic small towns, social homogeneity, and slow-paced, pastoral life. In that sense, the Midwest and the notion of the Heartland often evokes a quasi-sacred image of America—as a place rooted to land. The sociologist David Jacobson argues that place and national identity became firmly associated with each other with the rise of the nation-state and the modern world. Belonging to a place became aligned with belonging to a people and attained a moral character as well as a social identity.

Jacobsen understands the Northwest Ordinance of 1787 as playing a pivotal role in American history in just this way. It was integral to the new American nation's expansion westward and set the stage for associations of national identity and land that resonated later in "manifest destiny" ideology. Republicanism (meaning representative government formed by free citizens) and nationhood came together to form an image of the United States as a "landed democracy."[3] Of course, that "northwest" territory in 1787 was the land that now forms the bulk of what we call the Midwest. Thus, the literal territory of the Midwest has been a crucial part of the symbolic architecture of the nation since the eighteenth century.

Along with the land, its settling, and its agricultural history, the people who now populate the Midwest also have the reputation and image of being at the center of national identity. The Midwest provided a home to countless numbers of European immigrants, especially from those northern European countries that became the assimilated backbone of white American society. The region's agricultural base, like its industrial cities, received great impetus from waves of European immigration, ranging from the Germans in the Ohio River valley to the Scandinavians on the Northern Plains. But the fact cannot be avoided that many of these immigrants to rural America were different from urban immigrants in that they were fair-skinned and Protestant.

As a result of this convergence of immigration patterns and national myths, the phrase "All-American boy" calls nothing to mind so much as the white, blond-haired, blue-eyed, small-town hero. Whether held up as cultural ideal or satirized as an emblem of provincial complacency, this symbol clings to a Midwestern identity. The social roots of this icon are not false—Midwestern states are full of small towns that are populated by the blond-haired descendants of German, English, and Scandinavian immigrants. On more than one occasion I have had visitors from the East Coast say to me, "there sure are a lot of blond people here." The symbolic significance of this representation of the Midwest is only a partial reflection of the social reality of the region, as it misses the diverse, multi-ethnic, industrialized urban spaces that also cover the region, but it is powerfully resonant in our national cultural imagination.

Further associated with the Heartland imagery is the Midwest's connection to American civil religion. Distinct from the sectarian religious commitments of particular churches or denominations, civil religious sentiment takes the nation as its sacred object and uses broadly political symbols as its religious iconography.[4] Significantly, Harry Stout has argued that the American Civil War—so important to the development of a Midwestern regional identity—also marked the birth of a widespread civil religion in the United States.[5]

Certainly there was civil religious sentiment in the Revolutionary and Early National periods. From the Massachusetts Bay colony on, many Americans saw themselves as the New Hebrews, leaving the Old World for an Edenic paradise and ready to create a New Jerusalem. But that was a vision associated with social elites, and most resonant in New England and areas with a Reformed-tradition Protestant heritage.[6] Such a vision was more controversial and less accepted in other parts of the country. Further, many in the colonies could "sit out" the War of Independence and thus the war's direct impact did not immediately permeate every strand of American society.

Not so the Civil War. The extent to which that conflict touched almost every American family was truly staggering. This in part explains its continued hold on the American popular imagination. But it was also a fertile source of religious imagery for a nation recently swept by the waves of evangelical Protestant fervor and religious vibrancy that marked the so-called Second Great Awakening, in the first half of the nineteenth century.

It was in the aftermath of the Civil War that the Midwest began to assume a distinct regional identity as the Midwest.[7] The frontier had moved, so it was no longer the West. And because of the identification with slavery and losing the war, the region was definitely not the South. After all, regiments from Illinois, Ohio, Indiana, Michigan, and the like filled the Union Army. And yet, the Ohio River valley states of Ohio, Indiana, and Illinois were not exactly the "North" if the north was to be identified with Yankees from New England, Puritan religious traditions, and colonial-era class systems.

Small farmers in the Midwest were against the expansion of slavery, as a threat to the land they might hope to one day settle. But they had little in common with the proto-industrial working classes, recent immigrants, and abolitionists who filled the ranks of eastern seaboard states and their military units. The Mason-Dixon line did not extend into the Midwest, and was thus not as salient in establishing regional identity.[8]

The post-bellum period also began the development of the Midwest's own distinct economic system. This was, almost from the beginning, a rationalized system of industrial capitalism in which economic production was performed on a large scale, by the most efficient means technologically feasible, for the purpose of generating profits (as opposed to, for example, a farming system that was aimed only at the subsistence of the farming community itself). The technology of work became more and more powered by non-animate sources, and the products that resulted from economic activity were more and more shipped off to distant markets, rather than consumed locally. As the historian William Cronon persuasively argues, in the developing Midwest the industrializing city and its agricultural feeder region developed together.[9]

At some level, one could contrast the city's development with that of the countryside, and in doing so the noise, dirt, impersonality, and money drive of cities seemed far from the changeless, personable tradition of rural life. But this misses the extent to which city and countryside were growing and developing in tandem. Cronon calls Chicago "nature's metropolis" and demonstrates that as it grew as a center of trade, transportation, livestock shipping, and industrial production, the forms of agricultural production in the fields of Illinois, Indiana, and Wisconsin changed also. Efficiency, large-scale production, and wage labor were also transforming life in the country. The transportation system that made Chicago the "hog butcher of the world" and a major city also transformed rural and small-town ways of life. Midwestern cities and their "hinterlands" grew together, knit together in an industrializing, rationalizing economic system.

It is true that some parts of the Midwest were more affected by these changes than others. Areas that did not develop major cities, such as parts of Kansas and Iowa, did not experience the same types of economic transformation, at least at the same pace. Nonetheless, what may be most distinctive about the Midwest is the fact that it was the first American region to be entirely created by rationally organized capitalism—from its cities laid out on grids, to its mechanized transportation systems (rails, ships, barges), to its large-scale agriculture built significantly on wage labor, to the eventual creation of its highway system. It is a "modern" American region, to its core.[10]

And yet, Midwestern and American cultural mythology idealizes a pastoral, pre-industrial past, a place of small towns, family farms, country churches, and a serene, neighborly way of life. The blond, fresh-faced, naïve small-town kid— just off the bus from Iowa or Wisconsin—is a staple of American fiction. If the East Coast is epitomized by great cityscapes and skylines, and the West Coast by ocean beaches and laid back lifestyles, the Midwest is a place of small town and rural homebodies. This shows up over and over in American fiction, cinema, and culture. For example, Dorothy's Kansas in *The Wizard of Oz* epitomizes "home"; Ray Kinsella's Iowa in *Field of Dreams* not only attracts baseball players (participants in the "national" pastime) from beyond the grave, it is itself sanctified ("Is this heaven? No, it's Iowa.").

Small-town rubes may be naïve to the place of comedy—as the denizens of River City, Iowa, sing with excitement at the arrival of the Wells Fargo wagon and fall for Professor Harold Hill's scam in *The Music Man*. But they also have such exemplary moral character, and are of such essential sweetness, that they reform even a professional con man. In *Hoosiers* a disgraced basketball coach, an alcoholic father, and a social misfit are all redeemed and brought back into the embrace of a small-town community. Lake Wobegon, the fictional site of Garrison Keillor's small-town Minnesota upbringing, was dubbed "America's Hometown" by *National Geographic Traveler* magazine.[11] Keillor's portraits of the town play exactly on this theme; they are sprinkled with a large share of characters and characteristics to laugh at, but the end of each Prairie Home Companion monologue reveals a sweet wisdom, woven out of community, tradition, experience, and interpersonal commitment.

While social critics may have distrusted small-town provincialism (as in Sinclair Lewis' *Babbitt* or *Main Street*) the defining imagery of the small-town Midwest is culturally central to American identity. It is white, neighborly, hardworking, and full of "traditional" values. Indeed, one might argue that the Midwest's symbolic identity and meaning as a place for small town and family helps explain why the cities of the Midwest—abandoned for the suburbs after World War II—have often struggled. As sites of industry and immigrants, cities have a history of being viewed with suspicion by their states' rural residents. Certainly, many state legislatures have had a consistent "city versus country" conflict when it comes to appropriations bills and the distribution of state governmental services. Some of this tension may also explain why many Midwestern cities continue to lose population and shrink into the classic "doughnut" pattern of suburban and exurban development.[12] While cities in other parts of industrial America have come back from their 1960s and 1970s doldrums, perhaps Midwesterners' desires to feel as though they still live in a homogeneous small town continues to fuel the region's urban sprawl and white flight.

Does this history and culture, therefore, mean that Midwestern *religion* is in some way distinct? Has the *region* shaped its *religion*, as the religious character of the people who settled and developed the area shaped the region and its identity? Some contrasts with other regions jump quickly to mind. New England had established state churches and a social elite of Reformed Calvinist clergy. The clergy were a national elite (admittedly when the nation was smaller), as well as regionally distinctive. The nineteenth century, of course, challenged their dominance with waves of Catholic and Jewish immigrants, but in their own way the Irish Catholic clergy became as publicly prominent in New England (and in American Catholicism) as the Federalist Calvinist clergy had been a half-century before.

The South had the mix of Anglican establishment churches and pietistic revivals of Methodists, Baptists, and Disciples, among others. The War of Independence dashed the former, and then the War Between the States made a pietistic Baptist religious ethos culturally hegemonic. The current American West is known for its singularly low levels of religious identification and involvement, but that region's dominant religious traditions are indeed mixed—Hispanic Catholicism, Protestantism through missionaries, Mormonism, and Native American and Asian religions.

On one hand, Midwestern religion could be seen as a microcosm of the nation itself, and as Philip Barlow points out in this volume, the Midwest's population is closer to "representative" of the nation's population than any other region. At the very least, Midwestern religion is a microcosm of how the nation would like to see itself. The Ohio River valley's first European settlement was Protestant, and generally Northern European. Some of the Mississippi River, of course, was visited and named by French explorers, but the major identity was Protestant. Those areas that made up the "western reserve" (as in northeast Ohio) had settlers from western New England, so there was a decidedly Congregationalist and generic Reformed Calvinist culture there (and, not coincidently, large numbers of liberal arts colleges that remain to this day).

The "first wave" immigration of the 1840s-60s is famous for bringing thousand of Irish Catholics to the cities of the East Coast and to Chicago. Less noticed is the large numbers of Germans, split between Catholic and Protestant, who filled the Ohio and Mississippi River valleys. Cities such as Cincinnati and Milwaukee got large numbers of German Catholics, and the beer industry they brought with them. Other German Catholics settled in rural areas—southern Indiana and Illinois have small towns such as New Baden and Germantown. The plains of the northern Midwest filled with German and Scandinavian Lutherans, bringing a social conservatism with them, but often mixed with an "economic populism" in agriculture that distrusted large businesses and the Eastern domination of the growing and increasingly integrated national economy. That influence can still be seen in Minnesota's Democratic-Farm-Labor (DFL) Party.

The last quarter of the nineteenth century saw the arrival of large numbers of Italians, Greeks, and other Eastern Europeans, most of whom were Catholic and some of whom were Jewish. The factories and neighborhoods of Cleveland, Detroit, Flint, Toledo, Chicago, Milwaukee, and the like filled with Catholics, implicitly undermining the notion of the Midwest as a Protestant area, and often explicitly challenging the dominance of Irish Catholicism in the American Church.

The twentieth century was most significant for the Great Migration of African Americans to northern factory jobs and residential ghettos, further enriching the diversity of the Protestant urban religion of the region. Finally, while the Midwest has not experienced as much of the most recent wave of immigration as have the coasts, Asian, non-Christian immigrants have begun to make their mark on the area. Similarly, Latinos are becoming a significant minority in many places in the Midwest, both in cities and, a bit more surprisingly, in many rural areas where formerly migrant agricultural labor is becoming a permanent population.

None of this should seem particularly surprising to those who know the rough outlines of the social and religious history of American immigration. And that is just the point. This story—the story of the Midwest—is often told in history textbooks and journalistic accounts as the story of the American experience. What is often seen as normative for the nation as a whole is, upon closer inspection, the Midwestern narrative. The Midwest is both distinctive—for its traditional ways, solid values, and small-town way of life—and seen as "typical." Perhaps this is not surprising for a region that once was "The West" became "The Heartland" and has never been closely or clearly defined.

To push the importance of place beyond any purported distinctiveness of the Midwest, we must ask about the influence of types of locations. Is there something distinctive about urban religion? Is the religion of rural life somehow a particular genre? And what of suburbs, perhaps the most maligned of residential locations, but a place quickly belying the stereotypes about sameness; indeed, suburbs may be too diverse to be contained much longer in a single conceptual term.

Religion and Place

Religion is intricately associated with place, in both its social dimensions and its physical settings. "Sacred space" has a literal meaning for many religious peo-

ple as geographic locations such as mountains or lakes can be objects of venera-
tion, as can the consecrated space of a building or other part of a built environment. But sites can also shape religion in that the religion practiced in a different
setting and among different people is often not the same religion it once was.
Whether religion is essentially "sited" is a question for others. But how place
matters to religion—in the form of urban, rural, and suburban Midwestern locations—is the purpose of this essay. Doctrine may stay the same over time and
space, and indeed religious traditions are by definition supposed to connect people with their pasts in what seems to be an unbroken chain. But everyday, lived
religion—religion as the myriad cultural expressions of people as they move,
grow, marry, die, and try to make sense of it all—depends crucially on place to
constitute what it is.

As illustrated in this volume in the chapter by Raymond Brady Williams, religious identity often takes on more salience for immigrants in their new homes
than it had for them at home; they use it to connect with others like themselves,
find comfort in familiar teachings and rituals of the faith, and through religion
find a way to negotiate a new land.[13] But that religious identity, while perhaps
retaining traditional elements, becomes something new. Immigrants must and do
adapt—adopting some new ways, transforming some old ways, giving new
meanings to the familiar and familiar meanings to new practices. The religion that
is actually practiced by an immigrant community is not the same social phenomenon that the immigrants knew in their countries of origin.

Nor is the religious landscape of the new location unchanged by the immigrants who settle there. Thus, the Midwest, as a region created by migrating
Europeans and then populated by later waves of immigrants from all over the
world, has long had a mix of traditional and innovative religious elements. For
example, the Catholicism that emerged in the Midwest, as Jay Dolan demonstrates in this volume, was a more "Americanized" version of the faith than what
had taken root on the East Coast, and was more open to organizational changes
and renewal movements. Midwestern Protestantism, as described here by Mark
Noll, is a mixture of denominational groups that play different roles in different
states and areas. Thus, Methodists have been both sectarian, pietistic upstarts and
establishment churches, and ethnic churches have ranged from the Great Plains
Lutherans who dominated their regions and communities to the sectarian and
world-resistant Mennonites and Amish.

The important general conclusion is that religious culture and identity have
always been influential in Midwestern public life and its regional self-under-
standing. Small-town residents often thought of church membership as identical
to social belonging, and Protestant-church membership was a sign of social and
status location. In the cities, Catholic ethnic parishes were integral to public and

personal identity—and provided some haven from a Protestant society. And in the rapidly expanding suburbs, where mobility has often ruptured many other types of social connections, the church is often the main mechanism for holding families into a semblance of community life. These religious patterns are shaped by region, and then again shaped by whether they exist in city, country, or in-between. Let's examine the latter dynamics in more detail.

Urban Religion

What is "urban religion"? Obviously, the term means more than just the religion that happens in urban settings; rather this is a consideration of whether urban religion is a particular genre of religious phenomenon, one that brings with it specific challenges and responses. What produces urban religion? Is there something about the city itself that is unique and thus creates something religiously different? In the United States, and this may be particularly true of the Midwest, the city has been the physical space and the social setting where America has had to confront the world.

There are obvious racial dimensions to this, as there has been some historic hostility to cities in American society, tied in part to cities being the first homes for many new immigrants, particularly those with darker skin—whether from Italy, African Americans from Mississippi, or now those from India or Mexico. Along with concentrated—and hence visible—minority populations, cities have also been places where one could see easily social problems such as personal vice and poverty. Because of these qualities, many have found cities to be challenges to the old Puritan notion of the New World as a potential new Eden, a garden of pastoral perfection safe from the polluting and threatening influences of "the world." As the historian Robert Orsi notes in the introduction to *Gods of the City*, cities have often been the "mirror" of the characteristics of "traditional" America—white, Protestant, heterosexual, virtuous, agrarian.[14] It is worth noting, however, that many of the recent books about "urban religion," whether Orsi's collection or others, focus most of their attention on the great cities of the East Coast, rather than the Midwest.[15] The Heartland retains an aura of the pastoral.[16]

However, the image of Protestantism as rural and small-town, even in the Midwest, contrasts with much of the reality of its social history. Midwestern cities were as likely to be dominated by a grand First Presbyterian Church as were many small towns. James Lewis has argued, using Gary, Indiana, as the case-study example, that in many ways twentieth-century Protestantism was indeed "at home in the city."[17] Meanwhile, German Catholic small towns were common in the Ohio River valley. Finally, it is important to remember that the social dynamic involved was not just a Protestant small-town America vs. a Catholic and Jewish city. Beyond the demographic fact that rural Catholics and urban

Protestants existed, the stereotypical contrast between a city and the country only took on a religious cast because it was in the cities where Protestants first lost their majority status and were challenged socially and politically.

Similarly, it is important to remember that people who exist easily in the city—those very immigrant and migrating people that form urban populations—had to confront an intense religious diversity. Urban life meant that one had to encounter the religious "other," whether that meant Catholics and Jews in the 1890s or Muslims, Sikhs, and Hindus in the 1990s. Even different ethnic groups within the same religious tradition had to negotiate a type of understanding, as the tensions among Irish, Italian, and Polish Catholics, or between German and Russian Jews, attest. No matter how distinct one considers oneself, and how many symbolic barriers one creates between one's in-group and others, on city streets one must see others every day and decide on a practical response to them. It may be that the response is not particularly "religious" in that groups largely ignore each other and rule out any possible challenge to the idea that one's religion is the one true faith. But the physical reality is that one must deal with "others."

Thus, a city is both a physical space that mandates encounters and a social space that makes total withdrawal into purity impossible and may emphasize the need for cultural and religious distinction. In Midwestern cities, as a general rule, the demographic fact of religious diversity eventually became expressed in the cultural value of religious "pluralism." Civil religious celebrations of freedom of religion—after all, many immigrants did come to the United States in search of religious freedom—combined with a political culture of liberalism to create a public expression of tolerance.

While ethnic and religious neighborhoods abounded, American mobility also meant that there were many opportunities for exposure and interaction with others. To be sure, discrimination and prejudice that has existed and was usually pointed at Catholics and Jews, and more lately at non-Christians such as Muslims or Sikhs. But religious diversity has continued to increase in the nation, and a public culture of celebrating pluralism is generally ascendant. Pogroms never developed in the Midwest, and particularly compared to American racial dynamics, the region's capacity to handle religious diversity is notable.

Thus, *pluralism* and *density* have produced the necessity of a religious response and the need to confront the implicit challenge to truth that the existence of others provokes. One result is that religious people have recognized that at least in practical terms they do not, alone, have a monopoly on truth. For some groups, the city has become a "mission" field in which one can convert nonbelievers; the Moody Bible Institute in Chicago is perhaps the most famous example. Nonetheless, pluralism and density interact to touch all those involved.

Everyone must respond and formulate an orientation to that response in interaction. Nothing can remain unchanged—or "pure"—after it has confronted and then developed alongside its "other."

In the second half of the twentieth century, of course, American cities began losing population with the creation of the suburbs, a story that will be told in more detail below. What is notable at this point is that many Midwestern cities, unlike those in the Sun Belt or many Eastern urban places, continue to lose population, or are not growing significantly. Metropolitan areas continue to grow, but not the central cities.

For example, while the greater-Cincinnati area added 200,000 residents between 1980 and 2000, the city itself lost 54,000. The Milwaukee area gained about 115,000 people, while the city lost 33,000. The corresponding numbers for Detroit are 100,000 and 300,000. Cleveland's central city lost 105,000 people in those two decades as the metro area population remained steady.

Part of this is tied to the continuing decline of industrial manufacturing in the American economy. These cities all grew in the nineteenth century on the backs of their factories. They continue to lose populations as that form of employment is not fully replaced. And yet, metro areas grow, suburbs sprawl, and small towns are increasingly hard places to make a living. The economic imperative for living near concentrated populations continues (the number of people who can commute electronically is still small), but in the Midwest that is increasingly not in the urban center.

There is a definite racial component to the continued population shift between cities and suburbs. Between 1980 and 2000, the non-Hispanic white population of Cincinnati declined from 65 percent of the central city to 53 percent. Milwaukee's white population was 73 percent of the city; it is now 49 percent. Detroit's non-Hispanic white population was cut in half, from 40 to 20 percent of the city, while Cleveland's went from 57 to 45 percent. The "white flight" phenomenon has religious implications. Residential expansion and the church building projects that go with them are less possible in central cities, where land is often more expensive, has existing structures, and has many zoning and building codes. Further, the poor and immigrant communities that often live in central cities may have fewer resources to put into construction. And the young urban professionals and artistic-bohemian populations that continue to live in urban centers are the least likely groups to be regular churchgoers.

Thus, urban religion has become "entrepreneurial" because it is least able to rely on tradition, ingrained memberships and behaviors, and organizational loyalty among members. Urban religion is often "storefront" religion, begun by a charismatic organizer, working within an ethnic population or a particular neighborhood. This type of religious scene is highly competitive and not able to rely on long-standing religious identification and affiliation patterns. Further, urban religion becomes syncretic as religious entrepreneurs mix doctrines, practices, and symbols from a variety of sources, and respond to the social and cultural pluralism of its setting. Again, pluralism and density produce a different style of religious experience—a melding of traditions that often does not become fully its own tradition.

Suburban Religion

If urban and rural are the subjects of story, imagery, and illusion, the very concept of the "suburb" is fully shrouded in myth. A recent creation, at least culturally, the suburb as we think of it today is a post-World War II phenomenon. Subdivisions fueled by G.I. Bill loans, widespread access to automobiles, and the developing highway system made them physically possible. As a symbol of social mobility and material success, as well as racial homogeneity and political conservatism, the suburbs became culturally significant. It is important to remember how rapid suburban development was. In 1930, two-thirds of the Americans who lived in metropolitan areas lived in the central city. By 1970 the majority of metropolitan residents were suburbanites—and for the first time in American history, there were more people in suburbs than in either central cities or non-metropolitan areas.[18]

Suburban religion grew with suburban populations, in both numbers and, according to many, influence. After two decades of Depression and war, there was a great deal of "pent-up demand" in the church-building field, just as there was in housing. With the opening of suburban vistas—and the inexpensive farmland that was being gobbled up around major cities—churches went up as rapidly as housing subdivisions.[19] The main centers of suburban growth were the Northeast corridor from Boston to Washington, the far-West cities of Los Angeles and San Francisco, and the industrial cities of the Midwest.

Two stories about this suburbanization are important for American religion. First, the exodus to the suburbs and the post-war prosperity mark the major period of the "mainstreaming" of American Catholics. White Catholics were moving out of urban ethnic enclaves, out of the tightly knit parish structure, and becoming more homogenized into American culture and society.

That "homogenization" had a definite Protestant cast to it. Cities such as Cincinnati and Milwaukee had significant Catholic populations, of course. But while the cities were Catholic, the imprimatur of the Church did not mark the Midwest region's identity as was true for the Boston-to-Philadelphia Eastern seaboard. As Jay Dolan observes, the Midwest was never the Catholic heartland. The Catholic cities of the Midwest were often "political islands" in states where the state capital was a medium-sized town, surrounded by Protestant small towns and rural counties, and located in the geographic, rather than population, center of the state.[20] Thus, Catholics' moves into the suburbs, while making them more mainstream, also meant that they were losing many of the characteristic qualities of American Catholicism such as the ethnic parish.[21] And in turn, cities lost more of their political influences in state legislatures.

Suburbanization lessened the Catholic city-Protestant town divide, but ironically meant that generic Protestantism and middle-class American culture were becoming ever more closely identified. The religious revival of the 1950s—driven largely by the building boom in the suburbs—was producing a generic denominational Protestantism and a "Protestantized" Catholicism. While the small town of the mythological Heartland—with its Methodist, Lutheran, Presbyterian, and Baptist churches—was being swallowed by metropolitan sprawl, it was possible to see the myth recreated in the suburbs of Midwestern cities.

Almost simultaneously with their growth, suburbs began to be regularly skewered for their homogeneity and lack of social diversity, their cultural blandness, their self-satisfied complacency, their lack of history, and their association with racial exclusion. Several works to this effect, such as Kenneth Jackson's classic *The Crabgrass Frontier*,[22] or William H. Whyte's *The Organization Man*,[23] excoriated the whole of suburban society, in particular linking it to American patterns of racism and the conformism that helped produce the McCarthy era. Other critiques focused specifically on the religion of the suburbs, most notably Gibson Winter's *The Suburban Captivity of the Churches*,[24] and Peter Berger's *The Noise of Solemn Assemblies*.[25] As James Hudnut-Beumler notes, this literature formed a type of "suburban jeremiad" that criticized suburban churches for their accommodation of middle-class worldly values and the loss of any sense of prophetic voice.[26] As it was suburban religion that was being criticized for becoming too comfortable with secular culture, it was Protestantism that was particularly subject to critique. As noted, Protestantism, with its religious style was the dominant religion—it was most representative of and aligned with the "religion of the American Way of Life" that Will Herberg identified.[27] To the extent Catholicism and Judaism were forming parts of this American amalgam, they were adapting more to Protestantism than it was to them. Protestantism was, particularly in the suburbs of the Midwest, "the establishment."

The cultural critiques of suburban life and suburban religion, however, did not stop Americans from moving to them. One stereotype about suburban growth is that it involved "white flight" from the central cities. As with many stereotypes, there is more than a grain of truth to that. A suburban ring of white populations around increasingly minority central cities is a staple form, particularly in the Midwest. And yet, class and economic resources have driven suburban growth even among minority groups.

As African Americans and immigrant groups achieve the economic means to join the suburban flight, they often do so. Indeed, in many places now, newly arriving immigrants—especially those with education and white-collar jobs such as Indians or Koreans—are moving directly to the suburbs, without the generational transition of living in a city neighborhood "port of entry" for a generation or two. Between 1980 and 2000 the percentage of non-Hispanic whites in many Midwestern suburban areas decreased. Often the decrease was not large—for example, Cincinnati's suburban areas went from 95 percent white to 91 percent, while Cleveland went from 92 percent to 86 percent and Detroit from 94 percent to 86 percent. Nonetheless, suburban populations are slowly diversifying.

As a result, the concept of "suburb" is now overly unified. Some commentators speak of "inner-ring" suburbs versus "exurbs." There are suburbs that have their own commercial centers—and the accompanying employment opportunities—and these stand in particular distinction to those areas that are only residential subdivisions. Older suburbs often have the infrastructural challenges of aging roads, bridges, and sewers, while the sprawl suburbs on the metropolitan fringe battle a growing population that overwhelms the two-lane roads that originally held sparse traffic. In any case, suburbs vary by class, race, density, and religious identity.

For all the caricatures of the suburbs, however, and perhaps in keeping with their actual diversity, scholars have not found a definable suburban "ideology." Whereas the city is celebrated for its diversity, culture, and excitement, the small town is revered for its serenity, neighborliness, and security. The suburbanites that the sociologist David Hummon interviewed drew on parts of both these descriptions to say why they valued suburbs. They viewed their town as having "the best of both worlds"—things to do without the dirt and hectic pace of the city and domestic security, but without the monotony said to be associated with the small town. In other words, the suburban ideology is one of contrasts—what suburbs are *not*.[28]

As suburbs continue to expand into what are now called exurbs, the aura of—and nostalgia for—the small town continues to move with them. And yet, subdivision suburbs are without the community institutions that were the heart of small-town life. One religious response to that situation is the rise of the "megachurch." These churches, often with several thousand members, form their own communities, with an internal organizational division among varying interest and demographic groups. They often provide a sense of belonging for members, but often do so through a certain amount of social homogeneity. And significantly, they do not necessarily draw on only a local population—they draw members from a more decentralized geographic area that minimizes the number of non-church contacts members can have with each other.

Nancy Eiesland found that many of the desires that drew people to the exurban area she studied—the desire for a slower lifestyle and more integrated community—are undermined by the large numbers of people moving out to seek those very qualities. The influx of population overwhelms roads, schools, and sewers. She concludes, "The community connections and sense of place that drew many exurban newcomers . . are increasingly strained by the increasing migration to ever more distant exurbs."[29]

Rural Religion

As much of this essay has been premised on an examination of a cultural myth of the pastoral Protestant Heartland, it is time to examine midwestern rural religion as a major part of that myth. There is, of course, some basis in sociological and historical fact to the myth. Midwestern small towns and rural areas have historically been more Protestant, more ethnically and racially homogeneous, and more socially and culturally conservative than the Midwest's cities. They have been bastions of Republican party strength from the beginning of that party—first supporting its anti-slavery platforms, then playing important roles in the temperance movement and voting for prohibitionist policies and candidates; both the Women's Christian Temperance Union and the Anti-Saloon League had Midwestern origins. The rural Midwest has also been generally pro-business and often animated, as with its temperance concerns, by anti-Catholic prejudice and suspicion of the alliance among ethnic Catholics, labor unions, and the Democratic Party.[30] The contemporary Christian Right's conservative social-issues agenda has a great deal of support in the rural Midwest, and in many states the current Christian Right has had electoral success and has notable achievements in defining the terms of public political debate.[31]

But that success and the conservatism it implies is not uniform. As noted above, Minnesota and Wisconsin have had a religiously based economic populism since the nineteenth century. And the conservatism of many Midwestern rural populations has been as suspicious of capitalist economic institutions and materialist cultural values as it has been wary of libertarian social attitudes. Indeed, much of the Midwest has been termed to have a "moralistic" political culture.[32] In such a culture there is a willingness—even a perceived religious duty—to use community power to intervene in private lives for the sake of the public good or civic well-being.

The raw profit motive, driven by capitalist efficiency and resting on cultural individualism, was seen by many to be as much a threat to their chosen way of life as were the gender, racial, and cultural changes of the 1960s. This "common good moralism" or what Garrison Keillor once called in a Lake Wobegon monologue "small-town socialism" emerged in large part from the communalist religious commitments of Lutherans, Catholics, Mennonites, and Amish. The emphasis on building a good community and supporting its institutions, rather than a more limited pietist focus on individual salvation, separates the traditional religious and social conservatism of the rural Midwest from more recent versions of those ideologies that are often found in the expanding suburbs.[33]

An excellent example of the source of this cultural ethos, and its changes and challenges, is in the anthropologist Sonya Salamon's studies of farming communities in Illinois. She characterizes the communities she studied as being either "German yeoman" or "Yankee entrepreneur."[34] While these are admittedly broad types, they do reveal an important sociological difference.

German yeoman communities represent ethnically and religiously homogenous—in this case German Lutheran and Catholic—small towns and their surrounding farms. The economic and social emphasis was on the family farm, extended kinship networks, and the church as the center of community life. The people who formed these communities had great commitment to the community and its public good, and thus were willing to tax themselves (both financially and in terms of time and energy) in order to assure the community's survival and well-being.

Yankee entrepreneur communities, on the other hand, were composed of Anglo-American Protestants (generally migrating to the Midwest from the eastern United States), who worked family farms but were more oriented to commerce and less likely to pass the farm through multiple generations of the family. The economic life of the towns was oriented outward toward commerce rather than inward toward community sustenance. In Yankee towns, there were usually several Protestant churches (most often Methodist and Baptist) that either competed for members or were stratified by social status within the town. Thus, the religious life of the community tended to be a source of competition rather than cohesion.

The fate of these two different types of communities varied as farming and small towns became more precarious economically in the 1980s and 1990s. Farming was shrinking as an occupation, thus those moving off farms and out of small towns were not always being replaced. This meant that the ethnic homogeneity of German yeoman communities was not being diluted. They remained solidly German—Lutheran or Catholic—and relatively independent as communities. Further, as it was younger people moving out, the communities were getting older as well. However, given the ethnic and religious solidarity of the communities, combined with the demographic reality that older people are more consistent voters, these rural Midwestern areas often retained much of their political clout.

Yankee communities, on the other hand, were more diverse and mobile, and have had a harder time with the decline in farming and small businesses. With less commitment to farming as a family heritage, and less ability to rely on central institutions such as churches for community cohesion, more families left the farm and the community. Many of these small towns have kept a fairly stable population because of an influx of new residents who work in nearby cities but want a small-town lifestyle or appreciate the available housing values. The dense network of overlapping relationships has become weakened, and the very sense of community and identity itself has declined. The community's churches often suffer in these towns, as newcomers are likely to also attend "magnet" or "niche" churches in other places.[35] Politically, these types of rural areas have often become more like the outer suburbs and exurbs of metropolitan areas.

Perhaps ironically, the decline of rural churches and their communities has often led to an outburst of organizational innovation within the churches. Without the population or resources to maintain the church as it once was—particularly since many small-town churches have substantial brick or stone physical structures—other arrangements are tried. Church mergers, shared pastorates, increasing use of laity in pastoral roles, and increasing use of women clergy and women in other authoritative roles, have been common in rural areas. Thus, the locations that often have the most traditionalism are often sites for institutional innovation.

Region, Place, and Public Religion in the Midwest

This essay has provided ample reason to recognize how difficult it is to say something definitive about religion and place in a region as diffuse as the Midwest. Generalizations have been followed by qualifications; claims to essential characteristics and patterns have been followed by pointing out the diversity and exceptions that also make up the region. So, what to say in conclusion about region, place, and religion in the Midwest?

The Midwest continues in many ways to define America. But it may do so culturally and symbolically now more than in terms of politics, economics, or demographics. "Will it play in Peoria?" is an all-purpose way to think of a large, loosely defined, white, more or less middle-class, cultural sensibility. The myths of the Heartland as true America continue to permeate films, TV, and political and commercial marketing. National TV news anchors, no matter where they come from, cultivate a flat Midwestern accent in their voices.

And yet, the center of the American economy has moved from the farms and steel cities of the Midwest to the post-industrial knowledge industries of the coasts. The railroads, which opened up the Midwest to population, and provided the jobs and infrastructure projects that pushed west, have succumbed to air travel, so that many Americans only see the Midwest from 35,000 feet.

Politically, the Midwest is not as essential as it once was either. While Ohio, Michigan, and Illinois are often portrayed as key battleground states in national elections, more attention goes to California, Florida, Texas, and the Sun Belt. Classic Midwestern political issues, such as temperance, are historical memories.

There hasn't been an elected President from the Midwest since Dwight Eisenhower, who was also a national military hero. Perhaps significantly, Eisenhower was also famous for his endorsement of public religion in American life, albeit a generic religion. He was reported to have said something on the order of, "our political system makes no sense without religion, and I don't care what religion it is." While derided by some, it seems like a perfect representation of Herberg's reputed "religion of the American Way of Life." Eisenhower himself was baptized only late in life, and seemed to have chosen his Episcopalian identification for convenience and its consistency with his social status. Indeed, how many actually know that Eisenhower is buried in Kansas? He was a national property, and his low-key, difficult-to-characterize, Midwestern personality seems perfectly suited to the region—its defining characteristic is its "typicalness."

This, it seems to me, is the Midwest in contemporary American public life and religion. It is a region of tensions and cultural contradictions. A place of tradition and innovation. A region marked by moral conservatism, but one that has been centered on community welfare, with strong labor union and populist traditions. It is tempting to think that the Midwest's time has passed, that its era of influence was from the turn of the century until the 1960s. But that would be to underestimate the power of cultural understandings and collective myths. The Midwest was the region in which the modern United States was built, from the ground up. And it continues to resonate in our founding stories, our public religious culture, and our national life.

Endnotes

1. Nancy L. Eiesland, *A Particular Place: Urban Restructuring and Religious Ecology in a Southern Exurb.* New Brunswick, New Jersey: Rutgers University Press, 2000, 204.

2. Perhaps a "full disclosure" note is in order here. I have lived at some point in my life in Indiana, Illinois, Missouri, and Ohio. But I have also lived in Colorado, New Mexico, Florida, Massachusetts, and Connecticut. Thus, I have direct experience as a Midwesterner, but have also encountered others' interpretations and attempts to understand the region from the outside.

3. David Jacobson, *Place and Belonging in America.* Baltimore, Maryland: Johns Hopkins University Press, 2002.

4. See N.J. Demerath III and Rhys H. Williams, "Civil Religion in an Uncivil Society," *The Annals of the American Academy of Political and Social Sciences,* 480 (July 1985), pp. 154-166; and Rhys H. Williams and Susan M. Alexander, "Religious Rhetoric in American Populism: Civil Religion as Movement Ideology," *Journal for the Scientific Study of Religion* 33 (March 1994), 1-15.

5. Harry S. Stout, "Baptism in Blood: The Civil War and the Creation of an American Civil Religion." *Books & Culture* Vol. 9, No. 4 (July/August 2003), 16.

6. See, for example, David G. Hackett, "The Social Origins of Nationalism: Albany, New York 1754-1835," *Journal of Social History* 21 (1988), 660-682; or Nathan O. Hatch, *The Sacred Cause of Liberty*. New Haven, Connecticut: Yale University Press, 1977.

7. See the analysis of the development of regional identity in Christopher Phillips, *Missouri's Confederate: Claiborne Fox Jackson and the Creation of Southern Identity in the Border West*. Columbia: University of Missouri Press, 2000.

8. Elizabeth Lynn makes the observation that for people in Midwestern states such as Indiana or Illinois, the "Mason-Dixon" line is always described as "about five miles south" of wherever they happen to be (personal communication). This accurately reflects the extent to which the southern parts of those states had considerable Southern sentiment (and often large-scale agricultural systems as an economic base). But more significantly, she notes, it is a way of people identifying themselves as "not south of Mason-Dixon" as opposed to identifying as northerners.

9. William Cronon, *Nature's Metropolis: Chicago and the Great West*. New York: W.W. Norton & Co., 1991.

10. Andrew Cayton and Peter Onuf argue that a material-capitalist ethos of bourgeois values was from the beginning characteristic of the settlers of the Old Northwest. Further, at least in part because of this, many of the Yankee entrepreneurs who settled the region thought of middle-class, commercial capitalist culture and American culture as synonymous. See Andrew R.L. Cayton and Peter S. Onuf, *The Midwest and the Nation: Rethinking the History of an American Region*. Bloomington: Indiana University Press, 1990.

11. "America's Hometown," *National Geographic Traveler*, July/August 1998, pp. 62-72.

12. Bruce Katz and Robert E. Lang, eds., *Redefining Urban and Suburban America: Evidence from Census 2000*, volume 1. Washington, D.C.: Brookings Institution Press, 2003.

13. See R. Stephen Warner and Judith Wittner, eds., *Gatherings in Diaspora*. Philadelphia: Temple University Press, 1998.

14. Robert Orsi, ed. *Gods of the City: Religion and the American Urban Landscape*. Bloomington: Indiana University Press, 1999, 5.

15. See also, John M. Giggie and Diane Winston, eds. *Faith in the Market: Religion and the Rise of Urban Commercial Culture*. New Brunswick, New Jersey: Rutgers University Press, 2002; Gerald Gamm, *Urban Exodus: Why the Jews Left Boston and the Catholics Stayed*, Cambridge: Harvard University Press, 1999; Tony Carnes and Anna Karpathakis, eds., *New York Glory: Religions in the City*. New York: New York University Press, 2001. An exception, of course, is Lowell W. Livezey, ed. *Public Religion and Urban Transformation: Faith in the City*, New York: New York University Press, 2000, which uses Chicago as its site.

16. This cultural association is revealed in a personal anecdote. As I was leaving the East Coast after graduate school, a professor told me, "you aren't moving to the Midwest, you are moving to Chicago." The region's largest and most influential city was thought not to really be a part of the region itself.

17. James W. Lewis, *The Protestant Experience in Gary, Indiana, 1906-1975: At Home in the City*, Knoxville: University of Tennessee Press, 1992.

18. David M. Hummon, *Commonplaces: Community Ideology and Identity in American Culture*. Albany: State University of New York Press, 1990, 95.

19. See the analysis in Robert Wuthnow, *The Restructuring of American Religion: Society and Faith Since World War II*. Princeton, New Jersey: Princeton University Press, 1988.

20. I thank Bronwyn Williams, at one time a reporter for the *Milwaukee Journal*, for this observation, and the political islands metaphor.

21. While historian John McGreevy shows that there was a great deal of conflict around the shifting boundaries of parishes and ethnoracial neighborhoods, it is undeniable that the second half of the twentieth century saw a significant decrease in ethnic consciousness among American Catholics and parishes. See John T. McGreevy, *Parish Boundaries: The Catholic Encounter with Race in the Twentieth Century Urban North*. Chicago: University of Chicago Press, 1996.

22. Kenneth T. Jackson, *The Crabgrass Frontier: The Suburbanization of the United States*. New York: Oxford University Press, 1985.

23. William H. Whyte, Jr. *The Organization Man* (Garden City, New York: Doubleday Anchor Books, 1956).

24. Gibson Winter, *The Suburban Captivity of the Churches: An Analysis of Protestant Responsibility in the Expanding Metropolis*, Garden City, New York: Doubleday, 1961.

25. Peter L. Berger, *The Noise of Solemn Assemblies: Christian Commitment and the Religious Establishment in America*, Garden City, New York: Doubleday, 1961.

26. James Hudnut-Beumler, *Looking for God in the Suburbs: The Religion of the American Dream and its Critics, 1945-1965*. New Brunswick, New Jersey: Rutgers University Press, 1994.

27. Will Herberg, *Protestant-Catholic-Jew*. Garden City, New York: Anchor Books, 1955.

28. David M. Hummon, *Commonplaces: Community Ideology and Identity in American Culture*. Albany: State University of New York Press, 1990.

29. Nancy L. Eiesland, *A Particular Place: Urban Restructuring and Religious Ecology in a Southern Exurb*. New Brunswick, New Jersey: Rutgers University Press, 2000, 209.

30. See, for example, Peter Williams, "Ohio: The One and the Many." *Journal for the Scientific Study of Religion* 30 (December 1991), 526-31.

31. See John C. Green, Mark J. Rozell, and Clyde Wilcox, eds., *The Christian Right's Long Political March* (forthcoming).

32. See Daniel J. Elazar, *American Federalism*, 2nd ed. New York: Thomas Y. Crowell, Harper and Row, 1972.

33. See, for example, Herve Varenne, *Americans Together: Structured Diversity in a Midwestern Town*. New York: Teacher's College Press, Columbia University, 1977. While Varenne finds much attachment to the contemporary value of individualism and individual freedom, it is tempered by and interpreted through a morality that holds community, togetherness, and individual moral duty in equally high regard.

34. Sonya Salamon, *Prairie Patrimony: Family, Farming, and Community in the Midwest*. Chapel Hill: University of North Carolina Press, 1992. See also, Sonya Salamon, "The Rural People of the Midwest." 352-365 in Emery N. Castle, ed. *The Changing American Countryside: Rural People and Places*. Lawrence: University Press of Kansas, 1995.

35. See Nancy Tatom Ammerman, *Congregation and Community*. New Brunswick, New Jersey: Rutgers University Press, 1997, for a comprehensive study of the fate of congregations in changing communities.

CHAPTER EIGHT

THE MIDWEST: CONCLUSION

Peter W. Williams

The Midwest, as has often been asserted in this volume and in many others, is more of a construct than a firm social or political reality. In the national media, anchored on either coast, it is usually presented as "flyover country," a rather dull place compared with the allegedly vibrant urban culture of the two coasts. As such, it is the stuff out of which sitcoms are frequently made: "WKRP in Cincinnati," "The Drew Carey Show," "Third Rock from the Sun," and, in at least one memorable version, "The Mary Tyler Moore Show," which is still celebrated in downtown Minneapolis with a statue of fictive newscaster Mary Richards's tossing her hat jubilantly into the air. As a counterpoint, it has also been the setting for (relatively) high drama, as in the long-running and phenomenally successful "E.R.," set in Chicago—as was its shorter-running rival, "Chicago Hope." The wealthy suburbs of urban centers such as Chicago and Detroit have been nominal backdrops for films such as "Traffic" and "The Virgin Suicides" but, as in most of the Midwest-based television programs, little distinctive by way of social and cultural backdrop emerges here. In most of these endeavors, the Midwest seems to be little but a synonym for "Mid-America," which, whether in its upper-middle-class or blue-collar versions, emerges as a generic—and uninspiring—concept at best.

These stereotypes, like many others, do contain some grains of truth. As the historians Andrew Cayton and Peter Onuf have demonstrated, the region's nineteenth-century origins as a commerce-oriented region were buttressed by a history-denying and region-negating ideology that saw the Midwest as an escape from the past that weighed down older regions of the nation, such as New England and the South, with inhibitors of progress.[1] The Midwest was burdened neither with Puritanism nor slavery; rather, it was to be a uniquely American place where all sorts of folk could settle for the main purpose and pleasure of that all-American preoccupation, the making of money. A society would emerge that was rational, orderly, well-settled, and not much concerned with social causes other than those that seemed conducive to the achievement of commercial success for the enterprising. The Midwest, in other words, was to be not just another American region, but a prototype for a nation in which the concept of region would become irrelevant, as a commerce-friendly standardization became a universal norm. Similarly, the Ohio- and Kentucky-based Restoration movement within early nineteenth-century Protestantism was premised on a denial of the denominational creedalism they saw as separating Christians of the day on issues of human rather than biblical origin, and thus emerged as a sort of anti-denomination. So also did the prophets of the Midwest see their foundation as an anti-region, as rooted in entrepreneurial capitalism as the Restorationists were committed to the Bible alone and unadorned.

Both the boundaries and whatever essence the phenomenon of the Midwest may possess are thus elusive, partly by design and partly through the lack of any political institutions that could provide some parameters for the task of definition. The South, for example, is generally defined as consisting of the 11 states that seceded to form the Confederacy during the Civil War, together with the border states in which slavery was also institutionalized. The Midwest has no such history, other than, perhaps, the claim that its constituent states did *not* support slavery—a claim it shared with many other states to its east and west. Its people have not always, or even usually, voted as a predictable bloc, since those of its states that have strong urban populations have not always identified with the interests of those that are agriculturally based.

This divergence in voting patterns suggests that the notion of a monolithic "Midwest" is politically not very helpful, as witnessed in the regional division between "blue" (Democratic) and "red" (Republican) states on the electoral maps used by broadcasters during the 2000 presidential contest. What this split does, perhaps, suggest is that two of the region's economic bedrocks—agriculture and heavy industry—have correlated in the past and, to some extent, continue in the present to correlate with distinctive political cultures. Even this generalization is to some extent an oversimplification, however; the complex ethnic and religious strains that undergird these "blue" and "red" political camps do not lend themselves to easy correlations.

If we are to say anything meaningful about the Midwest as a region, we need to:

1. begin with some broad historical sketches of basic regional themes;

2. take a look at the emergence of cultural and religious pluralism in the region as a distinctive regional characteristic; and

3. see how these themes have resulted in a distinctive regional religious and civic culture by the beginning of the twenty-first century.

Some Broad Themes

If the lack of a sense of history is characteristically American, then the Midwest may have some claim to being a distinctively *American* region. Although skirmishes between Anglo-Americans and the French and native peoples certainly took place during the late colonial era and into the early decades of the nineteenth century, the society that emerged as the latter century progressed owed little consciously to its regional predecessors. Although a few pockets of descendants of early French settlers can be found in places along the Mississippi, the most lasting evidence of a Francophone past can be found in the mispronounced place names that range from Detroit to Des Moines to St. Louis. (A shibboleth for detecting true Detroiters is to ask how they pronounce the name of one of that city's major arteries, "Gratiot."[2]) Similarly, at least to the east of the Mississippi River, living evidence of the once-abundant aboriginal dwellers in the region are few and far between, while the residence patterns of those now living further west usually represent the results of enforced resettlement during the nineteenth century.

What the French and native peoples had in common was the venerable notion that religious and socio-political identity were, and were supposed to be, coextensive, although they enacted this notion in very different ways. The English-speaking colonists to whom they gradually yielded, however, had already rejected this idea in both theory and practice. Although the British monarchy had made some attempts among the Atlantic colonies to impose the Church of England as the established church of its overseas colonies as well, this effort had failed nearly universally by the time of the Revolution, and the threat of its being realized more fully had actually provided fuel for the insurrectionary flames. Interestingly, the guarantees of religious liberty enshrined in the First Amendment to the U.S. Constitution for the entire nation had been anticipated in the Northwest Ordinance, enacted four years prior to the Bill of Rights as a governmental charter for that region to the west that would eventually constitute a major part of what would be called the Midwest. Unlike the original colonies, an "establishment of religion" had never been known in this emergent region, nor had there been enough of a colonial European-American presence to have resulted even in an informal religious hegemony. The result was a virtual *tabula rasa*, a blank slate on which any number of forms of individual and collective religiosity might be inscribed, as long as none tried to impinge on the rights of its neighbors. If religious freedom and pluralism can be taken as hallmarks of a distinctively American ethos, then the Midwest came into being even before the nation itself as a political incarnation of this new order of things.

Another broad motif of American religious history that is relevant to the emergence of a distinctively regional ethos is the related notion of the *voluntary principle,* or in a more American vernacular form, *voluntarism.* The federal government, and before too many years all of the state governments, were forbidden by fundamental law from either promoting or harassing particular religions. Those religious institutions that had in their Old World incarnations depended on the state for financial support, enforced attendance, and the elimination of competition now had to look to their own resources for survival. As Lyman Beecher—the Connecticut Congregationalist who went on to become president of Presbyterian Lane Seminary in Cincinnati—was to acknowledge, this ban on the establishment of religion by the government was to prove "the best thing that ever happened to the state of Connecticut." The same can be said, presumably, of Ohio and the other states of the Midwest, although the latter had never known the religious establishments that had prevailed in colonial Connecticut and other colonies of New England and the tidewater South.[3]

Beecher's fraternal denominational families, the Congregationalists and Presbyterians, approached the challenge of the western frontier in 1801 with an innovative arrangement brokered by Jonathan Edwards, Jr., the son of the Massachusetts evangelist and theologian of the Great Awakening of the 1740s. In the heady atmosphere of what Beecher and his confreres regarded as a Second Great Awakening, the "Plan of Union" ensured that these two groups of British Calvinist stock would avoid redundancy and competition in their attempted evangelization of the frontier by refraining from building a church of one denomination within five miles of that of the other, and by enabling clergy of either group to minister to one another's congregation.

The problem for both of these denominations, however, was that, like the Episcopalians, they were so wedded to such conventions as an educated ministry and a formal order of public worship—both having an appeal primarily to the "better" classes—that they believed they could easily reach out to the rough and ready sorts attracted by the promise of frontier life. As Mark Noll points out in his essay in this volume, it was, instead, the emergent Methodists who were best equipped to thrive in a region where settlers were scattered, higher education and wealth in short supply, and denominational allegiance not to be taken for granted.

The "circuit riders" who rode themselves into exhaustion and early deaths were remarkably effective in spreading an interpretation of Christianity that emphasized not doctrine but direct experience of divine grace. These dedicated, if not highly educated, folk were most adept at devising new techniques of evangelization and organization that could reach the people of the frontier quite literally where they were. The emphasis on knowledge acquired through direct experience, a pragmatic flexibility in favoring effectiveness over tradition, and a skepticism about the value of formal education, were the religious counterparts of the ethos that would later empower Midwestern Anglo Protestants such as Thomas

Edison, Henry Ford, and Wilbur and Orville Wright in their quests for personal fortune attained through hands-on experience, innovation, and disciplined individual effort.

Despite this diffuse Methodist ethos, another theme of this foundational period dominated by the spread of evangelical Protestantism from east to west was the importance of education. T. Scott Miyakawa pointed out some time ago that a variety of Protestant denominations spearheaded early efforts on the Midwestern frontier towards the establishment of civic, and especially educational, institutions in the region.[4] They were motivated in part at least by the desire to spread their versions of a Protestant Christianity in which religious information was conveyed primarily in verbal form, both spoken—from the pulpit—and written, in Scripture.

A telling example can be found in the career of William Holmes McGuffey, who, while a professor of ancient languages at Miami University in Oxford, Ohio, began to edit the series of "eclectic readers" that would become a preeminent means of instruction in literacy throughout the region and beyond into the twentieth century (and that continue to inspire nostalgia among cultural conservatives into the twenty-first). Although McGuffey included excerpts from authors of established literary reputation, as well as biblical passages and exemplary stories of virtue rewarded and vice punished, his emphasis was on the practical tools of literacy and elocution as a means to this-worldly ends, fortified by a generic but distinctively Protestant emphasis on discipline, individualism, and personal and public morality.[5] That Miami was, in its early days, essentially a Presbyterian institution dependent in part on public funding illustrates well both the importance that regional Protestants placed on education at all levels, as well as the rather blurry line between church and state in the realm of education at the time. (Indiana University had similar origins, in which religious goals and public funding went together with little protest.)

Even though education at all levels had its origins in a now-unthinkable mixture of religious and governmental initiative and support, the Midwest is distinguishable from other "benchmark" regions, such as the South and New England, because of the distinct pattern of higher education that emerged there during the nineteenth century. On the one hand, the "Yankee Exodus" out of New England brought with it as part of its cultural heritage a commitment to denominationally sponsored collegiate education. This resulted in a proliferation of colleges founded in the nineteenth century by Congregationalists (e.g., Marietta and Oberlin), Presbyterians (Albion, Knox, Wooster), Methodists (Ohio Wesleyan), Episcopalians (Kenyon), Roman Catholics (John Carroll, Marquette, Notre Dame), and many others. Most of these have survived to the present day, although denominational ties have in many cases become attenuated. On the other hand, the region has historically been the seat of state-sponsored higher education, aided in part by the Morrill Act of 1863, which provided federal support for land-grant schools. Although religious connections existed even here—in addition to Indiana and Miami, one might cite the Roman Catholic priest Gabriel Richard's role in founding what would become the University of Michigan—these faded over the years as well.

The "Big Ten" state universities, together with myriad campuses founded in the wake of the G.I. Bill following World War II, have thus provided the region with an alternate track for wide-scale higher education. By the turn of the twenty-first century, the role of religiously affiliated schools in emphasizing loyalty to a particular tradition had begun to diminish in importance (although Notre Dame, for example, has become a nationally respected institution with a high percentage of Catholic enrollment, the number of Catholic students attending state or originally Protestant schools rose dramatically in the post-Vatican II decades).

Variants on these latter themes can be adduced in the subsequent decades of nineteenth-century Midwestern history. Lyman Beecher's Lane Seminary, for example, was to be torn apart during the 1830s by a band of students led by Theodore Dwight Weld who were adamantly opposed to the poor condition of people of color in surrounding Cincinnati, as well as the even worse fortunes of those enslaved directly across the Ohio River in Kentucky. (It was while in residence here with her father that Harriet Beecher Stowe had a chance to make a first-hand acquaintance with the "peculiar institution.") Weld soon led an exodus of his followers to the more sympathetic Oberlin College in northeastern Ohio, from whence they spread out to organize antislavery societies throughout the region's communities and their churches. After the Civil War, the same organizational and lobbying tactics pioneered by "Weld's Band of Seventy" would be taken up by the advocates of temperance; two of its most vociferous promoters, the Women's Christian Temperance Union and the Anti-Saloon League, were founded, respectively, at Oberlin in 1874 and Cleveland in 1893.

The president of Oberlin at the time of the beginnings of organized antislavery in the region had been the evangelist Charles G. Finney. Finney, like Lyman Beecher, had earlier left Connecticut to put into practice an innovative, controversial, and highly effective series of "new measures" in his evangelistic preaching, directed especially at the displaced New Englanders who had left that region's harsh soil to seek their fortunes in upstate New York and a swatch across the lower Great Lakes region. Their spoor, still visible today, consists of the Federal and Greek Revival churches they built in the New England-style towns they founded, as well as in the plethora of liberal arts colleges originally based on firm religious principles. They were soon joined in this enterprise by Baptists, Catholics, Disciples, Episcopalians, Lutherans, Quakers, and other newcomers who shared their confidence in the efficacy of a combination of literacy and disciplined faith in building a new commonwealth, morally upright and economically prosperous.

A final note on the establishment of a pan-regional (and incipiently national) religious and moral ethos in the region makes the transition from a primarily rural and small-town population to an urban predominance, especially east of the Mississippi. Chicago, which was rapidly emerging after the Civil War as the region's metropolis, came to symbolize nationally the power of commerce and its related virtues—efficiency, grand scale, and the subordination of all but the most powerful individuals to the good of the common enterprise. All of this was based, perhaps ironically, on the belief that individual perseverance would inevitably pay off in fortune, a conceit wasted on the immigrant stockyard workers of Upton Sinclair's *The Jungle*. It is therefore not surprising that this most American of cities should become home base for the premier evangelists of the age, who practiced a calling distinctively American in origin and character.

During the 1870s, Dwight L. Moody forsook his job as a shoe salesman in Massachusetts for new opportunities in Chicago. Moody soon became successful not so much as a businessman but as a business-like promoter of evangelical religion, and before long became a free-lance religious professional. Following in Finney's footsteps, he and his musical director, Ira D. Sankey, attracted crowds in the tens of thousands through their combination of business-like efficiency, which attracted the support of newly rich tycoons with names like Armour and Wanamaker; "new measures," such as the calculated use of music in their programs; and a simplified, sentimentalized version of traditional Reformed Protestantism that appealed to the emotions and made few intellectual demands.

Moody's convert and successor, Billy Sunday, who began adulthood as a professional baseball player, continued in this strain by adding vaudevillian hi-jinks and an appeal to an emerging regional nativism to protract the success of Chicago-based evangelism into the World-War-I era. In his heyday, Sunday (derived, ironically, from the German *Sonntag*) played to the sensibilities of the time by denouncing the twin evil legacies of the "Hun": biblical criticism and beer. (He delighted his audiences by observing that, if Hell were turned upside down, one would find "Made in Germany" stamped on the bottom.) Sunday's popularity was eventually eclipsed in the 1920s by an incipiently national popular culture that was now neither religious nor anchored in the ethos of a particular region.

The Midwest as Microcosm and Mosaic

Another take on the Midwest arises from a consideration of its character as a mosaic of a wide variety of cultures in miniature, with each reflecting a continuing process of *immigration*—the in-coming of peoples from foreign climes—and of *in-migration*—the movement of peoples from one part of the American nation to another. Although both of these processes have been characteristic of the nation as a whole since its inception, their playing out in the Midwest has had a distinctive character that has been significantly constitutive of the region's unique configuration. More particularly, we might say that the Midwest has been—and, to a significant degree, continues to be—a place in which peoples from the widest variety of ethnic and religious backgrounds have come and, after having arrived, have continued to preserve distinctive life-ways even while becoming in other important ways Americanized. It is a region in which the apparently conflicting processes of resistance and accommodation to "mainstream" norms have paradoxically taken place simultaneously. This is, to be sure, a matter more of degree than kind—much the same could be said of the New York and Los Angeles metropolitan areas—but here the process has been as much rural as urban.

Ohio—the author's home for the past third of a century—is a particularly good example of this phenomenon in its mix of urban, suburban, and rural population. Since 80 percent or more of its people live in the first two environments, the state is typical of the divide, roughly corresponding with the Mississippi River, between the more urban and industrial states of the eastern Old Northwest, and the more agricultural character of life on the prairies and plains to the west (though this would include a fair amount of Illinois, Indiana, and Wisconsin as well) Ohio remains remarkable for the persistence of distinctive cultures, usually involving a sizable religious component, in its various "micro-cultures."

The northeast corner of Ohio was, in its earliest European-American phase, very intentionally a western extension of New England. This Western Reserve of Connecticut was comprised in part of "firelands" designated by that state as compensation to its residents who had suffered depredations by the British during the Revolution. Its primary city was named after Moses Cleaveland, a Connecticut man, and the region's early architecture and "churchscape" are deliberate echoes of a recently departed New England. These origins are illustrated vividly in the "typical New England meetinghouse on the village green" represented by the Congregational church in Tallmadge—a suburb of Akron—that graced the cover of *Life* magazine's Thanksgiving issue in 1944 as an icon of "traditional American values" during the years of world war.

Somewhat to the south and west, Holmes County is still home to the Amish people, whose landscape is notable for the absence of automobiles, telephone poles, and other artifacts of the technological culture these peaceably minded people (selectively) eschew in their nostalgia for the sixteenth-century Switzerland of their origins. Descending further to the south, one finds a continuing Quaker presence in Wilmington, as well as the descendants of Welsh Calvinists in Jackson and Gallia counties, where Greek revival chapels are still in occasional use for gymanfas—festivals of preaching and hymn-singing—now frequented mainly by Columbus-dwellers of Welsh origin. Westward and northward, several counties in west central Ohio—Greene, Mercer, Auglaize, Darke—boast landscapes consisting of flat, rich farmlands punctuated by aluminum-capped silos and a plethora of German Catholic churches designed in the fusion of Gothic and Romanesque styles popular in southern Germany at the time of this migration during the late nineteenth century.

Ohio's cities, much like their regional counterparts, are similarly complex in their mosaic-like ethnic qualities. Cincinnati, in the far southwest, shares with its Ohio River sister-city, Louisville, a fusion of British, German, and African-American cultural influences. Unlike the cities of the Great Lakes, the "New Immigration" of the late nineteenth century largely by-passed this area. Instead, the founding stocks included British Protestants, especially Presbyterians from Pennsylvania and Virginia; Germans of all religious persuasions, including Jews; Catholics, Lutherans, Reformed, freethinkers, and eventually American-generated German Methodists; Irish Catholics; and, in the twentieth century, significant numbers of African Americans from the South and white Appalachians, primarily from Kentucky and West Virginia, all heading north in an attempted escape from adverse social and economic conditions. The latter group, which has populated southern Ohio in increasing numbers since World War II began offering major employment possibilities, has brought with them the conservative evangelical strains of Holiness, Pentecostal, and Southern Baptist churches that have mushroomed in the region. They range in scale from tiny rural meeting houses to the giant megachurches that abound on the interstate highways and ring roads that surround Cincinnati and Dayton.

At the other end of the state, Cleveland—a city, like Detroit, eponymous with the collapse of "Rust Belt" urban centers beginning in the 1960s—is much more similar to its Great Lakes counterparts than to Ohio River valley communities. More like Chicago than Cincinnati, Cleveland is a mosaic of ethnic neighborhoods dating back to the "New Immigration" era of the late nineteenth and early twentieth century, when vast numbers of southern and eastern Europeans came to meet the high demand for unskilled and semi-skilled jobs that the region's nascent industries—steel in Cleveland and Pittsburgh, automobiles in Detroit, meat-packing in Chicago—were rapidly creating. These newcomers settled in neighborhoods that developed along ethnic lines—Poles, Slovaks, Hungarians, Lithuanians, Italians, Croatians, Greeks, Ukrainians—most of them Roman Catholic, Eastern Orthodox, or Uniate Catholic (i.e., in communion with Rome but using liturgies of Orthodox provenance). Churches were the main institutions in these neighborhoods, frequently vast in scale, dominating the skyline visually, and offering both a symbol of continuing identity as well as social services not readily available in the public realm.

Urban politics in such cities became an exercise in the building of service-able ethnic coalitions through the provision of relief, sympathy, and patronage positions in municipal agencies in return for unquestioning electoral allegiance. This "boss" system had developed earlier in East Coast cities such as Boston and New York, where the Irish perfected it to the degree that it became known as a political "machine." It was highly functional in these newer cities as well, and was often led by Irish Americans who had been, together with the Germans, the earliest of non-British Protestant stock to settle there. Chicago's Irish-American Richard Daley, the father of his namesake and eventual successor, was among the last of the big-city political bosses, who ruled unchallenged until his heavy-handed tactics and rhetoric against Vietnam War protesters aroused national revulsion during the 1968 Democratic convention.

Yet another pattern of urban polity developed in Toledo during the 1890s. Sam "Golden Rule" Jones, a Welsh-born Methodist, made a substantial fortune in manufacturing. In contrast with many of the regional industrialists of his era, however, he attempted to manage his enterprise following what were essentially Social Gospel principles, and placed a sign in his factory proclaiming:

> The Rule That Governs This Factory: "Therefore Whatsoever Ye
> Would That Men Should Do Unto You, Do Ye So Unto Them."[6]

Jones was elected mayor of Toledo, an ethnically mixed and financially troubled industrial city in northwest Ohio, in 1897. During his several terms in office, he attempted to apply a similar mixture of political progressivism and social Christianity to the city's affairs, with positive but limited results.

Washington Gladden, one of the best-known of the Social Gospel preachers, similarly used his base as pastor of the First Congregational Church located on Columbus's Broad Street—then as now a main artery boasting a variety of prestigious Protestant churches as well as the Catholic cathedral—to promote a similar application of Christian ethics to social issues. William T. Stead's best-selling *If Christ Came to Chicago* of 1894 is a prime Midwestern example of the Social Gospel novel genre, in which readers are urged to put Christian principles to work in the social interactions of everyday life.

Institutional churches, such as Chicago's Fourth Presbyterian and Cleveland's Plymouth Congregational, were another manifestation of the Social Christianity impulse. Such urban churches had facilities not only for worship but also for large-scale programming including cafeterias, both religious and secular education, and wholesome recreation such as billiards, bowling, and basketball. Although these programs were intended primarily as outreach, especially to the young, they have also been viewed as means of social control designed to co-opt workers rather than encourage them to address politically the root causes of their problems. The same appraisal has been applied to urban ventures such as

Chicago's Pacific Garden Mission, which combined material relief and spiritual evangelism to the poor. Protestant urban outreach, in any case, manifested itself in a variety of ways and presumably for a variety of motives, but seldom took very radical political form.

Urban churches served many of the same social functions as their rural counterparts, but in a much more intense and competitive fashion. As with organized labor, a movement that developed among the same urban ethnic constituency, the Roman Catholic Church offered "careers open to talent" as a parallel path for ambitious young men. Bishops and clergy of large parishes often became prominent and powerful community figures through various combinations of charisma, claims to spiritual authority, and political influence, especially on issues perceived as moral.

Perhaps the most conspicuous success in the broader political arena was Father Charles Coughlin of Royal Oak, Michigan, a northern suburb of Detroit. During the Depression era of the 1930s, Coughlin became nationally known as the "radio priest" who first avidly supported FDR's New Deal, then turned against Roosevelt and began to espouse anti-Semitic and pro-Nazi sympathies until he was silenced by his bishop. Catholic clergy throughout the region, such as Cincinnati's Peter Dietz and Chicago's Bishop Bernard Sheil, gained regional reputations as advocates of organized labor and helped educate their constituents in Catholic social teaching such as the "just wage" doctrine that had roots in Pope Leo XIII's encyclical letter *Rerum Novarum* ("Of New Things") in 1891.

Catholic outreach in the region's cities often took forms parallel to those maintained by Protestants, with an eye to protecting Catholics from Protestant influence. The earliest Catholic efforts in the realms of education and welfare were primarily responses of the needs of their—largely immigrant—constituencies, who could hope for little support from government at any level. Vast institutional complexes, staffed primarily by priests, brothers, and especially by orders of sisters, sprang up throughout both larger and smaller cities of the region and to some extent in rural areas as well.

Virtually every Midwestern city of any size boasted by the 1920s, and in many cases earlier, an institutional infrastructure consisting of churches and rectories, primary parochial schools and convents for teaching sisters, seminaries at both the high school and college levels maintained both by dioceses and religious orders, mother houses for orders of women religious, central Catholic high schools, private secondary academies staffed by religious orders, colleges for men and women, hospitals, orphan asylums, YM/YWCA-like urban shelters for newly arrived single young people, cemeteries, and in a few cases full-fledged universities.

The purposes of these complexes included the provision of social and cultural essentials both to the ordinary faithful, most of whom belonged to the immigrant working classes and were thus not sophisticated in the workings of the American social system, as well as to those in the particularly vulnerable situations of sickness and poverty. The Catholic leadership was sensitive to what they perceived as alternating Protestant hostility and outreach to these constituencies, and were notably successful in providing a set of alternatives to non-Catholic institutions to help insure group loyalty over the generations.

To a lesser extent Jews, who were generally content to utilize secular schools, mimicked Catholics in creating distinctively Jewish hospitals and cemeteries for their own people. In one significant court case, Jews, Catholics, and freethinkers made common cause in Cincinnati in 1869/70 in opposing the use of the King James Version of the Bible in the "common" (public) schools of that city and won on appeal to the Ohio Supreme Court. This decision resulted in a "deprotestantization" of the public-school system which like its counterparts in many American cities had been controlled by a non-denominational but nevertheless solidly Protestant group of middle-class citizens. Although Catholics enjoyed their symbolic victory they, like a number of traditional Jews and more conservative Lutherans and other evangelicals, nevertheless continued to maintain a parallel school system not only free of competing creeds but also aimed at instilling a positive, highly particularistic religious content.

Although Ohio at the state level and Chicago at the urban are particularly vivid examples of the mosaic character of regional settlement patterns, other examples easily adduce themselves and call attention to the heterogeneous character of ethnic and religious distribution across the region. Western Michigan, for example, is known as an enclave of Dutch settlement, as witnessed in tulip festivals and bumper stickers reading "If you're not Dutch, you're not much." Holland and Grand Rapids are also the homes respectively of Hope and Calvin colleges, affiliated with the more mainline Reformed Church of America and the strongly conservative Christian Reformed Church. This region tends to be strongly conservative in political issues, counterbalancing to some degree the overwhelmingly Democratic makeup of Detroit. Further west, other Dutch in Iowa and the Bohemians of Nebraska, which Willa Cather celebrated in her *My Antonia,* constitute significant regional ethnic enclaves.

As noted in essays in this volume by Lagerquist and Noll in particular, the most distinctive ethnic presences in the trans-Mississippi Midwest are those of Germans and various brands of Scandinavians, large numbers of whom continue to maintain allegiance to various branches of the Lutheran tradition. The numerical strength of German Americans, which also runs high in much of Ohio, is diluted in religious terms because of the division of Germans and their descendants into Catholic, Lutheran, Reformed, Anabaptist, Jewish, and freethinking camps. Scandinavians, though divided originally along ethnic lines (German,

Swedish, Norwegian, Danish, Finnish), tended overwhelmingly towards Lutheranism—a tradition much more of an effective public presence on the American scene today than in its European homelands, where its established status, together with broader patterns of secularization, have deprived it of much of its influence. Even so, the Lutheran influence in the upper Great Plains region is less than hegemonic, since Methodists and Catholics also have deep roots in the region and continue to command allegiance. This phenomenon of ethnic and religious balance continues to be one of the region's distinguishing features—unlike the South, where an informal alliance of Evangelical denominations has maintained a virtual lock on regional religious culture for two centuries.

Religious Cultures and Civic Culture in the Region

At the beginning of the twenty-first century, the Midwest, or "Rust Belt," was a region that had seemingly touched bottom after a lengthy and painful exodus of its citizens to the Sunbelt, the younger in quest of employment and the older fleeing harsh weather. Even harder hit than the industrial territory to the east was the farm country of the Plains, where many towns were losing even the minimal critical mass of population to maintain their independent identity. Serious proposals have been advanced by environmentalists that the region had never been suited for sustained agriculture, and small-scale experiments in letting the area revert to prairie grasses have been launched here and there.

Nevertheless, the Midwest is still in business, even though its demographics have been changing in ways reflecting similar trends elsewhere. As a way of summarizing contemporary trends, we might look *ad seriatim* at the persistence of traditional religious communities and the impacts respectively on in-migrants, primarily from the South, and immigrants, mainly from Asia, the Middle East, and Latin America.

Roman Catholics have from its beginnings played a major role in the settlement of the Midwest, with major concentrations in the cities abutting the Great Lakes, but widely distributed in farming communities as well. Philip Barlow's treatment of Midwestern demography notes that denominational numerical preponderance means—in every state in the region—a compound of Catholics and one or more other groups. Yet although the Catholic hierarchy has exerted considerable influence on civic affairs, especially in Chicago, and has built up an institutional infrastructure similar in scope to that of the Northeast, its ability to act as a hegemonic presence has been complicated by several factors.

In the first place, the Catholic population of the Midwest has been much more ethnically diverse than in the Irish-dominated Atlantic seaboard region. Beginning in the late nineteenth century, Germans and Poles, as well as smaller groups such as Lithuanians, have challenged the power of the Irish, especially in the sensitive areas of the creation and staffing of ethnic parishes in cities such as Chicago and Detroit. Germans and Poles both petitioned the Vatican to recognize this diversity officially, and by the early twentieth century Rome began to respond by appointing bishops of non-Hibernian descent. Although more extreme requests, as for separate ethnic dioceses, were ignored, a system of de facto ethnic parishes corresponding to urban settlement patterns was maintained for several decades. The shrill nativism of the Great War put an end to attempts to maintain the use of the German (or any other foreign) language in regional schools, including those maintained by the Catholic Church, and even German-descended bishops promoted administrative centralization and cultural standardization within their bailiwicks.

Another feature of Midwestern Catholicism that may correlate with this ethnic diversity has been the less imperial tone utilized by its spokesmen in public discourse. Although regional clergy and bishops could be no less authoritative (not to say authoritarian) towards their own flocks than their Northeastern counterparts, they have been less likely to emerge as nationally visible advocates for Catholic issues as, say, Cardinals Spellman and O'Connor in New York or Cardinals Cushing and Law in Boston. On the other hand, as Jay Dolan notes, moderate to liberal figures such as Chicago's late Cardinal Joseph Bernardin and Milwaukee's Archbishop Rembert Weakland—the latter embarrassed into resignation by the revelation of a youthful sexual peccadillo—have also added a note of moderation to regional discourse both on ecclesiastical and civic issues. A recent study of American Catholicism cites two Midwestern dioceses—Lincoln, Nebraska, and Saginaw, Michigan—as striking examples, respectively, of conservative and liberalizing forces at work in the American Catholic community.[7]

Regional Catholicism has also been affected significantly by broader demographic trends both within the Church and in the broader society. Chicago, Detroit, Omaha, and Toledo, to name only a few of the region's cities, have become hosts to a significant influx of Mexicans seeking work no longer primarily as migrant agricultural laborers but now in urban factories, such as meat-processing plants. These immigrants are predominantly Catholic and, following a time-honored pattern, have displaced older urban ethnic populations as the latter have moved to the suburbs. St. Stanislaus Kostka Church in Chicago, for example, still serves the substantial Polish-American population reflected in its name, but has added a side altar dedicated to the Virgin of Guadalupe as a balance to another named for Poland's Our Lady of Czestochowa. Here, an established but diminishing Polish-American community is sharing a parish with more recently arrived Spanish-speaking co-religionists. In other cases, parishes have been closed down or consolidated.

It is in the realm of education that the Catholic presence within the broader society has been most apparent, both in the Midwest and elsewhere. As noted earlier, the development of a separate Catholic-school system, from elementary through college, took place during the era in which Catholic-Protestant tensions were at a height in the region—Illinois and Wisconsin, around 1890, enacted laws, rapidly repealed, that placed significant limits on religiously sponsored education. The Catholic system flourished through the mid-twentieth century and expanded with the population explosion into the suburbs following World War II.

By the late 1960s, however, major changes were to become increasingly visible. The ecumenical spirit promoted by Vatican II, together with the election of a Roman Catholic president in 1960, began to defuse interreligious tension, and the need for an exclusively Catholic system of education designed to insulate children from the larger world began to seem doubtful. In addition, a precipitous decline in the number of Catholic religious professionals—teaching sisters as well as clergy—started to undercut the possibility of maintaining a cadre of celibate women dedicated to religious work and willing to teach at subsistence wages. The rapid flow of previously urban, ethnic Catholics out of the cities and into colleges—now increasingly state-supported—and the religiously heterogeneous, post-ethnic suburbs, did not so much erode Catholic loyalty to the Church as call into question the earlier "ghetto" mentality that undergirded a separatistic educational system. Catholic schools hardly disappeared; they did, however, become pricier as their staffs became increasingly secular and as their religious curriculum grew less rigid and defensive, and more social-ethics oriented.

Those parochial schools that remained in the urban cores began to shift their missions away from socializing the children of Catholic immigrants into the faith and toward providing inner-city youngsters, frequently non-Catholic African Americans, with a more disciplined educational experience than that perceived by their parents as available at local public schools. This broadening of social mission has correlated with the movement for government-funded vouchers that would enable families to enroll children in schools of their choice, whether publicly or religiously supported. Such programs were enacted in Milwaukee and Cleveland during the 1990s, and their constitutionality was upheld by the U.S. Supreme Court in 2002 in *Zelman v. Simmons-Harris*, a case in which the Cleveland program had been challenged. Although religious schools are maintained in the Midwest by a variety of religious groups, ranging from Reform Jews to Seventh-day Adventists to Black Muslims to Missouri- and Wisconsin-Synod Lutherans, the Catholic-school system is by far the largest and most likely to be affected should voucher programs expand significantly in future years. Catholics have perceived this not so much as a Catholic issue but, as in many other areas of public policy, one where their perception of civic right has allied them with other like-minded religious communities.

The Jews of the Midwest similarly have a history in some important ways distinct from that of their Eastern seaboard counterparts. During the nineteenth century, Cincinnati was a major area of German Jewish settlement as a river port where Jewish newcomers settled or from which they departed through the region, seeking their fortunes as itinerant merchants equipped with a backpack or wagon load of household goods. Those traveling retailers who did well frequently opened dry goods stores in the region's towns and cities, some of which—Lazarus and Elder Beerman, for example—grew into major department stores and chains. Cincinnati also became the eventual home of the Bavarian-born rabbi, Isaac Mayer Wise, who founded the nation's first rabbinical seminary and a variety of other pioneering organizations and institutions in the Queen City for the nation's emergent Reform movement. Although the headquarters of the Union of American Hebrew Congregations (renamed in 2003 the Union for Reform Judiasm) left Cincinnati for the more densely Jewish city of New York during the 1950s, Hebrew Union College retains the main campus of its seminary in its original Ohio venue.

Although Jews of a wide variety of origins and religious persuasions, including some Hasidim, eventually found their way to the Midwest, the character of the Jewish community in the region has never very closely resembled that of New York City, the national benchmark. The early and successful presence of German-speaking Jews was never rivaled by the later-arriving Eastern Europeans to the degree that it was further east, and the regional Jewish population base was never really sufficient or distinctive enough to provide a platform for the take-off of the wide variety of Jewish-American cultural production to which New York has been host for well over a century.

The demographics of Midwestern Jewry, however, have been similar to that of their counterparts across the nation in significant ways. The movement of virtually entire neighborhoods from the inner city to the nearer suburbs to more remote suburban regions is illustrated in many Midwestern cities. In Cincinnati, for example, Jews abandoned their Auburndale enclave during the 1960s for Amberley Village, which boasts at least four temples or synagogues, together with two Jewish-oriented country clubs, one for those of German descent and the other for "Russian Jews," as Eastern European immigrants were generally known. The older synagogues along Reading Road in Auburndale have been appropriated by African-American Baptist and Pentecostal congregations. Similarly, in Detroit, the racially based riots of 1967 led to a rapid and nearly total movement of the Motor City's Jewish community from the city's West Side north across Eight Mile Road into Troy, Birmingham, and other suburban communities.

On the whole, Jewish Midwesterners have maintained strong senses of local community. Non-religious organizations such as the Federation of Jewish Agencies have played a role in fostering such identity. So have housing patterns brought about in part by voluntary neighborhood formation, which ensured access to houses of worship and other communal needs, as well as by earlier patterns of discrimination, such as the "point system" employed by realtors in Detroit's posh suburb of Grosse Pointe to exclude Jews and other allegedly undesirable ethnic, religious, and racial groups. There have been a few instances over time in which Midwestern Jews have asserted themselves in the public realm. During the 1920s and 1930s, for example, Detroit Jews became quite vocal over the public anti-semitism displayed by Henry Ford and Father Charles Coughlin, and generally succeeded in forcing them to tone down their obnoxious rhetoric. Similarly, a march by Neo-Nazis in Skokie, Illinois, a Chicago suburb with a large population of Holocaust survivors, became something of a *cause celebre* in 1979, although the marchers were legally successful in holding their demonstration. Most of the time, however, the region's Jews have chosen to avoid the public spotlight, and have quietly maintained their roles as good citizens and frequently successful players in business and professional circles. Michigan's Senator Carl Levin is a good but rather unusual example of a Midwestern Jew who has achieved high political office.

African Americans have lived in the Midwest since early times—one is reputed to have been the founder of Chicago—but began to arrive in massive numbers during the World-War-I era, attracted by the promise of jobs as well as freedom from the virtual serfdom in which they had been forced to live in much of the South. They settled overwhelmingly in urban areas, close to employment and sheltered frequently in neighborhoods recently abandoned by white ethnic groups, as illustrated earlier in our discussion of Jewish demographic patterns. The hierarchy of black denominational clusters asserted itself here, with the middle class supporting the various Methodist churches, Baptists further down the pecking order, and storefront congregations of "sanctified"—Holiness and Pentecostal—churches at the bottom.

It was in Depression-era Detroit, however, that a considerably less traditional movement arose in a black neighborhood. It was here that half-legendary W.D. Fard—one of several variants of his name—briefly carried on a career as a door-to-door silk peddler, spreading the message of the Nation of Islam—the "Black Muslims"—as he went until he vanished. His movement was continued by Elijah Poole, who renamed himself Elijah Muhammad and went on to recruit his most famous, but ultimately disloyal, disciple, Malcolm Little—later Malcolm X—originally from the vicinity of Lansing, Michigan. Although the movement would flourish in New York, Boston, and other cities as well, Detroit and Chicago remained major centers until the movement split and dwindled after Elijah Muhammad's passing. Other leaders of new religious movements, such as Detroit's Prophet Jones, attracted short-run followings as well.

More successful, however, have been more "mainstream," usually Baptist, clergy such as Detroit's C.L. Franklin—father of the singer Aretha Franklin—as well as Chicago's Jesse Jackson, sometime candidate for the Democratic presidential nomination, father of a Chicago Congressman, and highly visible political activist. Large urban black churches and their clergy have frequently been active in municipal politics, especially as a number of regional cities—Cleveland, Detroit, Gary—developed predominantly black populations.

Predominantly white Protestant churches have generally followed national trends, although with some intraregional diversification. The "mainline" denominations, which once dominated urban thoroughfares such as Detroit's Woodward Avenue and Indianapolis's Meridian Street, often shifted their bases of operation to the suburbs as their congregations moved in that direction. Their old houses of worship, when not demolished, have often been taken over by newcomer groups, at times within the same denomination, or have occasionally managed to draw a substantial congregation from throughout a metropolitan area, as in the case of Chicago's Fourth Presbyterian Church. The impact their clergy once exerted on municipal affairs—as illustrated in Reinhold Niebuhr's pastorate of a German Reformed parish in Detroit in the 1920s—began to dwindle as their constituencies shifted and as the old mainline style of quietly working behind the scenes to influence civic leaders began to give way to the more confrontational and controversial tactics of the Civil Rights era. Nevertheless, the continuing reality of the "Lutheran Belt" west of the Mississippi, together with a quiet but persistent presence of middle-class religious folkways throughout much of the region—less dramatic than in the South but much deeper than in most of Protestant America—makes the mainline churches an on-going force in the shaping of regional public culture.

Another major challenge to mainline Protestantism has been the rise of evangelicalism, beginning especially in the 1970s with the rise of the New Religious Right. Fundamentalism was not without roots in the area, as demonstrated vividly in the career of William Bell Riley at Minneapolis's First Baptist Church during the 1920s. Indiana has also been for some time an enclave of religious and political conservatism, with much of the state's public life during the 1920s having been dominated by the Ku Klux Klan. The state's distinctive demographics, with much of its population arriving from the South rather than the North and East, has much to do with this phenomenon and accounts for similar tendencies in parts of southern Illinois and Ohio. In the latter state especially, extensive in-migration from Kentucky and West Virginia in recent decades has brought with it a proliferation of Southern Baptist and Pentecostal churches. Together with the southward outflow of Rust Belt refugees, who have tended to be ethnic Catholic and union-oriented (albeit with many "Reagan Democrats" among them), this demographic shift may account for the state's rightward tilt in politics in recent years.

Although Ohio's Republican leadership has tended towards the political center, the forces of the Religious Right have been substantial enough to result in extensive hearings on the inclusion of "intelligent design"—a variant of the earlier anti-evolution movement known as "creationism"—in the state's public school curricula in 2002, even though this movement was ultimately defeated. Such a policy was briefly adopted in Kansas in 1999, although it was speedily rescinded after the 2000 elections. In another sensitive area of public policy, a number of court challenges to the display of religious symbols, especially the Ten Commandments, on public property have arisen in the region. These challenges have been uniformly opposed by conservative evangelicals while being sustained by the courts. In most cases, however, these cases have arisen in Indiana and southern Ohio, areas that are more culturally aligned with the South than with other parts of the Midwest.

Even though many evangelical churches, especially in the southern reaches of the region, are small and rural, maintaining school buses to collect lower-income followers, the same terms can hardly be used to characterize religious enterprises such as the Willow Creek Community Church in the suburbs of Chicago. A "megachurch" by any set of criteria, with membership well into the five-digit range, Willow Creek is a study in cultural adaptation, with a physical plant and extensive programming designed in the light of market-research surveys conducted to see what would appeal to the middle- to upper-middle-class residents of the emergent surrounding area. Although Willow Creek's doctrinal statement is profoundly conservative, its staff publicly utilizes an idiom based on popular culture and psychology, with little outward emphasis on neo-Calvinist doctrine. Similar megachurches—often preferring terms like "Christian Life Center" rather than the more traditional "church" as self-descriptors—flourish in many other of the southern part of the region's metropolitan centers, especially along the interstate beltways that surround cities and provide easy on-off access to a widely distributed clientele. Sophisticated agents of evangelicalism can be found in Minneapolis, where Billy Graham's ministries are based, as well as in academically rigorous and respected colleges such as Wheaton near Chicago and Calvin in Grand Rapids, Michigan.

A final major theme in delineating the contemporary Midwestern religious landscape is the influx of religious traditions primarily from Asia and the Middle East that has resulted from the Hart-Cellar Act of 1965. Such religions are not entirely new to the region; in fact, the oldest Muslim mosque in the nation can be found in Cedar Rapids, Iowa, and the most significant long-established Muslim community can be found in the Detroit suburb of Dearborn. Much newer, though hardly confined to the region, is the phenomenon of the Islamic center, a distinctively American combination of worship space—that is, a mosque—with cultural, social, educational, and athletic facilities, on the model of the old urban Protestant institutional church, the Catholic parish, the Jewish synagogue-community center, and the more recent evangelical megachurch. It is not clear which example of this hybrid is the oldest in the nation, although the one that lies in the western suburbs of Indianapolis has been around for some time.

Of these ancient but, in the American context, relatively new religions, Buddhism is not conspicuous in the region, although small temples can be found in many metropolitan areas. Hinduism is more visible; such Hindu temples as those on the outskirts of Cincinnati and Dayton, Ohio, for example, follow the general patterns of American temple design analyzed by Joanne Punzo Waghorne in her seminal essay focused on an example in suburban Washington, D.C.[8] In these structures, the lower level functions as social and cultural space—on the model of the Islamic center and its precedents—while the upper level displays images of a variety of deities, reflecting regional patterns of worship in India and here arrayed in a juxtaposition unknown in the mother country.

Hindus, Buddhists, and Muslims are too new to the region to be significant players as yet in the various public discourses, alliances, and battles over political and civic culture. Sociologically, they tend to resemble the Jewish example, since many bring with them from their ancestral homelands considerable cultural capital in the form of education and success orientation that have permitted them to skip over the usual first-generation sojourn in the inner city and attain very rapidly instead a secure place in suburban prosperity. There are certainly exceptions to this generalization: the older Muslim communities, for example, are populated largely by blue-collar families who left the Middle East for the opportunities offered by Ford and other heavy industries, and by no means all of their descendants have successfully made the climb into the white collar world and beyond. The newer immigrants are in some ways caught between two political worlds: while their economic interests and traditionalist morals may ally them with conservative forces, their outsider status may make them sensitive to the sorts of nativist suspicions engendered by the September 11, 2001 debacle.

Concluding Unscientific Postscript

It would be easy to conclude that the Midwest is a figment of the imagination. As noted earlier, the region has no specific boundaries other than those imposed by the arbitrary political divisions represented by state lines. Eastern Ohio and Michigan have more in common with western Pennsylvania and New York than with North Dakota and Iowa, while the latter are in some respects cultural soulmates more of eastern Colorado and Montana than their Great Lakes counterparts. The Mississippi is arguably the most important regional dividing line.

Of course, ambiguous cultural boundaries to some extent characterize all regions. Hence, for pragmatic purposes in the Religion by Region series, a rather separate Alaska has been grouped with Washington and Oregon to form the "Pacific Northwest" region; landlocked Nevada has been paired with California to make up the "Pacific." Even comparatively and traditionally coherent New England requires discerning eyes to apprehend what remains distinctive about it and what is merely an expression of national trends. And like the Pacific, the Pacific Northwest, and every other region, New England can be variously divided into subregions. As Stephen Prothero makes clear in New England's contribution to this series, Essex County, Vermont, with 6,000 people, is a very different place than Fairfield County, Connecticut, with nearly 900,000.

So Midwestern identity may be distinctive for being indistinct, but it is not unique. And as previous chapters have demonstrated, the Midwest has its own subregions; as elsewhere, these could, for varying purposes, be conceived of as smaller regions in their own right. Keeping all this in mind allows context for generalizations concerning what we have defined as the Midwest that might otherwise be dangerous.

In the western (trans-Mississippi) Midwest of the plains and prairies, population is thin and getting thinner; agriculture—though challenged at the level of the family farmer—is still highly important; and cultural and religious diversity is less dramatic than farther east. Catholics, Lutherans, and Methodists are the largest religious groups; with the exception of Lutherans in the northern stretch of the region, however, none is dominant. The traditional, if eroding, division of the twin cities into St. Paul (the cathedral site) Catholics and Minneapolis Lutherans parallels that of Garrison Keillor's Lake Wobegon, where Catholics and Lutherans each drive the automobile brand, Fords or Chevys, sold by their coreligionist dealers. Although none of these groups is exactly noted for its irrepressible liberalism, the political independence of the region certainly reflects something of the spirit of civic responsibility and ability to coexist gracefully with theologically incorrect neighbors that has emerged out of generations of shared experience and cooperation.

The lower part of the western region is well populated with the same ethnic and religious mixes, but its political culture differs somewhat from its northerly counterpart. Although cities such as Kansas City and St. Louis remain reliably Democratic, reflecting their substantial minority populations, the rural dominance of the region is reflected in its increasingly conservative politics: the impulse of distrust of urban culture permeates much of the political and moral culture of this seedbed of William Jennings Bryan-style populism. Even here, the quirkiness of Iowa, home of the early Democratic caucuses, does not exactly counterbalance the region's ethos, but does demonstrate its complexity.[9]

The Great Lakes and Ohio River valley parts of the Midwest are even more complicated. As in the western region, the southern tier of Ohio, Indiana, and Illinois, abutting the Ohio and the former slave-holding border states to the south, tends towards religious and political conservatism anchored in a mix of German Catholic and evangelical Protestant religious cultures. The northern, Great Lakes area, which begins in Buffalo and culminates in Milwaukee, is a great urban expanse that has experienced dramatic economic and social decline followed by modest, scattered recoveries during the past few decades. Once dominated by labor unions and big-city political bosses supported by a broad ethnic mix and the Catholic Church, the region's "Reagan Democrats"—the product of a post-Vietnam era disillusionment of working people with the perceived cultural left turn of their traditional party, especially with regard to abortion and other issues of sexuality and sexual identity—have become something of a political wild card. Ohio has been especially affected by this rightward drift, most likely reflecting its growing Appalachian population. Illinois, Michigan, and Wisconsin, however, along with neighboring Pennsylvania and Minnesota, still contain enough residual social and economic progressive sentiment to make them resistant, for example, to the "red state tide" of the 2000 presidential elections.

What gives the Midwest whatever consistency it may possess as a region arises more out of a system and spirit of balances than any universal specific characteristics. City, country, and suburbs; manufacturing, farming, and commerce; immigrants from the Hmong in Minneapolis to Armenians in Detroit; Catholics, Jews, Muslims, and Hindus; and white evangelical, African-American, and mainline Protestants; all play their roles in the region in general and in many of its constituent states and metropolitan areas as well. Seldom radical, Midwesterners can be liberal, middle of the road, conservative, or quirky; Good Government Progressives or xenophobic urban populists. In short, don't expect readily and consistently to discover some Midwestern "essence;" look instead at the mix and at the dynamics at work within the particular mixture under examination.

While it is difficult to point to a Midwestern essence, the closer look made possible by the essays in this volume do reveal a region with its own character and its own manifestations of religion in this particular public culture. The Asian and Middle Eastern religionists who have poured into the region in the past generation have forced, by their presence, a renegotiation of the civic culture they found here. The negotiations are, as Raymond Williams correctly points out, local versions of a national story. Yet the immigrants' negotiate with more than a nation; they negotiate with local and regional neighbors.

These neighbors are not wholly interchangeable with those in other regions. Proportionately fewer immigrants and proportionately more long-term Americans than on the East and West coasts conduct this informal negotiation in the Midwest, and this mix changes the cultural consciousness from what it might otherwise be. Similarly, the Midwestern region into which the immigrants enter is more Caucasian than anywhere in the United States except New England. The region is, in a broad vertical band in its western side, more thoroughly religiously affiliated than the rest of America.

While not truly dominant in most places, every state in the region is nonetheless suffused with a Catholicism that is, by comparison, absent in the South. And the Catholics who reside in the Midwest are the different breed written about by Jay Dolan, a breed more German and with an (admittedly eroding) legacy more open to reform and experiment than, say, the Irish Catholic legacy that confronts other immigrants when arriving in New England. The Midwest immigrants encounter is also more diffusely Methodist than anywhere outside the South, and beyond even the South it is Methodist in such a way that makes Methodism the largest of all denominations in nearly 200 counties in a horizontal belt spanning the region from Kansas and Nebraska to Ohio. This diffusion of Methodism into the culture has expression in ways worth remarking and begging further inspection.

As the political scientists John Green and James Guth have put it, United Methodism is at once the "church of the golden mean" and the "church of the large standard deviation;" that is, it's a church that holds the middle ground while encompassing a wide range of viewpoints among its members. Methodism emphasizes personal spiritual discipline (like the more conservative evangelical denominations) and social reform (like the rest of the liberal mainline denominations). Traditional Methodists, Green and Guth have found, combine relatively conservative views on social issues like abortion, school prayer, pornography, and the "traditional family," with relatively liberal views on economic issues like social welfare spending and aid to minorities. All in all, Green and Guth propose, "the distinctive contribution of Methodism may well lie in its potential to both contain diverse social stands and knit together gaps within the social fabric."[10] This, it seems clear, precisely encapsulates the characteristic Midwestern style.

Furthermore, if Mark Noll's provocative speculation holds under further scrutiny, the Methodist (and even broader Holiness) sensibility may be finding its latter-day expression in the Midwestern megachurches that are influencing American notions of what denominations are. In the Midwest (though not necessarily in other parts of the country) this new form of community seems linked to a deeper impulse to subordinate partisan politics to community building—a theme treated, among other places, in DeAne Lagerquist's probe of Midwestern Lutherans and Raymond Williams's examination of recent religious immigrants.

Every region of the United States is idiosyncratic in the local variations of its religious composition; the Midwest is no exception. Such local differences naturally affect public policy and culture. In Ohio's Wayne County, south of

Cleveland, for example, the Amish and Mennonites outnumber all other denominations. Further south, in Holmes County, Old Order Amish alone constitute one-third of all religious adherents, while Amish and Mennonite groups combine to make up 63 percent, three times their proportion in Pennsylvania's celebrated Lancaster County. In Holmes and adjacent counties, in fact, resides the largest concentration of Amish in the world, 50,000 strong. Virtually no crime occurs in Holmes county; the first gun-related homicide since the 1950s took place in 2003. The Amish ordinarily shun state and national elections, but, encouraged in a particular stance by their bishops, they can control local ones when an issue important to them arises.

In 1998, public Highland High School in eastern Holmes County built a new gymnasium. Behind this success, though, was much community exertion. When the need for the gym was first pushed forward, the Amish, who cease schooling after eighth grade and deemed it unjust to have to pay for the gym, turned out in force to defeat a general levy. In response, non-Amish "English," in good Amish fashion, solved the problem by privately collecting funds. This precise event could not have occurred in Arizona or Vermont or Georgia.

Despite all local variations, though, the Midwest is perhaps the region that more than any other retains a strong influence of mainline Protestantism, anchored by the Lutheran and Methodist aspects earlier alluded to and augmented by the considerable presence of The United Church of Christ, American (northern) Baptists, Disciples of Christ, Presbyterian Church (USA), and, in smaller spheres, the Episcopal Church. The tolerant inclinations deriving in good part from this mainline influence, combined with the vertical and national "Bible suspender" of religious adherence to which Philip Barlow drew attention in laying out the region's demography, may even make it possible to assert something more. Perhaps the Midwest combines the pluralist religious ethos of the Mid-Atlantic with the churchgoing habits of the South.

When we add to all this the unique timing and history of the region's settlement, immigration patterns, and economic thrust; when we recall religion's competition with political and economic power in the great cities of the former "Rust Belt," exemplified here by Elfriede Wedam and Lowell Livezey's account of Chicago, "nature's (transforming) metropolis;" when we attend to the region's peculiar patterns of rural, urban, and suburban relations and their cultural and religious dynamics and implications explored by Rhys Williams; we can glimpse, at last, a distinctive cultural recipe. In the context of this recipe, the intersections of religion and the public realm provide the potential for striking and subtle fascinations that belie the region's reputation as bland.

Although there is, then, a distinctive region to be discerned within various artificial boundaries, it remains true that, more than any other region in the country, the Midwest's identity is blurred. As suggested in this volume's Introduction, this blurred identity is, at least in part, because the Midwest is so often taken, symbolically and demographically, by insiders and by those without, as America's embodiment, its most encompassing microcosm. In this construction, the Midwest is the "America" region, the country's "common denominator" (to call again upon the language of the sociologists Robert and Helen Lynd, who believed, almost a century ago, that they had found the nation's "Middletown" in Muncie, Indiana). And we have seen that the secular and religious Midwest does indeed reflect many American traits. It would be a mistake, however, for any Midwesterners to conclude that they are just like the rest of the country, and the rest of the country just like them. For the Midwest is measurably and intuitively distinct from the "Fluid Identities" of the Pacific region, the "None Zone" in the Pacific Northwest, the evangelical cast of the "Distinctive South," and every other region in the United States. If the Heartland is extraordinarily ordinary, it is so in relation to an imagined composite nation, not to any one of its constituent parts.

Endnotes

1. Andrew R.L. Cayton and Peter S. Onuf, *The Midwest and the Nation: Rethinking the History of an American Region* (Bloomington;: Indiana University Press, 1990).

2. The correct pronunciation is "GRAA-shitt"

3. Barbara M. Cross, ed., *The Autobiography of Lyman Beecher* (Cambridge: Harvard University Press, 1961), I, 253.

4. T. Scott Miyakawa, *Protestants and Pioneers: Individualism and Conformity on the American Frontier* (Chicago: University of Chicago Press, 1964).

5. See Elliott J. Gorn, eds., *The McGuffey Readers: Selections from the 1879 Edition* ((Boston: Bedford/St. Martin's, 1998).

6. Andrew R.L. Cayton, *Ohio: The History of a People* (Columbus: Ohio State University Press, 2002), 222.

7. Charles R. Morris, *American Catholic: The Saints and Sinners Who Built America's Most Powerful Church* (New York: Vintage Books, 1997), chapter 15.

8. Joanne Punzo Waghorne, "The Hindu Gods in a Split-Level World: The Sri Siva-Vishnu Temple in Suburban Washington, D.C.," in Robert A. Orsi, ed., *Gods of the City* (Bloomington and Indianapolis: Indiana University Press, 1999), 103-130.

9. See Randall Balmer, *Mine Eyes Have Seen the Glory: A Journey into the Evangelical Subculture in America* (3rd ed.) (New York and Oxford: Oxford University Press, 2000), chapter 8.

10. John C. Green and James L. Guth, "United Methodists and American Culture: A Statistical Portrait," in William B. Lawrence, Dennis M. Campbell, and Russell E. Richey, eds., *The People(s) Methodist, Vol. 2: Forms and Reforms of Their Life* (Nashville: Abingdon Press: 1998), 23, 43, 45.

APPENDIX

In order to provide the best possible empirical basis for understanding the place of religion in each of the regions of the United States, the Religion by Region project contracted to obtain data from three sources: the North American Religion Atlas (NARA); the 2001 American Religious Identification Survey (ARIS); and the 1992, 1996, and 2000 National Surveys of Religion and Politics (NSRP).

NARA For the Project, the Polis Center of Indiana University-Purdue University at Indianapolis created an interactive Web site that made it possible to map general demographic and religious data at the national, regional, state-by-state, and county-by-county level. The demographic data were taken from the 2000 Census. The primary source for the religious data (congregations, members, and adherents) was the 2000 Religious Congregations and Membership Survey (RCMC) compiled by the Glenmary Research Center. Because a number of religious groups did not participate in the 2000 RCMS—including most historically African-American Protestant denominations—this dataset was supplemented with data from other sources *for adherents only*. The latter included projections from 1990 RCMC reports, ARIS, and several custom estimates. For a fuller methodological account, go to *http://www.religionatlas.org*.

ARIS The American Religious Identification Survey (ARIS 2001), carried out under the auspices of the Graduate Center of the City University of New York by Barry A. Kosmin, Egon Mayer, and Ariela Keysar, replicates the methodology of the National Survey of Religious Identification (NSRI 1990). As in 1990 the ARIS sample is based on a series of national random digit dialing (RDD) surveys, utilizing ICR, International Communication Research Group in Media, Pennsylvania, national telephone omnibus services. In all, 50,284 U.S. households were successfully interviewed. Within a household, an adult respondent was chosen using the "last birthday method" of random selection. One of the distinguishing features of both ARIS 2001 and NSRI 1990 is that respondents were asked to describe themselves in terms of religion with an open-ended question: "What is your religion, if any?[1]" ARIS 2001 enhanced the topics covered by adding questions concerning religious beliefs and membership as well as religious switching and religious identification of spouses/partners. The ARIS findings have a high level of statistical significance for most large religious groups and key geographical units, such as states. ARIS 2001 detailed methodology can be found in the report on the American Religious Identification Survey 2001 at *www.gc.cuny.edu/studies/aris-_index.htm.*

NSRP The National Surveys of Religion and Politics were conducted in 1992, 1996, and 2000 at the Bliss Center at the University of Akron under the direction of John C. Green, supported by grants from the Pew Charitable Trusts.

Together, these three surveys include more than 14,000 cases. Eight items were asked in all three surveys (partisanship, ideology, abortion, gay rights, help for minorities, environmental protection, welfare spending, and national health insurance). The responses on these items were pooled for all three years to produce enough cases for an analysis by region. These data must be viewed with some caution because they represent opinion over an entire decade rather than at one point in time. A more detailed account of how these data were compiled may be obtained from the Bliss Institute.

Endnote

1. In the 1990 NSRI survey, the question wording was: "What is your religion?" In the 2001 ARIS survey, the phrase, "... if any" was added to the question. A subsequent validity check based on cross-samples of 3,000 respondents carried out by ICR in 2002 found no statistical difference between the pattern of responses according to the two wordings.

BIBLIOGRAPHY

Mary E. Bendyna and Paul M. Perl, Political Preferences of American Catholics at the Time of Election 2000 (Washington, D.C., 2000).

Andrew R.L. Clayton and peter S. Onuf, *The Midwest and the Nation* (Indiana, 1990).

Jay P. Dolan, *In Search of an American Catholicism: A History of Religion and Culture in Tension* (New York, 2002).

Edwin Scott Gaustad and Philip L. Barlow, *New Historical Atlas of Religion in America* (Oxford, 2000).

L. DeAne Lagerquist, *The Lutherans* (Greenwood Press).

Lowell Livezey, ed., *Public Religion and Urban Transformation: Faith in the City* (New York University Press, 2000).

James H. Madison, ed., *Heartland: Comparative Histories of the Midwestern States* (Indiana, 1998).

Robert R. Mathisen, ed., *The Role of Religion in American Life: An Interpretive Historical Anthology* (National Book Network, 1994).

J. Gordon Melton and John Krol, *National Directory of Churches, Synagogues, and other Houses of Worship: Midwestern States: Illinois, Indiana, Iowa, Kansas, Michigan, Minnesota, Missouri* (Gale Group, 1993).

Terry M. Moe, *Schools, Vouchers and the American Public* (Washington, D.C., 2001).

Mark Noll, *One Nation Under God: Christian Faith and Political Action in America* (Harper Collins, 1988).

Timothy L. Smith, "The Ohio Valley: Testing Ground for America's Experiment in Religious Pluralism," *Church History* 90 (December, 1991).

Peter W. Williams, *Houses of God: Region, Religion, and Architecture in the United States* (University of Illinois Press, 2000).

Raymond Brady Williams, *Religions of Immigrants from India and Pakistan: New Threads in the American Tapestry* (Cambridge University Press, 1998).

CONTRIBUTORS

Philip Barlow is professor of Theological Studies at Hanover College, Hanover, Indiana. His most recent book is the *New Historical Atlas of Religion in America*, co-authored with Edwin Scott Gaustad (Oxford University Press, 2002).

Becky Cantonwine teaches mathematics and literature at Southwestern High School in Hanover, Indiana.

Jay P. Dolan, past president of the American Catholic Historical Association and the American Society of Church History, is professor emeritus of History at the University of Notre Dame. He recently authored *In Search of an American Catholicism: A History of Religion and Culture in Tension* (Oxford University Press, 2002).

DeAne Lagerquist is associate professor and chair of the department of Religion at St. Olaf College, Northfield, Minnesota. Among her books is *In America the Men Milk the Cows: Factors of Gender, Ethnicity, and Religion in the Americanization of Norwegian-American Women* (Carlson Publishers, 1991).

Lowell W. Livezey is lecturer at the Harvard Divinity School; director of the Religion in Urban America Program, University of Illinois at Chicago; and editor of (New York University Press, 2000).

Mark A. Noll is McManis Professor of History at Wheaton College, Wheaton, Illinois. His books include *America's God, from Jonathan Edwards to Abraham Lincoln* (Oxford University Press, 2002).

Mark Silk is associate professor of religion and public life at Trinity College, Hartford, Connecticut, and founding director of the Leonard E. Greenberg Center for the Study of Religion and Public Life at Trinity. A former newspaper reporter and member of the editorial board of the *Atlanta Journal-Constitution*, he is author of *Spiritual Politics: Religion and America Since World War II* (1998; 2nd edition forthcoming) and *Unsecular Media: Making News of Religion in America* (1995).

He is editor of *Religion in the News*, a magazine published by the Greenberg Center that examines how the news media handle religious subject matter.

Elfriede Wedam is visiting lecturer at the Honors College, University of Illinois at Chicago; associate director of the Religion in Urban America Program at University of Illinois, Chicago; and a contributor to *Public Religion and Urban Transformation: Faith in the City* (New York University Press, 2000).

Peter W. Williams is Distinguished Professor of Comparative Religion and American Studies at Miami University in Oxford, Ohio. His publications include *Houses of God: Region, Religion, and Architecture in the United States* (University of Illinois Press, 1987).

Raymond B. Williams is LaFollette Distinguished Professor in the Humanities, emeritus, at Wabash College in Crawfordsville, Indiana, and director, emeritus, of the Wabash Center for Teaching and Learning in Theology and Religion. With Guinder Singh Mann and Paul Numrich, he has recently authored *Buddhists, Hindus and Sikhs in the United States* (Oxford University Press, 2001).

Rhys H. Williams is professor and department head of Sociology at the University of Cincinnati. Among other works, he is the editor of *Cultural Wars in American Politics: Critical Reviews of a Popular Myth* (Aldrire de Gruyter, 1997).

INDEX

abolition, 214; Lutherans and, 99
abortion: Catholics and, 130–31; immigrants and, 144; Lutherans and, 88, 99–101
abuse scandal, 29, 44, 119–22
Addams, Jane, 50, 159
adherents: claimed by religious groups, in Midwest versus United States, 17, 18*f*; term, 9
Adrian College, 72
advocacy, term, 102
African Americans: Catholic, 115–16, 177; in Chicago, 116, 162, 164, 173–74, 177, 182, 184–85; in Illinois, 41; in Kansas, 38–39; Lutheran, 87; in Michigan, 42; in Midwest, 23, 76, 189, 225–26; in Ohio, 217; and politics, 78; in suburbs, 201; in urban areas, 194
African Methodist Episcopal Church, 56
African Methodist Episcopal Zion Church, 56
age: in Midwest, 22; in South Dakota, 33
agriculture: Methodists and, 79; in Midwest, 23, 210; and rural religion, 202–4; in South Dakota, 34
Algren, Nelson, 159, 164, 178, 185
Alinsky, Saul, 117
Allegan County, MI, 44
Allen, Richard, 127
Amberley Village, 224
American Association for the Aging, 98
American Baptist Churches, 56; in Midwest, 63*t*, 65; seminaries of, 74
American Indian Movement, 34
American Islamic College, 152

Americanization, term, 150
American Protective Association, 27, 109
American Religious Data Archive, 88
American Religious Identification Survey (ARIS), 17, 39, 138, 235–36
Amish, 30, 51, 64–65, 76, 216, 232
Amway, 44
Anabaptists: in Kansas, 39; in Midwest, 30, 59–60; in South Dakota, 36
anti-Catholicism, 27, 109, 202
anti-German sentiments, 90, 112
Anti-Saloon League, 202, 214
anti-Semitism, 225
Apostolic Christian Church of America, 65
Appalachians, in Ohio, 217
Arab Americans: in Chicago, 173; in Michigan, 43
architecture: Hindus and, 228; Lutherans and, 92–94
Armenians, 230
Armstrong, Anton, 93
arranged marriage, 141–42
arts, Lutherans and, 92–94
Asbury, Francis, 66
Asian Americans: Catholic, 115; in Chicago, 182; in Illinois, 41; in Kansas, 38; in Midwest, 23, 227–28; in urban areas, 194
Assemblies of God, 58, 63*t*, 64–65
assimilation, 141
Associated Reformed Presbyterian Church, 44
Associated Talmud Torah, 183
Association of Chicago Priests, 118

241